Recipe Hall of Fame

Fresh from the
Farmers Market
Cookbook

★

*Winning Recipes
from Hometown America*

GREG CAMPBELL

Farmers markets are a traditional way of selling agricultural and home manufactured products. Produce found at farmers markets is renowned for being locally grown and very fresh, and allow farmers to pick produce at the peak of flavor.

Best of the Best

★★★★★★★★★★★★   ★★★★★★★★★★★★

Recipe Hall of Fame
Fresh from the
Farmers Market
Cookbook

────────── ★ ──────────

*Winning Recipes
from Hometown America*

EDITED BY

Gwen McKee
Barbara Moseley
AND
Terresa Ray

QUAIL RIDGE PRESS
Preserving America's Food Heritage

Library of Congress Cataloging-in-Publication Data

Recipe hall of fame fresh from the farmers market cookbook : winning recipes from
hometown America / edited by Gwen McKee, Barbara Moseley, and Terresa Ray.
        p. cm. — (Recipe hall of fame cookbook collection).
    Includes index.
    ISBN-13: 978-1-934193-71-6
    ISBN-10: 1-934193-71-2
1. Cooking, American. 2. Cooking—Competitions—United States. 3. Cookbooks.
I. McKee, Gwen. II. Moseley, Barbara. III. Ray, Terresa, 1970- IV. Title: Fresh
from the farmers market cookbook.
TX715.R2895 2011
641.5973—dc23   2011022082

ISBN-10: 1-934193-71-6 • ISBN-13: 978-1-934193-71-2

Cover photo by Greg Campbell
Printed in Canada

On the cover: Old Fannin Road Farmers Market, Brandon, MS.
Thanks to owners Jim and Cindy Hunt.

QUAIL RIDGE PRESS
P. O. Box 123 • Brandon, MS 39043 • info@quailridge.com
www.recipehalloffame.com • www.quailridge.com
www.facebook.com/cookbookladies

Contents

★★★★★★★★★★★★ ★★★★★★★★★★★★

GREG CAMPBELL

Editors Gwen McKee, Barbara Moseley, and Terresa Ray pick fresh vegetables from Barbara's container garden.

More than three decades ago, we began collecting the best recipes from cookbooks in every state in the nation. Now that we've completed our search for the nation's very best recipes (the BEST OF THE BEST STATE COOKBOOK SERIES), we have started searching for those recipes that go beyond being called the best, recipes that are so wonderful they belong in a category of their own—the RECIPE HALL OF FAME!

The nearly 400 recipes in this cookbook were already selected as winners, since they were chosen as favorites from each of their cookbooks. Now they've achieved an even greater status with their induction into the RECIPE HALL OF FAME. These recipes proudly uphold our slogan of Preserving America's Food Heritage. Since 1982, these recipes have come from cookbooks all over the United States—church cookbooks, Junior League cookbooks, community cookbooks, etc., many of which are now out of print. It is our pleasure, as well as our mission, to make sure these cherished recipes continue to be handed down through generations, and enjoyed for years to come.

Now, we are proud to present to you the BEST of the BEST OF THE BEST recipes utilizing fresh fruits and vegetables—the *Recipe Hall of Fame Fresh from the Farmers Market Cookbook*, the fifth volume in our RECIPE HALL OF FAME COOKBOOK COLLECTION. These recipes all feature fresh fruits or vegetables, and are arranged by courses such as appetizers, breakfasts, salads, desserts, etc. With nearly 6,500 farmers markets all across the United States, and a large consumer demand for fresh, locally grown food, we knew this cookbook would appeal to cookbook collectors nationwide.

Not only is this a collection of outstanding fruit and vegetable recipes, but a book that will serve a very practical purpose: putting great food on the table at any time, for any occasion. Cooking delicious meals for family and friends brings us so much enjoyment. It is a way of showing our love, and sharing our time as we sit down together and catch up on life's comings and goings. And although it isn't necessary, it's always nice to know that the meals we serve will produce a bounty of compliments...and these will!

Choosing recipes for this cookbook was indeed a challenge. As we chose recipes, we considered several things: First, the recipe had to be chosen as one of our favorites. (We voted with our taste buds!) Next,

★★

there had to be something about the recipe that stood out from the rest, that made it so wonderful that it deserved to be inducted into the RECIPE HALL OF FAME. And of course, the recipe had to include fresh fruits or vegetables. (You can alter the recipes by using frozen or canned ingredients, if you choose, perhaps some you have put up yourself.)

Barbara and I wish to thank all of the contributors who spent so much time making sure they were presenting their very best recipes for inclusion in our BEST OF THE BEST cookbooks. Thanks also to our incredibly dedicated staff (Holly Hardy, Melinda Burnham, Lacy Ward, Chris Brown, and Cyndi Clark) who worked long hours making sure this cookbook was the best that it could be. Terresa Ray, our incredibly competent assistant for the last ten years, was so much a part of this book's coming together, that we added her name with ours as a full-fledged co-editor.

We hope you enjoy the latest inductees into the RECIPE HALL OF FAME as much as we did.

Our best to you,
Gwen McKee and Barbara Moseley

P.S. Please note that the title of each contributing cookbook is listed below the recipe along with the state name in parentheses, indicating the BEST OF THE BEST STATE COOKBOOK where the recipe appears.

ROBERT HOLMES/CALIFORNIA TOURISM

More than 300,000 tons of grapes are grown annually in California vineyards such as this one in Napa Valley. From these grapes are produced more than seventeen million gallons of wine each year.

Strawberry-Kiwi-Banana Smoothie

8 ounces papaya juice, soy milk,
  or other fruit juice
5–6 strawberries, fresh or frozen

1 kiwi fruit, peeled
1 banana
3 ice cubes

Put juice in blender jar. Cut fruit into chunks; add to blender with ice cubes. Blend until smooth. Makes 1 (20-ounce) smoothie.

Note: This basic recipe is easily adapted to suit available fruit and individual tastes. Bananas provide a nice texture, as does frozen fruit. I like to add nutritional supplements such as soy protein, spirulina, and bee pollen.

A Taste of Fayette County (West Virginia)

Orange Mint

It is my honest conviction that having this recipe should be a requirement, and that it should be issued when your social security number is given.

2½ cups water
2 cups sugar
Juice of 2 oranges and
  grated rind of both

Juice of 6 lemons and grated
  rind of 2
2 handfuls fresh mint leaves

Make a simple syrup of the sugar and water by boiling them together for 10 minutes. Add the juice of the fruits and the grated rind of the oranges and lemons. Pour this over the mint leaves, which have been well-washed. (I like to bruise a few of the leaves so that the flavor is more pronounced.) Cover tightly and let this brew for several hours. Strain through a sieve, then through one thickness of cheesecloth.

This makes one quart of rich juice, which may be kept in the refrigerator indefinitely.

To serve, fill tall glasses with finely powdered ice and pour ¼ cup (4 tablespoons) of this juice over the snow-like ice, then finish filling the glass with either ginger ale or cold water.

Long Lost Recipes of Aunt Susan (Oklahoma)

Chocolate Strawberry Cooler

½ cup sliced strawberries
2 tablespoons sugar
1 tablespoon Hershey's Cocoa
1 cup milk, divided

½ cup club soda, freshly
  opened
Ice cream or whipped cream
2 fresh strawberries (optional)

In blender container combine sliced strawberries, sugar, cocoa, and ½ cup milk. Cover; blend until smooth. Add remaining ½ cup milk and club soda; cover and blend. Pour into 2 glasses. Garnish with ice cream or whipped cream and strawberry, if desired. Serve immediately. Makes about 2 (8-ounce) servings.

Hershey's Fabulous Desserts (Pennsylvania)

LeConte Sunrise Juice

2 cups orange juice
2 cups apple juice
½ cup chopped pineapple

1 cup capped strawberries
3 bananas

Blend all ingredients in food processor; place in freezer until almost completely frozen. Re-blend and serve. Serves 6.

Recipe from the Burning Bush Restaurant, Gatlinburg
Fine Dining Tennessee Style (Tennessee)

Lemon Strawberry Punch

1½ cups sliced strawberries
3 (6-ounce) cans frozen
  lemonade

3 (6-ounce) cans water
2 quarts chilled ginger ale

Blend strawberries, lemonade, and water in blender. Pour mixture in punch bowl. Add ginger ale and ice. Taste to see if some sugar is needed.

Costco Wholesale Employee Association Cookbook (Washington)

★★★★★★★★★★★   ★★★★★★★★★★★

Mardi Gras Madness

Adds to the fun in true Carnival colors of purple, green, and gold!

1 ice ring
1 (40-ounce) bottle grape juice
1 (48-ounce) can unsweetened
   pineapple juice
1 (2-liter) bottle lemon-lime
   soft drink

1 fifth vodka or more, to taste
2 oranges or lemons, sliced
2 limes, sliced

Place ice ring in bottom of punch bowl. Add liquids in order given. Float slices of oranges and limes on top. Makes 8–9 quarts, about 65 (½-cup) servings.

Louisiana LEGACY (Louisiana)

Editors' extra: The best way to keep your punch cold is with a large block of ice. A pretty way to do this is to make an ice ring filled with fruit or other garnishes. Here's how: Arrange your fruit or other garnishes (choose an item that is in the recipe or compliments it) along the bottom and side of a large Bundt cake pan. Fill only partially with water, so garnishes don't move. Freeze; when frozen, remove pan and fill to top with additional water. Freeze again. Run warm water around the pan to loosen the ice. Place ice ring in your punch and enjoy!

Rhubarb Punch

We used to call this "Missionary Lemonade" in Sitka. It was as close as we came to the real thing.

6 cups cut-up rhubarb stalks
4 cups water
1½ cups sugar
⅓ cup orange juice

¼ cup lemon juice
Dash of salt
Water or ginger ale

Cook rhubarb in water until soft. Strain through sieve. (Should have 5 cups of juice.) Add sugar and bring to a boil. Add orange juice, lemon juice, and a dash of salt. Chill the mixture or freeze. Dilute punch with equal parts water or ginger ale to serve.

All-Alaska Women in Timber Cookbook (Alaska)

Rhubarb was legally classified as a fruit in the United States in 1947, even though botanically it is a vegetable.

Mariposa

The name is Spanish for "butterfly." This frosty drink goes light on the tongue.

2 ounces white rum
½ very ripe banana
½ medium mango, cut into
  chunks
2 ounces coconut milk
1 teaspoon vanilla extract

2 tablespoons sugar (or
  equivalent artificial
  sweetener)
½ pint vanilla ice cream
6 ounces milk

Place all ingredients in a blender and blend until smooth. Makes 2 servings.

The Mongo Mango Cookbook (Florida)

Peach Bellini

4 large peaches, skinned
  and cut
4½ tablespoons powdered
  sugar, or to taste

Crushed ice (about 2 cups)
1 bottle champagne

Process peaches in blender until frothy. Blend in powdered sugar. Add crushed ice; blend just until mixed. Pour into pitcher and add champagne. Stir slowly until combined thoroughly. Yields 16–18 servings.

With Great Gusto (Ohio)

The juice from peaches makes a wonderful moisturizer, and it can be found in many brands of cosmetics.

★★★★★★★★★★★   ★★★★★★★★★★★

White Sangria

This is a refreshing summertime drink and it won't stain carpets or linens like red wine sangria.

½ gallon dry white wine
2 apples (cored, sliced, and
   unpeeled)
½ lemon, sliced thin
1 orange, sliced thin
1 lime, sliced thin

2 fresh peaches, sliced (when
   available)
½ gallon (2 quarts) soda water
½ cup frozen lemonade
   concentrate, or ½ cup sugar

Mix all ingredients and chill.

It's a Long Way to Guacamole (Texas)

Blackberry Wine

4 quarts blackberries
10 quarts water
10 pounds sugar
Juice of 3 lemons

Juice of 4 oranges
1 yeast cake
3 pounds ground raisins
10 quarts water

Boil blackberries in 10 quarts water for 15 minutes. Add sugar while the mixture is hot. Cool and add juice from lemons and oranges, then stir in yeast and mix well. Put in a large crock. Stir twice a day for 7 days. Add ground raisins and 10 quarts water. Stir twice a day for 10 days until yeast stops working. Strain and bottle with loose caps.

Wildlife Harvest Game Cookbook (Iowa)

The state of Oregon is the world's largest producer of blackberries, harvesting more than forty million pounds a year.

★★★★★★★★★★★★ ★★★★★★★★★★★★

Chunky Guacamole

1 large ripe avocado
1 medium tomato
1 small onion
1 small bell pepper

3 long green chiles
Juice of ½ lemon
Salt to taste

Chop all the ingredients fine. Do not mash. Use freshly roasted and peeled chiles, but, if they are not available, use canned or frozen. Mix together with the lemon juice and add salt to taste. Serve as a dip or as a salad with lettuce and corn chips.

The Best from New Mexico Kitchens (New Mexico)

Fresh Avocado Salsa

6 green onions, chopped
2 medium tomatoes, chopped
1 (4-ounce) can green chiles
⅓ cup chopped fresh cilantro

2 large or 3 medium avocados,
  cubed
1 tablespoon fresh lemon juice
1 teaspoon garlic salt

Combine all ingredients; let sit at least 1 hour for juices to combine. Serve as sauce for tacos, tostadas, or steak, or use as a dip with tortilla chips.

Pleasures from the Good Earth (Arizona)

Florida was the site of the first U.S. avocado trees in the 1830s. However, today, nearly 80% of the nation's avocados come from California.

Red Star Salsa

¾ cup crushed tomatoes
3 large tomatoes, chopped
   small
1 medium red onion, chopped
   small
1 medium mango, chopped
   small

¼ cup minced cilantro
1 tablespoon chipotle paste
2 ounces red wine vinegar
½–1 teaspoon cream of
   coconut, or to taste

Mix all ingredients together. Serve with tortilla chips.

Caring and Sharing (South Carolina)

Editors' Extra: If you can't find chipotle paste at your grocery store, just buy canned chipotle peppers in adobo sauce, and purée only the peppers (not the sauce), but make sure to remove the seeds first, as they pack a lot of heat.

Simply Sensational Strawberry Salsa

½ Vidalia onion
½ red bell pepper
½ green bell pepper
½ yellow bell pepper
½–1 jalapeño pepper to taste
1 large ripe tomato

½ cup apple cider vinegar
1½ teaspoons garlic powder
1½ teaspoons parsley flakes
12 large ripe strawberries, cut
   small
1 package Equal sweetener

Dice onion, peppers, and tomato. Marinate ½–1 hour in vinegar. Toss in garlic powder and parsley flakes. Sweeten strawberries with Equal and add to vegetable mixture. Serve very cold with tortilla chips or warm over chicken. Also good as a marinade.

Pungo Strawberry Festival Cookbook (Virginia II)

Eggplant Caviar

1 medium eggplant, peeled
and cut into ½-inch cubes
⅓ cup chopped green bell
pepper
1 medium onion, chopped
3 garlic cloves, crushed, or
½ teaspoon garlic powder
⅓ cup olive oil
1 (4-ounce) can mushrooms,
drained
1 (6-ounce) can tomato paste
⅛–¼ cup water
2 tablespoons red wine vinegar
½ cup sliced stuffed green
olives
½ teaspoon seasoned salt
1 teaspoon sugar
½ teaspoon pepper
½ teaspoon oregano

Mix the eggplant, green bell pepper, onion, garlic, and olive oil in
a pan. Cover and cook slowly for 30 minutes. Then add the
remaining ingredients. Cover and simmer another 30 minutes.
Serve hot or cold with pita bread or crackers. Easy. Can do ahead.
Serves 6–8.

Cooking in Clover (Missouri)

Pretty Platter Dip

1 (9-ounce) can bean dip
1 (31-ounce) can refried beans
3 or 4 ripe avocados, mashed
2 teaspoons lemon juice
Salt to taste
1 cup sour cream
1 package taco seasoning mix
4 tomatoes, diced
2 (4-ounce) cans sliced black
olives
2 bunches green onions, diced
1½ cups finely grated Cheddar
cheese

Mix bean dip and refried beans; spread on round serving platter.
Mix avocados, lemon juice, and salt and spread on bean layer.
Combine sour cream and taco seasoning and spread on avocado
layer. Place diced tomatoes around outer edge; black olives next
circle; green onions next circle and cheese as center. Serve with
dipping chips.

The Garden Patch (Arizona)

Cucumber Spread with Lemon Thyme

1 medium cucumber, peeled
  and seeded
½ medium onion
1 (8-ounce) package cream
  cheese, softened
Dash of salt

Dash of hot pepper sauce
1 drop green food coloring
  (optional)
1 tablespoon chopped fresh
  lemon thyme, or to taste

Grind cucumber to a pulp in blender or food processor. Place on a double layer of cheesecloth and squeeze out juice. Grind onion in blender or food processor. Add cucumber, cream cheese, and remaining 4 ingredients. Blend until fairly smooth. Refrigerate overnight. Serve with fresh vegetables or crackers. Yields about 1 cup.

Today's Herbal Kitchen (Tennessee)

Hawaiian Fruit Kabobs

1 (14-ounce) can pineapple
  chunks, drained, reserve
  juice
1½ teaspoons finely chopped
  fresh mint leaves

1 tablespoon lemon juice
1 large banana
1 large papaya
Maraschino cherries (optional)

Combine reserved pineapple juice, mint leaves, and lemon juice. Cut peeled banana and papaya into 1-inch chunks. Marinate fruit in juice for 5 or more minutes. Alternate fruit on cocktail skewers. Serve chilled. Makes 18–24 kabobs.

Pupus from Paradise (Hawaii)

Editors' Extra: Okay to use fresh pineapple. Use more lemon juice to marinate fruit.

Pineapples can weigh up to twenty pounds, though the average size sold in grocery stores is two to five pounds.

Cranberry Glazed Brie

3 cups cranberries
¾ cup brown sugar
⅓ cup dried currants
⅓ cup water
⅛ teaspoon dry mustard
⅛ teaspoon ground allspice
⅛ teaspoon cardamom
⅛ teaspoon cloves
⅛ teaspoon ginger
1 (2.2-pound) brie cheese
  wheel

In a saucepan, combine cranberries, brown sugar, currants, water, and spices. Cook over high heat for 5 minutes. Remove from heat to cool. Cover and refrigerate. (This may be made up to 3 days in advance.) Set brie on a heat-proof platter. Using a sharp knife, cut a circular top off rind, leaving ½-inch border. Spread cranberry marmalade over brie and refrigerate for 6 hours. Remove from refrigerator 2 hours before serving and bring to room temperature. Bake at 300° for 12 minutes. Serve with fresh fruit slices such as apples or pears, and/or crackers. Serves 12.

Recipes of Note for Entertaining (Minnesota)

Starboard Stuffed Mushrooms

1 pound medium mushrooms
1 stick butter or margarine,
  melted
¼ cup minced green onions
¼ cup water, white wine, or
  sherry
1 cup herb-seasoned stuffing

Wash mushrooms; remove stems. Dip caps in melted butter and place upside down on baking pan. Finely chop ¼ of stems and sauté with green onions in remaining butter. Add water or wine. Stir in stuffing. Spoon into mushroom caps. Bake in 350° oven about 10 minutes. Makes about 18 hors d'oeuvres.

How to Make a Steamship Float (Michigan)

Stuffed Mushrooms

1–2 packages fresh mushrooms
1 (5-ounce) bottle soy sauce
1 pound ground chuck
½ cup chopped green bell
  pepper

4 tablespoons bread crumbs
2 egg yolks
2 tablespoons minced onion

Remove stems from mushrooms and chop; set aside. Soak caps in soy sauce for one hour.

Drain caps; save soy sauce. Mix remaining ingredients with chopped stems. Stuff and mound meat mixture into caps. Brush with soy sauce. Bake at 350° for 20–25 minutes, or broil for 8–10 minutes.

The Crooked Lake Volunteer Fire Department Cookbook (Wisconsin)

Deep-Fried Mushrooms

1 pound fresh mushrooms
2 eggs, slightly beaten

Flour
Bread crumbs

Wash and clean mushrooms. Cut large ones in half. Dip in flour, eggs, and bread crumbs. Deep-fry in oil. Serve with mustard dip.

MUSTARD DIP FOR VEGETABLES AND FRIED MUSHROOMS:

1 cup sour cream
1 cup Miracle Whip salad
  dressing
3 tablespoons Dijon mustard
¼ cup chopped onion

1 garlic clove
Dash of salt
3 dashes Worcestershire
Paprika

Combine all ingredients. Sprinkle paprika on top. Serve with raw vegetables. Delicious with fried mushrooms.

Hullabaloo in the Kitchen (Texas)

Mushrooms are grown commercially in nearly every state in the nation, however Pennsylvania accounts for roughly 55% of total U.S. production. As a matter of fact, Kennett Square, Pennsylvania, is known as the Mushroom Capital of the World.

C D Cajun Mushrooms

This has always been one of the most often requested recipes at the Continental Divide. It's great as an appetizer, luncheon entrée, or a midnight supper.

3 tablespoons butter, divided
3 cups quartered mushrooms
½ cup chopped sweet red
   bell pepper
½ cup chopped green onions
1 tablespoon thyme
1 tablespoon granulated garlic

1 tablespoon Worcestershire
1 tablespoon Tabasco
Salt to taste
3 cups whipping cream
2 tablespoons chopped fresh
   parsley

In a hot sauté pan, add 1 tablespoon butter and cook the mushrooms. Set aside in a baking dish. Melt the rest of the butter and add the pepper, onions, thyme, and garlic. Sauté until slightly cooked and add the rest of the ingredients, except parsley. Cook for about 7 minutes on high heat until the cream is partially reduced. Salt to taste. Pour the mixture over the mushrooms and place in a hot oven until the cream mixture begins to thicken and bubble. Sprinkle the chopped parsley over the top and serve with crunchy French or Cuban bread to dip in the mixture. Serve with a crisp Sauvignon Blanc or very cold dry champagne.

Recipe by Jay and Karen Bentley, Continental Divide, Ennis, Montana
Montana Celebrity Cookbook (Big Sky)

The button mushroom, better known as the white mushroom, is the most widely cultivated, harvested, and distributed mushroom in the world. This edible fungus is eaten so commonly by such a wide variety of people that the term "mushroom" conjures up the image of a button mushroom in most people's minds. In the United States alone, 90% of all mushrooms sold are button mushrooms. An average person consumes over two pounds of button mushrooms a year. The button mushroom has a classic mushroom-like appearance, with a short, thick stalk and a white cap.

★ ★ ★ ★ ★ ★ ★ ★ ★ ★ ★ ★ ★ ★ ★ ★ ★ ★ ★ ★ ★ ★ ★ ★

Spinach Cheese Squares

1 (10-ounce) bag fresh spinach
3 eggs
1 cup flour
1 cup milk
1 teaspoon salt

1 teaspoon baking powder
¾ pound sharp Cheddar
  cheese, grated
¼ cup margarine (not butter)

Wash spinach, drain, remove stems, and cut up into small pieces, using a knife or scissors. Beat eggs in a bowl; stir in flour, milk, salt, and baking powder. Add grated cheese and spinach, stirring until ingredients are well mixed. Melt margarine in a 9x13-inch baking pan. Pour spinach mixture into pan and smooth over. Bake at 350° for 30 minutes. Leave in pan and cut into bite-size pieces. Serves 45–50.

Can be frozen. Separate pieces and place in freezing bags. If frozen, thaw and heat at 300° for 10–15 minutes.

The Bloomin' Cookbook (Pennsylvania)

Zucchini Appetizers

1 cup biscuit mix
3 cups unpeeled and thinly
  sliced zucchini (about 4 small)
½ cup finely chopped onion
¾ cup grated Parmesan cheese
2 tablespoons snipped parsley

4 eggs, beaten
½ teaspoon salt
½ teaspoon seasoned salt
Couple dashes of pepper,
  both black and cayenne
½ cup vegetable oil

Mix all ingredients and spread in a greased 9x13-inch pan. Bake at 350° for about 30 minutes, or until golden brown. Serve hot out of the oven. Can be made ahead and reheated. Makes about 4 dozen 2x1-inch appetizers.

Collectibles III (Texas II)

★★★★★★★★★★★ ★★★★★★★★★★★

Cucumber Sandwiches

1 large package dry ranch
  dressing mix
1½ cups mayonnaise

¾ cup buttermilk
Bread rounds
2 large cucumbers, sliced thinly

Combine the dressing mix, mayonnaise, and buttermilk. Blend until smooth and of good spreading consistency. Spread each bread round with dressing mixture. Top with a slice of cucumber and finish with a dollop of dressing. Chill before serving.

Bouquet Garni (Mississippi)

Bacon and Tomato Tarts

3 tomatoes, chopped and
  drained
1 pound bacon, cooked crisp
  and crumbled
1 cup mayonnaise
½–1 tablespoon Italian
  seasoning, or to taste

1½ cups shredded Swiss
  cheese
1 Vidalia onion, chopped
2 (15-count) packages
  miniature phyllo shells

Mix tomatoes, bacon, mayonnaise, seasoning, cheese, and onion in a bowl. Spoon into phyllo shells. Arrange on a baking sheet. Bake at 350° for 15–20 minutes or until golden brown. Serves 30.

Par 3: Tea-Time at the Masters® (Georgia)

Kathleen's Vidalia Onions

Vidalia onions are indigenous to Georgia. Any sweet regional onion may be substituted.

12 small Vidalia onions, thinly sliced
2 cups water
1 cup sugar

1 cup vinegar
¼–½ cup mayonnaise
1 teaspoon celery salt
Party rye bread

Combine first 4 ingredients. Marinate overnight in refrigerator. When ready to serve, drain and pat dry. Toss with mayonnaise and celery salt. Serve on party rye bread. Easy, must prepare ahead. Preparation time: 15 minutes. Serves 10–12.

Atlanta Cooknotes (Georgia)

The Vidalia onion is a Georgia-grown onion known for its sweet, mild flavor. Its history began in 1931 in Toombs County when farmer Mose Coleman discovered the onions he planted were not hot...they were sweet! His sweet onions were a struggle to sell at first, but Coleman persevered and managed to sell those first crops for $3.50 per 50-pound bag. In the 1940s, the state of Georgia built a Farmers Market in the town of Vidalia, which greatly aided in spreading the word about "those Vidalia onions," and that is how they got their famous name. Throughout the 50s and 60s, production grew at a slow but steady pace, but by 1977, the onion had achieved such success that it merited its own festival!

Today, Vidalia onions have developed an international reputation as the "world's sweetest onion." Their mild flavor is due to the unique combination of soils and climate found in the 20-county production area, the only place in the world that true Vidalia onions can be grown. Vidalia onion enthusiasts can now explore the history of Georgia's beloved state vegetable and the growing region that has made it so famous at the Vidalia Onion Museum, which opened its doors to the public on April 29, 2011.

Bread & Breakfast

★★★★★★★ ★★★★★★★

CHRISTIANE TAS, WWW.WIKIPEDIA.ORG

Corn is the most widely grown crop in America, and Iowa leads the nation in the production of corn, soybeans, and pork. Ninety-two percent of Iowa's land is devoted to agriculture.

Veggie-Stuffed French Loaf

1 (11-ounce) package French
   bread dough
1 zucchini squash, sliced
1 yellow squash, sliced
1 (4-ounce) can sliced black
   olives
½ green bell pepper, sliced or
   chopped
1 (8-ounce) package sliced
   mushrooms
Mozzarella cheese (grated or
   sliced)
Velveeta or American cheese
   slices

Place a rectangle of aluminum foil in long baking pan. Spray foil
with nonstick spray. Unroll dough onto foil. Arrange slices of
veggies and cheeses in layers. Roll up like a jellyroll. Pinch ends
together. Make sure seam side of dough is down. Bake at 350° for
35 minutes. If dough browns before 35 minutes, pull foil up
around the roll and continue baking.

Recipe submitted by author Mary Morrow, Richmond
Kentucky Authors Cook (Kentucky)

Sweet Onion Cornbread

2 cups self-rising cornmeal
1 tablespoon sugar
1 teaspoon baking powder
2 cups milk
1 egg
4 tablespoons vegetable oil,
   divided
2 cups finely chopped sweet
   onions

Preheat oven to 350°. In a large mixing bowl, combine the cornmeal, sugar, and baking powder. Add the milk, egg, and 2 tablespoons of oil, mixing well (the batter will be quite thin). Stir in the
onions and mix well. Grease a 10-inch iron skillet with the remaining oil, pour in the batter, and bake for 30–35 minutes or until light
brown. Let cool 10 minutes before serving. Makes 8 servings.

Breads and Spreads (Georgia)

Bread in an Onion Ring

2 large onions
  (Idaho-Eastern Oregon)
¼ cup yellow cornmeal
½ cup all-purpose flour
½ teaspoon salt
¼ teaspoon cayenne pepper

2 teaspoons sugar
1½ teaspoons baking powder
½ cup milk
1 egg
¼ cup bacon drippings or
  vegetable oil

Peel onions and cut crosswise into ½-inch slices. Remove centers of slices to leave ½-inch-thick rings. Prepare batter by mixing rest of ingredients in order given. Place onion rings on griddle that has been coated liberally with oil and heated to 350° (medium heat). Fill each onion ring with batter and cook on one side. Turn and cook on other side. Serve hot. Very good with fish and coleslaw.

Onions Make the Meal Cookbook (Idaho)

Onion Ring Loaf

This is better than Blooming Onions!

4–6 mild white onions or sweet
  onions
1 cup milk
3 eggs, beaten

Salt to taste
Approximately 2 cups pancake
  or baking mix
Oil for deep-frying

Slice onions crosswise and separate into rings. Soak rings in mixture of milk, eggs, and salt to taste in bowl for 30 minutes. Dip each onion ring in pancake mix and fry in 375° oil until golden brown. Pack fried onion rings solidly, but without pressing, into an 4x8-inch loaf pan. Bake at 400° for 10–15 minutes. Turn onto serving plate. Makes 4 servings.

Country Chic's Home Cookin (Mid-Atlantic)

★★★★★★★★★★★ ★★★★★★★★★★★

Banana Oatmeal Bread

This is the best banana bread we have ever baked, and goodness knows, in 41 years a lot of over-ripe bananas have been destined for a batch of quick bread. This one is favored because it is made with oatmeal, which keeps it moist. Each time the subject turns to bananas, we recall the day we took six banana baked goods to the ape house at the Toledo Zoo. Along with cookies, bread, cakes, etc., we took a table, lace cloth, and candelabrum to add to the photo setup. When everything was in place, and the monkey stared down at the table in disbelief, the photographer said, "Are you going to get any more crazy ideas?"

That was in January. The next summer we took cold soups to be photographed with the polar bears at the zoo. Fortunately, it was a different photographer, which may have saved the food editor's life.

½ cup shortening	½ teaspoon salt
1 cup sugar	½ teaspoon cinnamon
2 eggs	1½ cups mashed bananas
½ teaspoon vanilla	(about 3 medium)
1 cup all-purpose flour	¼ cup milk
1 teaspoon baking soda	½ cup chopped raisins

Cream shortening and sugar. Add eggs and vanilla and beat until fluffy. Combine dry ingredients and add to first mixture alternately with bananas and milk. Mix well and fold in raisins.

Bake in greased 5x9-inch loaf pan 50–60 minutes in 350° oven. Cover for 5 minutes after being removed from oven to keep the moisture in the bread.

Aren't You Going to Taste It, Honey? (Ohio)

Bananas were first introduced to the American public at the Philadelphia Centennial Exposition of America in 1876.

★★★★★★★★★★★ ★★★★★★★★★★★

Hawaiian Macadamia Nut Bread

¼ cup butter, softened
¾ cup light brown sugar
2 eggs, beaten
1¾ cups all-purpose flour
2 teaspoons baking powder
¼ teaspoon baking soda

½ teaspoon salt
¾ cup chopped macadamia
  nuts
1 cup shredded fresh
  pineapple, with juice

Cream butter and sugar; beat in eggs. Combine flour, baking powder, baking soda, and salt. Stir in nuts. Stir ½ the flour mixture into creamed mixture. Gently stir in pineapple and remaining flour mixture. Turn batter into greased 5x9x3-inch loaf pan. Bake one hour in preheated 350° oven, or until it tests done.

Seasoned with Aloha Vol. 2 (Hawaii)

Cranberry Apple Nut Bread

3 eggs
1 teaspoon vanilla
¾ cup vegetable oil
½ cup milk
3 cups all-purpose flour
1¾ cups sugar
1 teaspoon baking soda

1 teaspoon salt
½ teaspoon cinnamon
3 cups diced Granny Smith
  apples
1 cup chopped walnuts
1½ cups cranberries (Alaskan
  low-bush)

Mix liquids together in one bowl and dry in another. Gradually add dry to liquid until mixed, and beat on low speed for 3 minutes. Stir in apples and nuts. Last, fold in cranberries. Spoon into sprayed loaf pans (any size) to about ½ full. Bake at 350° for about 1 hour, or until browned, and bread pops back when touched. Spoon Glaze over top, if desired. Yields 16 servings.

GLAZE:
1 cup powdered sugar

2 tablespoons lemon juice

Recipe from Alaskan's Lazy Daze B & B, North Pole
Favorite Recipes from Alaska's Bed and Breakfasts (Alaska)

Bread in a Jar

2⅔ cups sugar
⅔ cup vegetable shortening
4 eggs
⅔ cups water
2 cups fruit (mashed bananas or
   applesauce)
3½ cups all-purpose flour

¼ teaspoon ground cloves
1 teaspoon cinnamon
1 teaspoon baking powder
2 teaspoons baking soda
1 teaspoon salt
1 cup chopped nuts or raisins

Cream together sugar and shortening. Beat in eggs and water. Add fruit. Add flour, cloves, cinnamon, baking powder, soda, salt, and nuts. Mix well and set aside.

    Grease inside of 6 wide-mouth pint canning jars. Don't grease the rims. Pour one cup of batter into each prepared jar. Do not use more or it will overflow jar. Place open jars evenly spaced on cookie sheet. Place in 325° preheated oven. Bake about 45 minutes or until toothpick inserted comes out clean. Remove jars one at a time. Wipe rim around top. Place metal disk on top in place, then twist ring on to secure. It will seal.

Measures of Love (New York)

Editors' Extra: This can also be baked in two 5x9-inch loaf pans at the same temperature for about 1 hour. Check with a toothpick to make sure it's done.

Blueberry Lemon Bread

⅓ cup butter
1 cup sugar
3 tablespoons lemon juice
2 tablespoons lemon rind
2 eggs
1½ cups all-purpose flour
1 teaspoon baking powder

1 teaspoon salt
½ cup milk
1 cup blueberries, coated with
   flour
½ cup chopped walnuts or
   almonds

Mix butter, sugar, lemon juice, and rind. Beat in eggs. In separate bowl mix flour, baking powder, and salt. Alternately add flour mixture and milk. Fold in blueberries and nuts. Pour into 2 (5x9x3-inch) loaf pans and bake at 350° for 60 minutes.

Cooks Extraordinaires (Wisconsin)

Blueberry-Lemon Scones

2 cups unbleached all-purpose
  flour
1 tablespoon baking powder
3 tablespoons sugar
  (reserve a little for top)
¼ teaspoon salt
1 teaspoon lemon zest
5 tablespoons cold, unsalted
  butter, cut into small pieces
1 cup heavy cream (reserve a
  little for top)
½ cup fresh blueberries

Adjust oven rack to middle position. Preheat oven to 425°. Place flour, baking powder, sugar, and salt into large bowl. Cut in lemon zest and butter until it resembles coarse meal. Stir in cream and blueberries just until a dough begins to form. Transfer to countertop and knead briefly. Form 8-inch circle and cut into 8 wedges. Brush wedges with cream and sprinkle with sugar. Transfer to ungreased cookie sheet. Bake for 12–15 minutes until tops are light brown. Cool on wire rack for at least 10–20 minutes.

Recipes for the House that Love Built (North Carolina)

Double Chocolate Banana Muffins

½ cup butter, softened
1⅓ cups sugar
2 eggs
1⅓ cups sour cream
2 teaspoons vanilla
2 cups all-purpose flour
¼ cup cocoa
1 teaspoon baking powder
1 teaspoon baking soda
Pinch of salt
2 ripe bananas, mashed
1 cup semisweet chocolate chips
½ cup coarsely chopped
  walnuts

Preheat oven to 350°. Grease or line muffin pans. In a large bowl, mix butter, sugar, eggs, sour cream, and vanilla. Add flour, cocoa, baking powder, baking soda, and salt all at once. Mix just until ingredients are blended. Stir in bananas, chocolate chips, and walnuts.

Fill muffin cups ⅔–¾ full. Bake 18–20 minutes or until a toothpick comes out clean—be careful not to hit a melted chocolate chip! Cool 5 minutes, then remove muffins from tins, and place on a rack to cool completely. Serve warm or at room temperature. Makes 24 regular muffins or 7–8 dozen mini muffins.

Culinary Memories of Merridun, Volume 2 (South Carolina)

Cherry Crumb Muffins

MUFFINS:

4 cups all-purpose flour
2 teaspoons salt
½ cup sugar
½ teaspoon cinnamon
¼ teaspoon nutmeg

2 eggs
½ cup margarine, melted
2 cups buttermilk
1⅓ cups fresh cherries, pitted

Preheat oven to 400°. Sift all dry ingredients together in large mixing bowl. Add liquids to dry ingredients and mix with approximately 5–6 strokes using a wooden spoon. Chop pitted cherries and add to batter, mixing only until combined. Do not overmix or the muffins will be tough. Pour batter into lined muffin tins, filling ⅔ full. Makes 24 muffins.

CRUMB TOPPING:

¼ cup brown sugar
⅛ cup all-purpose flour
⅛ cup regular oats

1½ tablespoons margarine
1½ tablespoons chopped nuts

Combine all ingredients until crumbly; sprinkle over muffins. Bake 20–25 minutes. Let muffins cool slightly and turn out onto cooling rack. Let cool completely. Serve with Orange Honey Butter.

ORANGE HONEY BUTTER:

½ pound butter, softened
½ cup orange blossom
   clover honey

Zest from 3 oranges

Simply combine butter and honey with wooden spoon until well blended and very soft. Add zest of oranges and stir until combined. Serve with Cherry Crumb Muffins or your favorite pancakes.

Ships of the Great Lakes Cookbook (Michigan)

Pumpkin Apple Streusel Muffins

2 cups sugar
2½ cups all-purpose flour
1 teaspoon baking soda
¼ teaspoon salt
¼ teaspoon cloves
¼ teaspoon nutmeg

2 teaspoons cinnamon
½ teaspoon ginger
2 eggs, slightly beaten
1 cup pumpkin
½ cup vegetable oil
2 cups peeled and diced apples

Mix dry ingredients in large bowl. Combine eggs, pumpkin, and oil; add to dry ingredients. Mix only until moistened. Stir in apples. Spoon into greased or paper-lined muffin tins, filling ¾ full. Sprinkle with Streusel Topping. Bake at 350° for 35–40 minutes or until toothpick comes out clean.

STREUSEL TOPPING:
2 tablespoons all-purpose flour
¼ cup sugar

½ teaspoon cinnamon
4 teaspoons butter

Combine dry ingredients; cut in butter until mixture is crumbly.

Apples, Apples, Apples (Missouri)

Apple facts:
• Fresh apples float because 25 percent of their volume is air. Makes for good Halloween apple bobbing!
• The average person eats 65 apples per year.
• Apple trees don't bear their first fruit until they are four or five years old.

Cinnamon Breakfast Squares

1 cup peeled, seeded, and
  shredded zucchini
¼ cup oil
1 teaspoon vanilla
1 egg
¼ cup brown sugar
¼ cup white sugar

1 cup all-purpose flour
1 teaspoon baking soda
½ teaspoon salt
½ teaspoon cinnamon
1 tablespoon grated orange rind
  (optional)
Butter or honey butter

Combine zucchini with oil and vanilla. Stir in unbeaten egg. Add sugars and blend. Sift dry ingredients together and add to mixture. Stir until well mixed (do not beat). Blend in orange peel. Spread into a greased 8x8-inch pan. Bake at 350° for 30 minutes. Cool 10 minutes. Cut into squares and break open like muffins; spread with butter (honey butter is best).

How to Enjoy Zucchini (Utah)

Blueberry Cream Cheese Fingers

1 cup butter, softened
1 (8-ounce) package cream
  cheese, softened
2 cups plus 1 tablespoon
  all-purpose flour, divided
3 tablespoons sugar, divided

1 cup fresh blueberries (or
  frozen unsweetened
  blueberries, thawed)
1 egg yolk, beaten
1 tablespoon water

In a mixer bowl, cream butter and cream cheese until well blended. Combine 2 cups flour and 2 tablespoons sugar; beat into butter mixture. Divide pastry in half and wrap in wax paper or clear plastic wrap; chill for 1–2 hours or until easy to handle.

In shallow plate, combine remaining flour and remaining sugar; roll blueberries in mixture. On a lightly floured surface, roll half the pastry into a 10x25-inch rectangle. Cut into 10 (5-inch) squares. On each square near one edge, arrange 8–10 coated blueberries in a row. Roll up pastry jellyroll style; pinch ends together. Place on an ungreased cookie sheet seam side down. Combine egg yolk and water; brush onto tops of pastries. Repeat with remaining dough. Bake pastries in a 350° oven for 20 minutes.

Alabama Blueberry Festival Recipes (Alabama)

Strawberry Cheesecake French Toast

1 cup ricotta cheese
3 tablespoons powdered sugar
1 tablespoon vanilla extract
16 (⅓-inch) slices French or
   Italian bread
2 large eggs

1 cup milk
1½ tablespoons butter
2 cups sliced strawberries
Strawberry syrup
Powdered sugar for garnish

Stir together ricotta cheese, powdered sugar, and vanilla until smooth. Spread 8 bread slices with mixture; top with remaining bread, like a sandwich. In bowl, beat eggs and milk. Add butter to frying pan over medium heat. Dip bread in egg mixture to saturate. Fry on each side until golden brown, about 5 minutes for each side. Place strawberry slices on top. Pour syrup over sandwich, and dust with powdered sugar. Makes 4–8 servings.

Recipe from Myrtledene Bed & Breakfast, Lebanon
Another Sunrise in Kentucky (Kentucky)

Stuffed French Toast with Strawberries

8 slices white or wheat bread,
   cut 1 inch thick
1 (8-ounce) package cream
   cheese, softened
6 tablespoons strawberry
   preserves
1⅓ cups milk

4 eggs
2 teaspoons sugar
2 teaspoons vanilla
1 teaspoon cinnamon
4 cups sliced strawberries
4 tablespoons powdered sugar

Cut each bread slice in half crosswise. With a sharp knife, cut a horizontal slit in each half slice to make a pocket. In a medium bowl, combine cream cheese and preserves. Spread ¹⁄₁₆ of the mixture inside each bread pocket. Pinch edges of bread together to hold filling. In a shallow bowl, whisk together milk, eggs, sugar, vanilla, and cinnamon. Dip filled bread slices in egg mixture to coat. Cook about 6 minutes or until golden brown, turning once. Top with strawberries and sprinkle with powdered sugar.

Pleasures from the Good Earth (Utah)

Apple Cinnamon French Toast

5 tablespoons butter
2 whole baking apples, peeled, cored, and sliced
1 cup firmly packed brown sugar
2 tablespoons corn syrup

1 teaspoon cinnamon
9 pieces French bread, sliced 1 inch thick
3 large eggs
1 cup milk
1 teaspoon vanilla extract

Day before serving: In skillet, melt butter at medium heat. Add apple slices and cook until tender. Add brown sugar, corn syrup, and cinnamon. Cook, stirring until brown sugar dissolves. Pour into greased 9x13-inch pan and spread evenly. Arrange bread in one layer on top of apples. Mix eggs, milk, and vanilla. Pour over bread. Cover and refrigerate overnight.

Bake at 375° for 30–35 minutes. Mixture should be firm and bread golden. Cool in pan for 5 minutes. Invert a tray over French toast and carefully turn both over to unmold so apple layer is on top. Spoon any remaining sauce and/or apples over French toast. Serve immediately topped with sweetened whipped cream. Makes 6 servings.

Recipe from Fox Hollow Bed & Breakfast, Bozeman, Montana
A Taste of Montana (Big Sky)

Huckleberry Waffles

1½ cups cake flour
¼ cup oat bran
2 teaspoons baking powder
1 tablespoon sugar

3 eggs, separated
¼ cup butter, melted
1½ cups milk
1½ cups huckleberries

Sift together flour, bran, baking powder, and sugar. Beat egg yolks; add butter and milk. Stir into dry ingredients until dry particles are just moistened. Beat egg whites stiff. Fold into batter along with huckleberries. Bake on preheated waffle iron. Serves 4.

The Rocky Mountain Wild Foods Cookbook (Idaho)

★★★★★★★★★★ ★★★★★★★★★★★

Baked Apple-Oatmeal

Wonderful!

2 cups milk	1 cup rolled oats
3 tablespoons brown sugar	1 cup diced, peeled apple
1 tablespoon butter	½ cup raisins
¼ teaspoon salt	Milk or cream
¼ teaspoon ground cinnamon	

In a saucepan combine milk, brown sugar, butter, salt, and cinnamon; heat just to boiling. Stir in the oats, apple, and raisins; heat until bubbles appear at the edge of the pan. Spoon into a buttered 1½-quart casserole and cover. Bake in a 350° oven for 30 minutes. Cover loosely with foil and keep warm in a low oven until ready to serve. Serve hot with milk or cream. Makes 4 servings.

From the High Country of Wyoming (Big Sky)

Baked Mushroom Delight

½ pound fresh mushrooms, sliced	3 cups (12 ounces) shredded Monterey Jack cheese
2 tablespoons butter or margarine	8 eggs, beaten
8 strips bacon, fried crisp, drained, and crumbled	Salt and pepper to taste

Preheat oven to 275°. Sauté mushrooms in butter; place on bottom of a well-greased 8-inch square baking dish. Top with bacon and then the cheese. Combine eggs, salt and pepper; pour over layered ingredients. Bake 45 minutes or until top is golden brown. Do not overcook. Serves 6–8.

To Prepare in Advance: Assemble up to the point of pouring the egg mixture over the layered ingredients. This "Delight" can also be frozen after baking and reheated.

Becky's Brunch & Breakfast Book (Texas)

Milwaukee Breakfast

1 small potato
2 eggs
1 small tomato, diced
1 small piece green bell pepper,
  diced

1 small piece onion, diced
2 button mushrooms, diced
1–2 pats butter

Cook potato in microwave on HIGH for 3–4 minutes, until you can get a fork in easily. Peel and dice potato into ¼-inch pieces. Beat eggs until smooth. Combine all ingredients and add to beaten eggs. Cook on HIGH for one minute, then stir and cook for one more minute; stir again. If eggs are a little wet, let sit for about 10 seconds and then stir again. Do not overcook unless you like it dry.

Taste and See (Wisconsin)

Brunch Strata

3 cups sliced fresh mushrooms
3 cups chopped zucchini
2 cups cubed fully cooked ham
1½ cups chopped onions
1½ cups chopped green bell
  peppers
2 garlic cloves, minced
⅛ cup vegetable oil
2 (8-ounce) packages cream
  cheese, softened

½ cup half-and-half
12 eggs
4 cups cubed day-old bread
3 cups shredded Cheddar
  cheese
1 teaspoon salt
½ teaspoon pepper

In a large skillet, sauté first 6 ingredients in oil until vegetables are tender. Drain and pat dry; set aside. In a large mixing bowl, beat cream cheese and half-and-half until smooth. Beat in eggs. Stir in bread, cheese, salt, pepper, and vegetable mixture. Pour into 2 greased 7x11-inch baking dishes. Bake uncovered at 350° for 35–40 minutes or until a knife inserted near center comes out clean. Let stand 10 minutes before serving. Makes 16 servings.

Asthma Walk Cook Book (Ohio)

Sausage Ring

1 pound bulk sausage, hot
1 pound bulk sausage, mild
1 large onion, chopped

2 apples, peeled and chopped
1 cup crushed cornflakes

Mix all ingredients together and pack into 1½-quart ring mold. Place mold on cookie sheet and bake (350°) for 20 minutes. Drain grease off mold and bake another 20–30 minutes or until done. Fill center with scrambled eggs. Serves 10–12.

Heavenly Hostess (Alabama)

Blue Knoll Cheesy Apple Egg Bake

2 cups sliced peeled Granny
  Smith apples
2 tablespoons cinnamon-sugar
6 slices crisp-cooked bacon,
  crumbled

2 cups shredded Cheddar
  cheese
2 cups milk
6 eggs
2 cups baking mix

Layer apples, cinnamon-sugar, bacon, and cheese in order listed in a 9x13-inch baking dish sprayed with nonstick cooking spray. Whisk milk and eggs in a bowl until blended. Add baking mix and stir until smooth. Pour egg mixture over prepared layers. Bake at 375° for 40 minutes or until set. Serve with warm maple syrup. Yields 8 servings.

Recipe from Blue Knoll Farm Bed & Breakfast, Castleton
Vintage Virginia (Virginia II)

Editors' Extra: To make your own cinnamon-sugar, combine ½ cup sugar with 1½ tablespoons cinnamon. Store in a clean spice jar with a shaker top.

Contrary to popular belief, there is no mention in the Bible of the apple being the forbidden fruit that was eaten by Adam and Eve in the Garden of Eden. The fruit is referred to as "fruit of the Tree of Knowledge of Good and Evil," with no specification as to which kind of fruit. The apple was first implicated as the forbidden fruit in Hugo van der Goes' 1470 painting, *The Fall of Man*. After that, it continued to be known and depicted as the forbidden fruit.

★★★★★★★★★★★ ★★★★★★★★★★★

Breakfast in the Skillet

6 bacon slices
2 tomatoes, diced
½ cup grated cheese
6 eggs, beaten

1 tablespoon snipped chives
1 tablespoon snipped parsley
1 tablespoon Worcestershire
Salt and pepper to taste

In large skillet, cook bacon until crisp, then drain on paper towels. Add tomatoes to bacon fat; sauté 3 minutes. With a wooden spoon, blend in grated cheese, then pour eggs into skillet. Cook mixture over low heat, lifting it occasionally from bottom of skillet with pancake turner, until eggs are set but still very soft. Break bacon into small pieces and add to eggs along with chives, parsley, Worcestershire, and salt and pepper. Toss lightly. Makes 2 generous servings.

Mackay Heritage Cookbook (Idaho)

Easy Broccoli Quiche

2 cups finely chopped
  broccoli
⅓ cup chopped onion
1 cup chopped ham
1 cup shredded Cheddar
  cheese

½ cup biscuit mix
3 eggs
1 cup milk
¼ teaspoon salt
¼ teaspoon pepper

Cook broccoli and onion covered in a small amount of boiling water 10 minutes; drain. Place in lightly greased 9-inch pie plate; sprinkle with ham and cheese. Combine remaining ingredients in blender or mixing bowl. Blend or mix until smooth. Pour over broccoli mixture; bake at 375° for 25–30 minutes or until set. Let stand 5 minutes before serving.

Feeding the Flock / First Baptist Church, Boiling Spring Lake
(North Carolina)

Apple Raisin Quiche

A favorite bed and breakfast recipe.

Pastry for 9-inch pie (1-crust)
3¾ cups peeled, cored,
  and thinly sliced Granny
  Smith apples (about
  3 medium)
½ cup raisins
¼ cup packed light brown
  sugar

2 teaspoons cinnamon
3 cups (12 ounces) shredded
  Monterey Jack cheese
3 eggs
1 cup whipping cream

Preheat oven to 400°. Line 9-inch pie plate with pastry. Crimp edge and prick bottom and sides with fork at ½-inch intervals. To prevent shrinkage, bake only 6 minutes with pie shell covered snugly with aluminum foil. Remove foil and bake about 10 minutes until shell is lightly browned. Layer ½ the apples, raisins, sugar, and cinnamon in pie shell; repeat layers. Cover completely with cheese.

Beat eggs with cream. Make a small hole in cheese; pour egg mixture into cheese. Cover hole with cheese. Bake about an hour, until top is browned and apples are tender when tested with pick. Cool 10–15 minutes before cutting into wedges. Serve with sausage or Canadian bacon.

A Taste of Twin Pines (Indiana)

Spinach Scrambled with Eggs

3 pounds fresh spinach,
  washed
2 cups salted water

1 tablespoon butter
Black pepper to taste
2 eggs, beaten

Cook spinach in salted water just until tender. Remove from stove and pour out as much liquor as possible. Chop spinach. Lightly brown 1 tablespoon butter in skillet, then add spinach. Sprinkle with black pepper and cook until there is no remaining juice. Add eggs and scramble until eggs are done. Serves 6.

Queen Anne's Table (North Carolina)

★★★★★★★★★★★★ ★★★★★★★★★★★★

Asparagus Cheese Omelet

6 fresh asparagus spears
6 eggs
2 tablespoons cold water
Salt and pepper to taste

⅓ cup grated sharp Cheddar
  cheese
2 tablespoons olive oil

Clean and steam asparagus until tender; drain. Beat together eggs, water, salt, and pepper until frothy. Pour egg mixture on a hot oiled griddle; lower heat. Place asparagus spears on half of omelet. Sprinkle with cheese and fold other half over filling. Cook about 5 minutes or until eggs are done and lightly brown. Lift onto serving plate with wide turner. Serves 2–3.

A Court and Willow Restaurant recipe
The Bloomin' Cookbook (Pennsylvania)

Ham and Potato Omelet

¼ cup butter or margarine
2 cups diced, uncooked potatoes
¼ cup chopped onion
1 cup diced ham
6 eggs
1 tablespoon dried parsley
  flakes

½ teaspoon salt
Dash of pepper
2 tablespoons water
½ cup shredded Cheddar
  cheese

Melt butter in 9- or 10-inch nonstick frying pan. Add potatoes and onion; cover and cook over medium-high heat, stirring occasionally to brown evenly, for about 20 minutes or until potatoes are tender and golden. Add ham and cook a few minutes longer until lightly browned. Reduce heat.

Beat together eggs, parsley flakes, salt, pepper, and water until well blended. Pour egg mixture over potatoes and ham. Cover and cook until eggs are almost set (about 10 minutes), slipping spatula around edge of pan occasionally to allow egg mixture to run down. Sprinkle with cheese and cover again until cheese melts. Cut in wedges to serve. Makes 4–6 servings.

Oregon: The Other Side (Oregon)

★★★★★★★★★★★ ★★★★★★★★★★★

Travis' Mexican Omelette

Chorizo or a spicy sausage
¼ cup sliced green onions
1 cup sliced fresh mushrooms
1 tomato, chopped
4 eggs, beaten
¼ cup milk

Salt and pepper to taste
1 cup shredded Cheddar
  cheese
Sour cream
Salsa

Sauté sausage, onions, mushrooms, and tomato. Add eggs, milk, salt and pepper, and scramble. Fold in the cheese. Serve topped with sour cream and salsa.

A Taste of Prairie Life (Great Plains)

Tennessee Tomato Gravy

Tomato gravy is a hill country favorite. This particular recipe adaptation comes from, and with my thanks to, Lynne Tolley and Pat Mitchamore, authors of "Jack Daniel's The Spirit of Tennessee Cookbook." The tomato gravy can be cooked after frying salt pork, bacon, pork chops, or ham.

2 tablespoons drippings
¼ cup finely chopped onion
2 tablespoons all-purpose flour
2 cups peeled, seeded, and
  chopped tomatoes

Chicken stock and water as
  required
½ teaspoon powdered thyme
1¼ teaspoons sugar
Salt and pepper to taste

In a frying pan containing around 2 tablespoons of drippings, sauté onion until tender. Mix in flour and cook several minutes. Add tomatoes; stir well. Water or chicken stock may be required here (to reach desired consistency), depending on the liquid available from the tomatoes. Season with thyme, sugar, salt and pepper. Cook over low heat, stirring occasionally, until gravy thickens. Yields 2 cups gravy.

Smokehouse Ham, Spoon Bread, & Scuppernong Wine (Tennessee)

Pepper Jelly

1 cup ground bell pepper
2 tablespoons ground hot
  peppers
1½ cups cider vinegar

6½ cups sugar
1 (6-ounce) bottle liquid
  fruit pectin
Green food coloring

Mix everything except fruit pectin in saucepan and bring to a boil. Let boil for 5 minutes, remove from heat and add fruit pectin, stirring until mixture starts to jell. Pour into sterile jelly jars and seal. (This is good spooned over a brick of cream cheese and served with ginger snaps.)

The Farmer's Daughters (Arkansas)

Apricot Pepper Jelly

¼ cup jalapeño peppers, with
  stems and seeds removed
3 cups thinly sliced bell peppers
  (assorted colors)
2 cups apple cider vinegar

1½ cups dried apricots, cut
  into thin strips
6 cups sugar
1 teaspoon vegetable oil
1 pouch liquid pectin (3 ounces)

Process jalapeño peppers in blender until fine. Combine bell peppers, vinegar, jalapeño peppers, dried apricots, and sugar in a large saucepan. Bring to a boil. Add oil to prevent foam from forming. Boil for 10 minutes. Remove from heat. Stir in pectin. Place in sterilized canning jars and process in boiling water bath for 10 minutes. Yields 6 half-pints.

Sounds Tasty! (California)

A relative of the peach, the apricot is smaller and has a smooth, oval pit that falls out easily when the fruit is halved.

Ice Box Peach Jam

2½ cups peaches (2 pounds   5 cups sugar
    or 7 large)   ¾ cup water
2 tablespoons lemon juice   1 box Sure-Jell fruit pectin

Peel peaches, chop or grind and mix with lemon juice. Add sugar.
Mix well and let stand 10 minutes. In small pan, mix water and
Sure Jell. Boil 1 minute stirring constantly. Add this to the fruit
mixture and continue stirring for 3 minutes. Ladle into screw-top
jars or plastic containers with snap lids. Makes 5 cups. Cover and
let stand at room temperature for 24 hours to set. Refrigerate.
Surplus can be frozen.

Seems Like I Done It This A-Way III (Oklahoma)

Heavenly Jam

5 cups finely cut rhubarb   1 (20-ounce) can crushed
5 cups sugar   pineapple
Juice of 1 lemon   2 boxes strawberry Jell-O

Boil rhubarb, sugar, lemon juice, and crushed pineapple. Remove
from heat and add to regular boxes of strawberry Jell-O. Stir until
dissolved. Pour into jars and seal with paraffin wax or freeze.

Home Cookin' Is a Family Affair (Oklahoma)

Most rhubarb is frozen for commercial and institutional use, most commonly for
medicinal purposes; of the crops grown in the United States, only about a quarter is
sold fresh. The stalks of rhubarb are the only parts used for cooking.

Pear Preserves

16 cups peeled, sliced pears
2 pounds (4 cups) sugar

Juice of 1 lemon
2 cups water

Place pears, sugar, and lemon juice in a large pot and add water. Cook over moderate heat until pears are tender and syrup is thick. Ladle preserves into hot, sterilized half pint jars and seal. Process for 5 minutes in boiling water bath, if desired. Makes 8–10 half pints.

Note: I like to add about 3 drops of red food coloring to the syrup because it makes the pears look more appetizing.

Aunt Freddie's Pantry (Mississippi)

Strawberry Fig Preserves

3 cups peeled mashed figs
3 cups sugar

2 (3-ounce) packages
strawberry Jell-O

Mix well in saucepan; cook for 10 minutes. Pour mixture into jars and seal.

Flatlanders Cook Book (Georgia)

The flower of the fig is inside the fruit, sort of like an inside out strawberry, so there are no blossoms on fig trees. Figs are rich in calcium, potassium, phosphorus, and iron.

Soups, Stews & Chilies

★★★★★★★ ★★★★★★★

© WILLIAM H. MULLINS OUTDOOR PHOTOGRAPHY

Idaho's higher elevations, ideal climate, and light, volcanic soil tend to produce superior potatoes. It is no surprise that Idaho is ranked first in potato production, with more than 30% of the nation's potatoes grown there. Washington ranks second.

Hot Apple Soup

4 Granny Smith apples
4 McIntosh apples
2½ cups water
2 tablespoons lemon juice
¼ teaspoon nutmeg

½ teaspoon cinnamon
1 cup light cream or
  half-and-half
Unsweetened whipped cream
  for garnish

Peel, core, and quarter apples. Combine all ingredients except creams in saucepan and bring to boil. Simmer 15 minutes till apples are soft. Purée; return to pan, add cream, and heat through, but don't boil. Garnish each serving with a dollop of whipped cream and sprinkle with cinnamon sugar. Serve with graham crackers. Serves 4.

Recipes from the Heart (Big Sky)

Chilled Peach Soup

Peach soup, a family favorite, adapts to any dining situation—poolside, picnic, with bread or muffins as a main course, or as a dessert, with pound cake and fresh blueberries or raspberries.

10 medium-size fresh peaches,
  peeled and pitted, or
  2 (1-pound) bags frozen
  peaches
1½ cups softened vanilla ice
  cream

½ cup half-and-half
¼ cup white wine
¼ teaspoon freshly ground
  nutmeg
½ cup sugar (approximately)

Pureé the peaches in food processor or blender. Add ice cream, half-and-half, wine, and nutmeg; blend until smooth. Add sugar to taste, and chill at least 2 hours before serving.

Outdoor Cooking (Arizona)

You can buy two main varieties of peaches: clingstone (the flesh sticks to the stone) and freestone (the stone is easily separated from the flesh).

Zesty Gazpacho

4 large ripe tomatoes, peeled
  and chopped
⅓ green bell pepper
⅓ cucumber, peeled
¼ onion, chopped
2 garlic cloves
3 tablespoons red wine vinegar
2 tablespoons olive oil

1 tablespoon salt
3 cups cubed French bread
  (crust removed), soaked in
  water
Garnish: minced onion, green
  bell pepper, cucumber, sour
  cream, black olives

In processor/blender purée tomatoes, green bell pepper, cucumber, onion, and garlic. Blend in vinegar, oil, salt, and bread crumbs in batches. Transfer to a bowl, thin it to desired consistency with ice water. Chill covered.

Garnish with minced onion, green bell pepper, cucumber, and a dollop of sour cream with black olive curls. Makes 6 cups and serves 4–6. Yum!

Ship to Shore II (North Carolina)

Yellow Tomato Gazpacho

Olive bread is a nice accompaniment.

1 pound yellow bell peppers
1½ pounds yellow tomatoes,
  peeled and seeded
1 pound cucumbers, peeled
  and seeded
½ cup chopped sweet onion,
  preferably Vidalia
2 medium garlic cloves,
  coarsely chopped
⅓ cup mayonnaise

2 tablespoons olive oil
2 tablespoons white wine
  vinegar
1½ slices white bread,
  crusts removed
1 teaspoon salt
⅓ teaspoon white pepper
3 dashes hot sauce
1 red tomato, finely chopped
  for garnish

Roast peppers over open flame until blackened; remove skin, interior ribs, and seeds. Put all the ingredients, except red tomato for garnish, in a food processor, and process until smooth.

Store soup in the refrigerator for several hours. If too thick, thin with a few ice cubes. Garnish with the red tomato.

A Traveler's Table (Georgia)

★★★★★★★★★★★★   ★★★★★★★★★★★★

Barbecued Bean Soup

2½ cups pinto beans
8 cups water
2 cups chopped carrots
1 cup chopped onion
1 meaty ham bone

1 (16-ounce) can tomatoes
¼ cup vinegar
2 tablespoons brown sugar
2 tablespoons Worcestershire
2 teaspoons prepared mustard

Wash and soak beans. Cook with water, carrots, onion, and ham bone for 2½ hours. Add the rest of ingredients and cook ½ hour more or till beans are tender. Remove ham bone; cut meat off of it and return meat to soup. Mash some of the beans in the blender to help thicken soup. Makes 8–10 servings.

Per serving: Calories 442.5; Prot. 24g; Sugars 10.6g; Fiber 24.37g; Sat. Fat 3.56g; Poly. Fat 1.1mg; Chol. 37.5mg; Sod. 384.37mg; Potas. 1177mg.

More Than Soup Bean Cookbook (Colorado)

Black Belt Butterbean Soup

2 cups shelled fresh butterbeans
2 tablespoons butter
2 tablespoons flour
1 cup scalded milk

2 cups chicken stock or chicken
  consommé
1 tablespoon onion juice
Salt and pepper to taste

Cook butterbeans in salted water until tender. Drain and put through colander. Melt butter in heavy skillet; stir in flour and add scalded milk, stirring constantly. Add stock or consommé and blend until smooth. Combine with prepared beans and add onion juice and seasonings. Heat and combine well. Sprinkle and serve with paprika. A pat of butter may also be added to each bowl of soup, if desired.

Treasured Alabama Recipes (Alabama)

Lentils & Carrot Soup

My husband Stephen and I could live on soup, especially in the cold winter months. This soup is not only delicious, but an immune system booster. I usually use vegetable broth instead of chicken broth. During cold and flu season, I use chicken broth. When served with a leafy green salad or Waldorf salad and crusty bread or cornbread, what more could you possibly want?

2 tablespoons olive oil
1 large yellow onion, chopped
2 large carrots, sliced
2 large garlic cloves, minced
1 cup dried lentils

2¼ cups chicken or vegetable
** broth**
1 teaspoon dried marjoram
Sea salt and pepper to taste

Heat oil in a heavy-bottomed pan over medium heat. Add onion, and sauté until soft. Add carrots and garlic; sauté 2 more minutes. Add lentils, then broth. Mix in marjoram, salt and pepper. Cover lentils and simmer until tender and broth is almost absorbed. Add water, if you prefer a soupier soup.

Recipe submitted by Barbara Popyach, Richmond
Kentucky Authors Cook (Kentucky)

Carrots are usually sold without their tops because the tops draw moisture from the roots. Many people buy carrots with tops to ensure the product is fresh, but that's not a good idea. For carrots to last longer, the tops should be removed.

★★★★★★★★★★★ ★★★★★★★★★★★

Mexican Corn Soup

4 cups fresh corn kernels
¼ cup chopped onion
2 tablespoons butter
2 tablespoons flour
Salt and pepper to taste
2 cups chicken broth

2 cups milk or cream
1 cup grated Cheddar cheese
1 (4-ounce) can green chiles,
  chopped (optional)
Tortilla chips
½ cup crumbled crisp bacon

Sauté corn and onion in butter until tender. Add flour, salt and pepper; cook 1 minute. Gradually add broth, alternating with milk or cream, until thickened. Add Cheddar cheese and green chiles; do not overheat. Serve soup in individual bowls, stirring in 4 or 5 tortilla chips; garnish with crumbled bacon.

Lone Star Legacy (Texas II)

Champagne, Oyster, and Corn Soup

5 ears of corn
30 oysters
¼ cup light olive oil
4 large shallots, peeled, minced
1 teaspoon minced garlic
1 potato, peeled, finely chopped

¾ cup champagne
4 cups chicken or fish stock
1 cup cream
Salt and pepper to taste
¼ cup chopped parsley

Shuck the corn; remove kernels from cobs with sharp knife. Shell oysters and drain, reserving the liquor. Combine olive oil and shallots in large sauté pan. Cook over medium-high heat until shallots are translucent. Add garlic and potato. Cook for 2 minutes, stirring constantly. Add the champagne. Cook for 1 minute. Stir in the corn, reserved oyster liquor, and chicken stock. Bring to a boil and cook for 7 minutes. Stir in cream and heat thoroughly. Add oysters. Cook until edges of oysters have curled. Season with salt and pepper. Stir in parsley and serve immediately. Yields 4–6 servings.

Recipe by Anne Rosensweig, chef/owner of Lobster Box, New York City
Champagne...Uncorked! The Insider's Guide to Champagne
(New York)

★★★★★★★★★★★ ★★★★★★★★★★★

Chicken Corn Soup

1 (3- to 4-pound) chicken
1 tablespoon salt
¼ teaspoon pepper
1½ cups chopped celery
1 medium onion, chopped
2 tablespoons chopped fresh
  parsley

4 cups whole-kernel corn
6 ounces medium noodles,
  cooked, drained
Chopped fresh parsley for
  garnish
Chopped hard-cooked egg for
  garnish

Place chicken in a large stockpot. Season with salt and pepper. Add enough water to cover. Cook until chicken is tender and falls from bones. Remove chicken from stockpot, reserving broth. Cut chicken into small pieces, discarding skin and bones. Bring reserved broth to a boil. Add celery, onion, 2 tablespoons parsley, and corn. Cook 15 minutes or until tender. Add chicken and noodles. Cook until heated through. Ladle into soup bowls. Sprinkle with chopped fresh parsley and hard-cooked egg. Yields 6–8 servings.

The Bounty of Chester County Heritage Edition (Pennsylvania)

Chicken-Noodle Soup

1 (3-pound) chicken, cut up
1 tablespoon salt
Water to cover
1½ cups chopped celery
  with leaves

1 cup sliced carrots
½ cup chopped onion
½ teaspoon poultry seasoning
2 cups uncooked noodles

Simmer chicken in salted water in covered saucepan until tender. (A frying chicken will take 45 minutes.) Remove chicken from broth; cool enough to handle. Remove skin and bones; chop meat. Skim most fat from broth; measure broth. Add water, if needed, to make 5 cups; bring to a boil. Add chicken, vegetables, and poultry seasoning. Simmer, covered, 20 minutes. Add noodles; simmer, uncovered, 10 minutes or until noodles are tender. Yields 6 servings.

Cookin' & Quiltin' (Tennessee)

Cheeseburger Soup

½ pound ground beef
¾ cup chopped onion
¾ cup shredded carrots
¾ cup diced celery
1 teaspoon dried basil
1 teaspoon dried parsley
　flakes
4 tablespoons butter or
　margarine, divided

3 cups chicken broth
4 cups diced peeled potatoes
½ cup all-purpose flour
1 (8-ounce) block Velveeta
　cheese, cubed
1½ cups milk
¾ teaspoon salt
¼–½ teaspoon pepper
¼ cup sour cream

In a 3-quart saucepan, brown beef; drain and set aside. In same saucepan, sauté onion, carrots, celery, basil, and parsley in 1 tablespoon butter until vegetables are tender, about 10 minutes. Add broth, potatoes, and beef; bring to a boil. Reduce heat; cover and simmer 10–12 minutes or until potatoes are tender.

　Meanwhile, in a small skillet, melt remaining butter. Add flour; cook and stir 3–5 minutes or until bubbly. Add to soup; bring to a boil. Cook and stir 2 minutes. Reduce heat to low. Add cheese, milk, salt, and pepper; cook and stir until cheese melts. Remove from heat; blend in sour cream. Yields 8 servings.

Feeding the Flock (Shiloh Baptist Church) (North Carolina)

Tennessee Cheddar Soup

1 cup finely chopped onion
1 cup finely chopped carrots
1 cup finely chopped celery
½ cup margarine
1 cup all-purpose flour
1 quart chicken stock or
　bouillon

3 cups grated Cheddar cheese
1 quart milk
1 teaspoon salt
½ teaspoon white pepper

Sauté vegetables in margarine until soft. Add flour and mix until smooth. Add chicken stock. Bring to a boil; reduce heat and simmer 15 minutes. Add cheese; cook 10 minutes longer. Add milk, salt, and pepper. Heat to serving temperature. Makes 2 quarts, approximately 12 servings.

Dining with Pioneers Volume II (Tennessee)

Ham and Vegetable Soup

¼ cup butter
2 cups shredded cabbage
1 onion, chopped
¼ cup all-purpose flour
1 teaspoon salt
½ teaspoon paprika
½ teaspoon dry mustard
⅛ teaspoon black pepper

1 (15-ounce) can chicken broth
2½ cups milk
2 cups chopped cauliflower,
  cooked
1 cup chopped broccoli, cooked
1 cup thinly sliced carrots,
  cooked
1½ cups diced ham

Melt butter in a 3-quart saucepan. Add cabbage and onion; sauté until tender. Stir in flour and seasonings. Blend until smooth. Gradually stir in chicken broth and milk. Bring to a boil, stirring constantly. Add the cooked vegetables to the soup. Add ham. Heat thoroughly. This recipe freezes well.

Blessed Be the Cook (Wisconsin)

Fresh Cabbage Soup

5 slices bacon, diced
1 pound cabbage, chopped
2 carrots, diced
2 potatoes, diced
1 stalk celery, sliced

1½ quarts water
2 tablespoons flour
2 tablespoons butter or
  margarine, softened
Salt and pepper to taste

Fry bacon until golden in large saucepan; drain fat. Add vegetables and water; bring to boil, then simmer 20 minutes or until vegetables are tender. Blend flour into butter until smooth; stir into soup. Bring soup to boil, stirring well. Shut off heat, add seasoning, stir, and serve.

Historically Delicious (Michigan)

Dilled Tomato Soup

2 medium onions, chopped
1 garlic clove, chopped
2 tablespoons margarine
4 large fresh tomatoes,
    peeled and cubed
½ cup water

1 chicken bouillon cube
2½ teaspoons fresh dill,
    or ¾ teaspoon dry dill
¼ teaspoon salt
⅛ teaspoon pepper
½ cup mayonnaise

In a 2-quart saucepan over medium heat, sauté onions and garlic in margarine for 3 minutes. Add the next 6 ingredients; cover and simmer for 10 minutes. Remove from heat and cool. Blend half in blender. Mix the second half with mayonnaise. Combine both mixtures. Cover and chill overnight. Soup is good served hot or cold. Makes 5 cups. Garnish with additional dill.

Still Gathering (Illinois)

Cream of Turnip Soup

6 cups quartered turnips
1 teaspoon sugar
1 teaspoon salt
3 cups water
2 tablespoons butter

1 tablespoon chicken bouillon
    granules
2 tablespoons cream of wheat
2 cups evaporated milk
Buttered croutons

Peel and quarter turnips. Combine turnips, sugar, salt, and water in medium saucepan. Cover and simmer until tender, about 15 minutes. Add butter. Pour into blender. Purée. Return to saucepan. Add chicken bouillon and cream of wheat. Stir. Simmer, stirring, for 5 minutes until mixture is thickened. Add milk. Heat, but do not boil. Taste for seasoning.

Garnish each serving with buttered croutons. Makes 6–8 servings.

Elsah Landing Heartland Cooking (Illinois)

Turnips are the original jack-o'-lantern, actually used in Ireland as lanterns. However, Irishmen migrating to America soon learned that turnips were not nearly as plentiful as were pumpkins, so they quickly adopted the pumpkin as the top choice for their jack-o'-lantern.

★★★★★★★★★★★ ★★★★★★★★★★★

Onion Wine Soup

¼ cup butter
5 large onions, chopped
5 cups beef broth
½ cup celery leaves
1 large potato, sliced
1 cup dry white wine

1 tablespoon vinegar
2 teaspoons sugar
1 cup light cream
1 tablespoon minced parsley
Salt and pepper to taste

Melt butter in large saucepan. Add chopped onions; mix well. Add beef broth, celery, and potato. Bring to a boil, cover, and simmer 30 minutes. Purée mixture in blender. Return to saucepan; blend in wine, vinegar, and sugar. Bring to a boil; simmer 5 minutes. Stir in cream, parsley, and salt and pepper to taste. Heat thoroughly, but do not boil. Yields 6–8 servings. (Takes 20 minutes to prepare; 30 minutes to cook.)

Recipe by Nancy Reagan
Philadelphia Main Line Classics (Pennsylvania)

Gourmet Cream of Zucchini Soup

3 cups sliced onions
3 tablespoons margarine
4 medium zucchini, sliced
4 garlic cloves, minced

1 cup chopped parsley
5 teaspoons chicken bouillon
6–8 cups water
Dash of pepper

In a large kettle, sauté onions in margarine till transparent. Add rest of ingredients. Cook until tender; cool; run through blender. Terrific with homemade cubed bread, fried in margarine until crusty.

Note: Can add more chicken bouillon to suit your taste.

Oma's (Grandma's) Family Secrets (Iowa)

Cream of Broccoli Soup

1 small head broccoli	¼ cup all-purpose flour
1 medium onion	2 teaspoons salt
½ teaspoon thyme	½ teaspoon pepper
1 quart chicken broth	4 cups milk
4 tablespoons butter	1 cup shredded Cheddar cheese

Cook together broccoli, onion, thyme, and chicken broth until tender. In other pan, melt butter; stir in flour, salt, and pepper. Add milk and cook until bubbly. Mix with broccoli. Stir in cheese until melted.

Unbearably Good! Sharing Our Best (Wisconsin)

Broccoli-Cauliflower Soup

3 chicken bouillon cubes	1 bunch broccoli, florets only
3 cups water	3 cups milk
3–4 carrots, diced	⅓ cup butter, melted
3–4 stalks celery, diced	⅓ cup all-purpose flour
1 green bell pepper, diced	2–3 cups cubed Velveeta cheese
1 head cauliflower, florets only	

Dissolve bouillon cubes in water. Cook all vegetables in this broth until tender. Add milk. Cream butter and flour until smooth. Add to mixture, stirring to keep smooth. Turn heat to low. Add Velveeta cheese; heat until cheese melts, stirring to prevent sticking.

Kitchen Keepsakes (Minnesota)

Broccoli is a member of the cabbage family, and a close relative of cauliflower. The average person in the United States consumes four and one-half pounds of broccoli per year.

Squash Bisque

This soup is delicious cold, too!

2 medium onions, chopped
2 tablespoons butter
1 quart chicken broth
4 cups sliced squash
¾ cup sliced carrots
2 medium potatoes, diced

1 teaspoon salt
1 teaspoon thyme
2–4 teaspoons Worcestershire
1 (16-ounce) carton
  half-and-half

In a large saucepan, sauté onions in butter. Add chicken broth, squash, carrots, potatoes, salt, and thyme, and cook only until vegetables are tender. Cool. Purée in food processor. Return to saucepan and add Worcestershire and half-and-half. Heat on low and serve. (High heat will make the soup curdle.) Makes 2 quarts.

Celebrations on the Bayou (Louisiana II)

Red Pepper Bisque

8 red bell peppers
2 yellow onions, chopped
¼ cup butter (½ stick)
2 teaspoons minced garlic
½ cup minced basil leaves

6 cups rich chicken stock,
  divided
2 cups heavy cream
Salt and pepper to taste

Seed red bell peppers and cut into 1-inch pieces. Cook peppers and onions in butter in a large skillet or saucepan over medium heat until onions are translucent, stirring frequently. Add garlic, basil, and 2 cups chicken stock. Simmer about 10 minutes or until red bell peppers are tender, stirring occasionally. Process mixture in batches in blender or food processor until smooth. Strain into a soup pot and blend in remaining chicken stock. Simmer 10–15 minutes or until slightly thickened, stirring occasionally. Blend in heavy cream gradually. Add salt and pepper. Heat to serving temperature; do not boil. Ladle into soup bowls. Yields 2½ quarts.

Celebrations (Alabama)

Onion Bisque

Our most requested soup, Murphin Ridge's Onion Bisque was awarded "Best Soup" by Cincinnati *magazine. On top of that, it's easy to make. Feel free to substitute vegetable stock or even water for the unsalted chicken stock.*

**6 onions, or 1 sweet or Vidalia
   onion per person, sliced
½ cup butter
2 tablespoons sugar
Unsalted chicken stock to cover
   (at least 4 cups)**

**½ cup heavy cream
1½ cups grated Parmesan
   cheese
Bowl-sized croutons, toasted
   with butter and sprinkled
   with Parmesan cheese**

In a large saucepan, sauté onions in butter until they become limp; sprinkle onions with sugar while they sauté. Cover onions with stock and cook slowly, 30–45 minutes, watching to see that the stock does not boil away. Turn off heat, and taste soup for seasoning. Purée soup in batches in food processor, or blend soup in saucepan with an immersion blender. Leave some small bits of onion for texture. Return soup to saucepan. Add cream and cheese and heat soup through slowly. Serve with croutons on side. Yields 8–10 servings.

A Taste of the Murphin Ridge Inn (Ohio)

According to an old English rhyme, the thickness of an onion skin can help predict the severity of the winter. Thin skins mean a mild winter is coming, while thick skins indicate a rough winter ahead.

★★★★★★★★★★★   ★★★★★★★★★★★

Southern Corn Chowder
(Microwave)

½ cup chopped salt pork
  (may substitute 4 slices bacon)
1 medium onion, chopped
½ cup sliced celery
½ cup diced green bell pepper
¼ cup all-purpose flour
2 cups milk

2 potatoes, microwaved and
  diced
1 teaspoon salt
1 bay leaf
½ cup light cream
2–3 cups fresh corn, cut
  from cob

Microwave salt pork 2–3 minutes on HIGH. Add onion, celery, and bell pepper. Microwave 2–3 minutes. Mix flour with small amount of the milk and add to above mixture along with the diced potatoes. Add remaining milk, salt, and bay leaf, and heat on HIGH until thickened. Add cream and corn. Microwave again on HIGH 4–6 minutes.

Simply Scrumptious Microwaving (Georgia)

Oregon Coast Clam Chowder

4 slices bacon, diced
1 tablespoon pan drippings
1½ cups chopped onions
¼ cup all-purpose flour
¼ cup grated carrot
¼ cup chopped celery
3 cups peeled, diced potatoes

1 teaspoon salt
⅛ teaspoon pepper
2 (8-ounce) cans chopped
  clams, drained (reserve
  liquid)
1 cup evaporated milk

In large saucepan, cook diced bacon until lightly browned; drain, reserving 1 tablespoon. In reserved drippings, sauté onions until translucent. Stir in flour; add bacon, carrot, celery, potatoes, and seasonings. To reserved clam liquid, add enough water to make 3 cups. Stir into vegetable mixture; bring to a boil. Reduce heat and boil gently, uncovered, 20 minutes, stirring occasionally. Add clams; cook 5 minutes longer. Stir in milk; reheat. Makes 7½ cups.

Oregon Cook Book (Oregon)

Shrimp and Sausage Gumbo

1 cup canola oil
2½ cups all-purpose flour
½ pound andouille sausage,
  or ½ pound smoked sausage
2 red bell peppers, diced small
2 green bell peppers, diced
  small
2 Vidalia onions, diced small
4 ribs celery, diced small
¼ cup minced garlic

½ pound okra, sliced
4 tomatoes, peeled, chopped
2 quarts chicken or clam stock*
¼ cup gumbo filé
Salt and pepper to taste
2 bay leaves
1 tablespoon chopped fresh
  thyme
1 pound shrimp, peeled,
  deveined

In large Dutch oven, heat oil until very hot. Carefully add flour, and stir with a wooden spoon almost constantly, until it is nutty smelling and the color of light brown sugar. Add sausage and vegetables, except tomatoes, and stir to cook. Add remaining ingredients, except shrimp. Stir occasionally and simmer 20 minutes. Add shrimp, and adjust seasoning and consistency with more stock, if needed. Yields 2 quarts.

*May substitute canned broth, bouillon, or water for stock.

Recipe by Chef Chip Ulbrecht, The Beaufort Inn
Soups, Stews, Gumbos, Chilis, Chowders, and Bisques
(South Carolina)

Originating in Africa, the okra plant is cultivated in tropical, subtropical, and warm temperate regions around the world. Known as "ladies' fingers" in most English-speaking countries outside of the United States, okra is grown mostly in the hot southern states. Best known as an important ingredient in the famous southern gumbos, okra is also delicious sautéed, parboiled, fried, or even pickled. If possible, choose pods under three inches long, as they are more likely to be tender.

★★★★★★★★★★★ ★★★★★★★★★★★

Dead Heat Kentucky Burgoo

1 fat hen, at least 4 pounds
1–2 pounds lean stew meat
  (beef, veal, and/or lamb)
3–4 pints water
1½ teaspoons coarsely
  ground pepper
½ teaspoon cayenne pepper
2 (15-ounce) cans tomato
  purée
12 potatoes, peeled and cut
  in chunks
4 large onions, chopped

1 large head cabbage, finely
  chopped
6–8 medium tomatoes, peeled
  and chopped, or 3 (1-pound)
  cans tomatoes
6–8 ears corn, cut off cob, or 2
  (15-ounce) cans whole-kernel
  corn
1 pound fresh carrots, sliced
1–2 tablespoons salt
1 teaspoon pepper
½–1 cup Worcestershire

Cook chicken and other meat in water with coarsely ground pepper and cayenne pepper until chicken will leave the bones and meat is very tender, about 40 minutes. Remove bones, shred meat, and return to liquid. Add tomato purée, potatoes, onions, cabbage, tomatoes, corn, and carrots. Season with salt, pepper, and Worcestershire. Cook slowly 2–3 hours, until consistency of a thick stew, stirring from the bottom to keep from scorching. Add water, if necessary, to keep from sticking. If you like additional vegetables, add 2 cups fresh butterbeans, 2 cups sliced fresh okra, and/or 2 green bell peppers, finely chopped. Serves 10. Serve with Petite Syrah, a Zinfandel, a Rhône red, or a Chianti.

The Kentucky Derby Museum Cook Book (Kentucky)

Eating five servings of fruits and vegetables each day is a good way to stay healthy and strong.

Four-Hour Stew

1 pound beef stew meat
1 package Lipton Onion
  Soup Mix
1 (10¾-ounce) can tomato soup
1 (10¾-ounce) can cream of
  mushroom soup

2 cans water
6 carrots
4 large potatoes
3 stalks celery
½ cup frozen English peas

In large Dutch oven, put stew meat, onion soup mix, tomato soup, cream of mushroom soup, and water. In 350° oven, bake without lid for 2 hours. Then add vegetables (your choice—vegetables can vary with taste; use your imagination), stirring, and bake with lid on for 2 more hours (4-hour stew). No salt and pepper, no thickening for gravy. Very easy, very good!

Country Lady Nibbling and Scribbling (Iowa)

Edisto Stew

2 (12-ounce) cans beer
6–8 ears corn
2 teaspoons crab boil seasoning
1 teaspoon chili powder

1 teaspoon black pepper
1 teaspoon Tabasco
1 pound link sausage, sliced
1 pound shrimp, unpeeled

Bring beer and enough water to cover corn to a boil; add corn and seasonings. Let simmer 5 minutes, then add sausage and simmer 5 minutes. Add shrimp and cook until pink. Drain and spread on newspaper. Dive in; pretend you're on the island.

Recipes & Memories (South Carolina)

★★★★★★★★★★★★   ★★★★★★★★★★★★

Creamy Shrimp and Spinach Stew

8 ounces fresh or frozen shrimp,
  peeled, deveined
1 cup sliced fresh mushrooms
1 medium onion, chopped
  (½ cup)
1 garlic clove, minced
2 tablespoons margarine or
  butter
3 tablespoons all-purpose flour
1 bay leaf

⅛ teaspoon ground nutmeg
⅛ teaspoon pepper
1 (14½-ounce) can vegetable
  broth
1 cup half-and-half, light
  cream, or milk
2 cups torn fresh spinach
¾ cup shredded Gruyère
  cheese (3 ounces)

Thaw shrimp, if frozen; rinse and set aside. In medium saucepan,
cook mushrooms, onion, and garlic in margarine or butter until tender. Stir in flour, bay leaf, nutmeg, and pepper. Add vegetable
broth and half-and-half, light cream, or milk all at once. Cook and
stir until mixture is thickened and bubbly. Add shrimp. Cook for
2 minutes more. Add spinach and Gruyère cheese. Cook and stir
until spinach wilts and cheese melts. Remove and discard bay leaf.
Makes 4 servings.

Recipes from the Children's Museum at Saratoga (New York)

Did you know…
• that spinach became the third most popular children's food, after turkey and ice
  cream, when cartoon character Popeye the Sailor Man made his debut on January
  17, 1929? He was portrayed as having a strong affinity for spinach, becoming
  physically stronger after consuming it.
• that spinach grows quickly? It can be harvested and eaten after only 37 to 45 days!
• that when cooked, spinach will shrink in size by 90%?

★★★★★★★★★★★ ★★★★★★★★★★★

Turkey Chili

3 pounds ground turkey
2 onions, diced
8 tomatoes, diced
1 (8-ounce) can tomato sauce
1 (10-ounce) can Rotel tomatoes
2 cups canned kidney beans
2 tablespoons minced garlic
8 ounces fresh mushrooms, diced
Splash of Tabasco and Worcestershire

1 package taco seasoning
1 red bell pepper, diced
1 (16-ounce) can Budweiser beer
1–2 tablespoons chili powder
2½ ounces shredded Lite Line Cheddar cheese (approximately 1 tablespoon for each serving)

Brown ground turkey and onions in large pan. Add remaining ingredients (except cheese) to browned mixture. Cook for approximately 2 hours over low heat. Stir every 15–20 minutes. When ready to serve, sprinkle shredded cheese on top. Serves 20.

Note: Chili always tastes better after being refrigerated for 24–36 hours. Let those flavors mingle!

Amount per serving: Calories 133; Grams of fat 1.72; Cholesterol 41.4mg; Sodium 232mg; % of Fat 12%.

Eat To Your Heart's Content! (Arkansas)

Tomatoes are a natural source of the antioxidant "lycopene," which may help prevent heart disease. According to scientists, more lycopene is absorbed by the body from cooked tomatoes than from fresh tomatoes.

★★★★★★★ ★★★★★★★

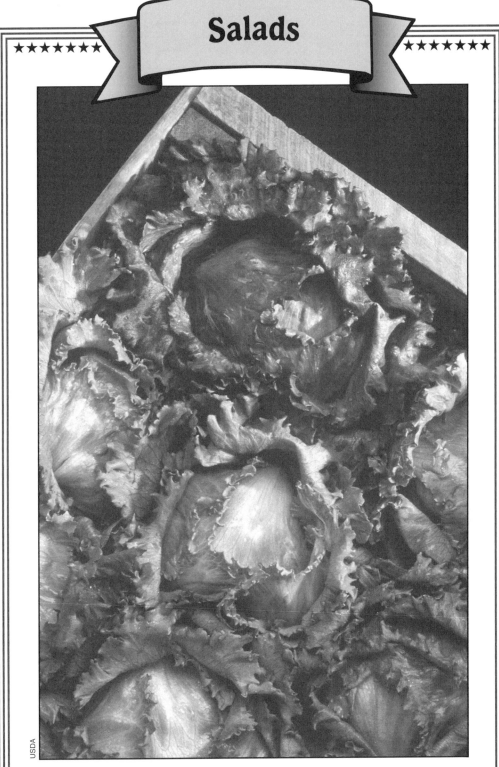

USDA

Lettuce is a vegetable that is pretty much immune to any form of preservation. You can't freeze it, can it, dry it, or pickle it. Darker green lettuce leaves are more nutritious than lighter green leaves.

Romaine, Grapefruit, and Avocado Salad

2 heads romaine lettuce,
  torn into bite-size pieces
2 avocados, sliced

¼ cup sliced ripe olives
2 cups fresh grapefruit
  sections

Combine romaine, avocados, olives, and grapefruit in a large bowl. Add Red Wine Vinaigrette, tossing to coat. Serve immediately. Serves 8–10.

RED WINE VINAIGRETTE:

½ cup olive oil
¼ cup red wine vinegar
¼ cup sugar
½ teaspoon salt

½ teaspoon celery seeds
½ teaspoon dry mustard
½ red onion, grated

Whisk together all ingredients.

Blackened Mountain Seasonings (North Carolina)

Mardi Gras Salad

This lively salad features the traditional Mardi Gras colors of purple for justice, green for faith, and gold for power.

1 head lettuce
1 cup sliced purple cabbage

1 cup sliced yellow bell pepper

Wash and dry lettuce. Tear into pieces. Place in large salad bowl. Sprinkle cabbage and bell pepper on top. Pour one cup Creole Mustard Salad Dressing over salad. Toss and serve. Serves 12.

CREOLE MUSTARD SALAD DRESSING:

2 tablespoons Creole Mustard
2 tablespoons vinegar (cane,
  red wine, or rice)

¾ cup oil

Blend mustard and vinegar. Slowly add oil; blend until smooth. Pour over salad.

The Cookin' Cajun Cooking School Cookbook (Louisiana II)

Almond Orange Garden Salad

Try this delicious dressing on all of your salad favorites.

SUNLIGHT SALAD DRESSING:

1 cup vegetable oil
¼ cup white wine vinegar
¼ cup sugar
1 teaspoon salt

1 teaspoon black pepper
3 teaspoons freshly chopped
parsley, or 1 teaspoon dried
parsley

Combine dressing ingredients in a jar, and shake until well mixed.

SALAD:

¼ cup sugar
1 cup sliced almonds
½ head iceberg lettuce
½ head romaine lettuce
6 green onions, chopped

1½ cups fresh oranges, peeled
and sectioned, or 2 (10-ounce)
cans Mandarin oranges,
drained

Add sugar to frying pan with almonds, and cook over medium heat, stirring and watching closely. When almonds are browned, pour them onto foil and let cool. Tear clean lettuce into bite-size pieces and place in a salad bowl. Add onions and oranges. Pour Sunlight Salad Dressing over salad to taste, and toss lightly. Top with almonds and serve. Yields 8 servings.

A Slice of Paradise (Florida)

Almonds are actually stone fruits related to cherries, plums, and peaches. The world's largest almond factory in Sacramento, California, processes two million pounds of almonds a day.

Feta Cheese, Apple & Spiced Pecan Salad

SPICED PECANS:

3 tablespoons unsalted butter
1 teaspoon salt
1 teaspoon cinnamon
¼ teaspoon cayenne pepper

Dash of hot pepper sauce
  (like Tabasco)
1⅔ cups pecans (6 ounces)

Melt butter; mix in seasonings. Pour butter mixture over pecans; toss. Spread on heavy cookie sheet. Bake until crisp, about 15 minutes at 300°. Cool completely.

2 tablespoons wine vinegar
1 tablespoon + 1 teaspoon
  Dijon mustard
½ cup olive oil
Salt and freshly ground
  pepper to taste
1 head red leaf lettuce, torn
  in pieces

1 head Boston lettuce (or ½
  Boston and ½ romaine),
  torn in pieces
1 red Delicious apple, finely
  chopped
½ pound feta cheese,
  crumbled

Mix vinegar and mustard in large bowl. Gradually whisk in oil. Season with salt and pepper. Add lettuce and toss to coat. Sprinkle apple, cheese, and Spiced Pecans over salad and serve. Serves 8.

A Taste of Twin Pines (Indiana)

Lettuce is the second most popular fresh vegetable in the United States behind potatoes. The average American eats approximately thirty pounds of lettuce each year, which is five times what was eaten in 1900.

Summer Sunrise Melon and Spinach Salad

The bright, sunrise orange of cantaloupe and leafy green of spinach make this salad beautiful, while bits of scallions and toasty sesame seeds make it delicious. Serve it in August, when melons are at their market peak. (Or substitute fresh strawberries earlier in the summer.)

1½ pounds fresh spinach	**1 teaspoon paprika**
2 tablespoons sesame seeds	**½ teaspoon Worcestershire**
⅓ cup red wine vinegar	**⅓ cup vegetable oil**
2 tablespoons minced green onion	**2–3 cups cantaloupe chunks (or hulled strawberries)**
1 tablespoon sugar	**Freshly ground black pepper**

Wash spinach. Tear into bite-size pieces, removing stems. Dry in a salad spinner or clean towel. Chill spinach. Toast sesame seeds in a small, dry skillet over medium heat until golden, about 3–4 minutes. Do not scorch.

Mix vinegar, green onion, sugar, paprika, and Worcestershire in a bowl; whisk in oil in a thin stream. Just before serving, toss spinach, sesame seeds, dressing and fruit in a large glass bowl. Pass the pepper mill. Makes 6–8 large servings.

Fresh Market Wisconsin (Wisconsin)

A cantaloupe is actually called a muskmelon. This familiar fruit with orange flesh and khaki-colored, netted skin provides the most beta-carotene in the entire melon family.

Christmas Salad Supreme

This beautiful salad draws rave reviews.

JAM VINAIGRETTE:

2 tablespoons raspberry or apple cider vinegar
⅓ cup vegetable oil

2 tablespoons raspberry or other fruit jam

Whisk all ingredients together. Place in small jar and refrigerate. Shake well before using.

SALAD:

¾ pound fresh spinach, torn
1 cup fresh or frozen raspberries, divided
10 fresh strawberries, halved

3 large kiwi, peeled and sliced thin, divided
¾ cup chopped pecans (or macadamia nuts)

About one hour before serving, combine spinach, ¾ of the berries, and 2 kiwi. Drizzle with Jam Vinaigrette. Toss and place in container with a tight lid. Chill, turning once. (If you use frozen berries, add them just before serving, or they will be too limp).

Just before serving, toss again with rest of berries and pecans, and garnish with last sliced kiwi.

Friends and Celebrities Cookbook II (Hawaii)

The difference between raspberries and blackberries is that raspberries have a hollow core in the middle while blackberries do not.

★ ★ ★ ★ ★ ★ ★ ★ ★ ★ ★   ★ ★ ★ ★ ★ ★ ★ ★ ★ ★ ★

Sunny Fruit Fiesta

1 cantaloupe, halved and
   seeded
½ honeydew melon, halved
   and seeded
¼ cup sugar
2 tablespoons fresh lemon
   juice

¼ cup fresh lime juice
1 tablespoon orange liqueur
   (optional)
1½ teaspoons grated lime peel
1 cup fresh strawberries
1 cup seedless grapes

Using a melon baller, scoop cantaloupe and honeydew into balls (reserve melon halves). In a large bowl, combine the sugar, lemon juice, lime juice, orange liqueur, and lime peel. Stir well to dissolve sugar. Add the cantaloupe and honeydew balls, strawberries, and grapes. Toss gently to combine. Cover bowl with plastic wrap and refrigerate for at least one hour to blend flavors; stir once or twice. Spoon into melon half. Serves 6.

What's Cookin' in Melon Country (Colorado)

Fresh Fruit Salad à la Watermelon

1¾ cups sugar
2½ cups water
½ cup fresh lemon juice
   (2–3 lemons)
1 teaspoon almond extract
2½ cups cubed watermelon
   (keep juice)

Fresh fruit, cut into bite-size
   pieces: strawberries,
   melon, pineapple, pears,
   peaches, kiwi, oranges, etc.
¼ cup fresh orange juice
   (one orange)
½ teaspoon Kirsch (optional)

Bring the sugar and water to a boil, and boil for 5 minutes. Set aside to cool. Add lemon juice, almond extract, watermelon cubes, and any watermelon juice. Put into blender and mix. Put in 2-quart ring mold, stir twice, and then freeze.

Unmold; fill center with other fresh fruit cut into bite-size pieces. Moisten salad with orange juice and Kirsch. Serves 8–10.

A Great Taste of Arkansas (Arkansas)

★★★★★★★★★★★   ★★★★★★★★★★★

Wedding Bell Pear Salads

1 (5-ounce) jar Old English
  cheese
1 (3-ounce) package cream
  cheese, softened
2 tablespoons finely chopped
  celery
1 tablespoon minced parsley

⅛ teaspoon tarragon
1 tablespoon minced green
  onion
12 Bartlett pear halves
Green onion for garnish
Salad greens

Cream together Old English and cream cheese, celery, parsley, tarragon, and minced green onion. Spread on cut sides of pear halves; place halves together in pairs to form whole pears. Garnish with piece of green onion to resemble stem. Chill. To serve, place pears upright on greens on a platter. Makes 6 salads.

What's New in Wedding Food (North Carolina)

Slice of the South Salad

2 (3-ounce) packages blackberry
  gelatin
2 cups blackberries

1 cup chopped pecans
  (optional)

Mix gelatin according to package directions (if berries are frozen, decrease cold water to ½ cup). Add berries and nuts to gelatin and let chill until set.

TOPPING:

1 (8-ounce) package cream
  cheese, softened
¼ cup cold milk
½ cup sugar

1 teaspoon vanilla
2 cups whipped topping
Pecans, chopped (optional)

Mix cream cheese with milk, sugar, and vanilla; fold mixture into whipped topping. Spread on gelatin and chill. Sprinkle pecans on top as a garnish. Yields 15 servings.

Upper Crust: A Slice of the South (Tennessee)

Green Bean Tossed Salad

Buck and Judy Lovett of Mountain Spring Farms in Myrtle Creek saw a need for a farmers' market in their area, so they started the Douglas County Farmers Market in 1994 in addition to their community supported agriculture (CSA) project based on their farm. For the ultimate salad, use young, tender green beans.

DRESSING:

2 garlic cloves, minced
½ cup chopped and packed
   fresh basil
2 tablespoons white wine vinegar

1 tablespoon grated Parmesan
   cheese
Salt and pepper to taste

Mix Dressing ingredients together and set aside.

SALAD:

1½ pounds fresh green beans,
   blanched
8 sun-dried tomatoes, sliced,
   with some of the oil

½ cup pine nuts, toasted (toast
   on cookie sheet at 300° for 5
   minutes)

Mix Salad ingredients and toss with Dressing. Serve on chilled plates.

                Oregon Farmers' Markets Cookbook and Guide (Oregon)

Marinated Zucchini and Mozzarella Cheese Salad

12 ounces mozzarella cheese
1 large tomato
1 medium zucchini
¼ cup oil
¼ cup white vinegar

1 garlic clove, chopped
1 tablespoon fresh basil (or
   ½ teaspoon dried)
¼ teaspoon salt
½ teaspoon sugar

Cut cheese into 6 slices. Place in 8-inch square dish. Cut tomato into 6 slices. Place tomato slices on top of cheese. Slice zucchini into ¼-inch slices. Arrange slices in dish. Combine remaining ingredients and shake. Pour over zucchini. Cover dish and refrigerate until ready to serve.

                Treasured Recipes from Mason, Ohio (Ohio)

★★★★★★★★★★★ ★★★★★★★★★★★

Asparagus Vinaigrette

Favorite warm weather vegetable dish. Perfect for patio lunch or supper and very pretty!

1 pound fresh asparagus
Bibb lettuce
3 slices cooked bacon, crumbled

1 hard-cooked egg, chopped fine

Boil or steam asparagus until done, but crisp (about 10 minutes). Cool and arrange on bed of Bibb lettuce. Sprinkle with bacon and egg. Just before serving, put Vinaigrette Dressing over all.

VINAIGRETTE DRESSING:
½ cup olive oil or Wesson oil
3 tablespoons vinegar
1 teaspoon salt
½ teaspoon freshly ground
** pepper**
Dash of cayenne pepper
¼ teaspoon paprika

1 tablespoon chopped pimento
1 tablespoon chopped
** cucumber pickle**
¾ tablespoon chopped green
** bell pepper**
½ teaspoon chopped parsley
½ tablespoon chopped olives

Combine oil, vinegar, salt, pepper, cayenne, and paprika. Heat thoroughly. Add chopped pimento, pickle, green bell pepper, parsley, and olives. Serves 4.

The Historic Roswell Cook Book (Georgia)

Asparagus grows very quickly; under ideal conditions, an asparagus spear can grow 10 inches in a 24-hour period! California grows more than 50,000 tons of asparagus each year, which is about 70% of all the asparagus grown in the United States.

★★★★★★★★★★★ ★★★★★★★★★★★

Cucumber and Onion Salad

6 cucumbers   6 large onions

Chill thoroughly, peel, and slice in alternate layers. Just before serving, mix with Dressing.

DRESSING:

½ cup vinegar   1 teaspoon salt
1 tablespoon butter   2 whole eggs
½ cup sugar   Whipped or sour cream
2 tablespoons flour

Heat vinegar and butter until hot. In top of double boiler, mix well the sugar, flour, salt, and eggs. Add heated vinegar and cook over boiling water until thick. When cool, add whipped cream in equal quantity, using either sweet or sour cream, and mix well.

Inverness Cook Book (Mississippi)

Cucumber Salad

1 large cucumber   1 teaspoon sugar
½ tablespoon minced onions   2 tablespoons vinegar
1 garlic clove, minced   1 tablespoon oil
1 tablespoon chopped parsley   1 tablespoon sour cream

Take a large cucumber and peel and slice it thinly. Put into a bowl and salt lightly. Let stand for about ½ hour. Then press the slices between your hands to press out all of the water. Put the pressed slices into a bowl and add remaining ingredients. Mix well. Sprinkle with paprika and serve.

Grandmother's Cookbook (Pennsylvania)

No wonder cucumbers are a summertime favorite...the inner temperature of a cucumber can be up to twenty degrees cooler than the outside air. Maybe that's where the phrase "cool as a cucumber" comes from.

★★★★★★★★★★★★ ★★★★★★★★★★★★

Nutty Broccoli Salad

½ pound bacon
4 cups chopped tender broccoli
1 (2-ounce) package sliced
　almonds
1 cup white raisins

1 medium red onion, chopped
1 (4-ounce) package salted
　sunflower seeds, or 1 cup
　unsalted roasted peanuts

Fry bacon and crumble. Combine all ingredients and refrigerate. One hour before serving, add Dressing.

DRESSING:
2 tablespoons red wine vinegar
2 tablespoons sugar

1 cup mayonnaise

Mix and pour over salad.

Golden Moments (Mississippi)

Pat's Cauliflower Salad

1 head cauliflower, cut into
　bite-size pieces
½ cup fried and crumbled
　bacon
½ cup shredded Cheddar
　cheese
4 green onions, chopped
2 teaspoons Lawry's Seasoned
　Salt

¼ cup vinegar
1 teaspoon black pepper
2 tablespoons sugar
1 cup mayonnaise
1 cup sour cream
2 tablespoons milk

Place cauliflower, crumbled bacon, cheese, and onions in a large bowl. Mix together in another bowl the seasoned salt, vinegar, pepper, sugar, mayonnaise, sour cream, and milk. Pour just enough of the sauce over the cauliflower mixture to moisten slightly. Keep chilled.

Kitchen Chatter (Nevada)

Always Requested Cornbread Salad

Wonderful!

1 (9x13-inch) pan cooked
  cornbread, crumbled
1½ cups mayonnaise
2 cups sliced celery
1 green bell pepper, seeded and
  chopped
1 (5-ounce) jar green olives
  and pimentos, drained,
  rinsed, and chopped

¾ cup chopped green onions
¾ cup chopped pecans, toasted
2 large tomatoes, chopped
1 teaspoon sage
Pepper to taste
10 slices bacon, fried crisp
  and crumbled
1 jalapeño pepper, seeded
  and chopped

In bowl, combine all ingredients. Refrigerate 3–4 hours before serving. Serves 12.

Great Flavors of Texas (Texas II)

A tomato is technically a fruit because it is a ripened ovary of a plant. But for trade purposes, a tomato is considered a vegetable. The identity crisis stems from an 1893 Supreme Court ruling that classified the tomato as a vegetable so it could be taxed under tariff law.

White Potato Salad

5 pounds new potatoes
½ cup water
½ cup white vinegar
½ cup sugar
3 small onions, minced

2 cups Hellmann's mayonnaise
  (do not substitute)
¼ cup heavy cream
1 tablespoon salt
Olive oil

The night before, boil unpeeled potatoes for 20 minutes from boiling point. Do not let them get too soft. Boil water, vinegar, and sugar together. Pour over onions. Let stand until potatoes are peeled and sliced very thin. Pour onion mixture over potatoes. In separate bowl, mix mayonnaise, cream, and salt till smooth and creamy. Pour over potatoes and mix carefully together. Be sure all potatoes get saturated. Dribble olive oil over top. Cover and let stand in refrigerator overnight. Do not cover with foil. Salad will appear watery when you finish, but will absorb moisture overnight. Salad will keep in refrigerator 4–5 days. Serves 16.

A Century of Recipes Through the Windows of Time (Michigan)

Southern-Style Potato Salad

4 pounds potatoes (about 4
  large potatoes)
3 hard-cooked eggs, grated
1 cup mayonnaise
½ cup sour cream
¼ cup finely chopped celery
2 tablespoons finely chopped
  onion
2 tablespoons sweet pickle
  relish

1 tablespoon mustard
1 tablespoon salt
½ teaspoon freshly ground
  pepper
½ pound bacon, cooked,
  crumbled
Chopped fresh parsley for
  garnish
Grape tomatoes for garnish

Cook potatoes in boiling water 40 minutes or until tender; drain and cool. Peel potatoes; cut into 1-inch cubes. Stir together potatoes and eggs. Stir together mayonnaise and next 7 ingredients; gently stir into potato mixture. Cover and chill.

Sprinkle with bacon just before serving. Garnish with parsley and tomatoes, if desired.

Best Kept Secrets (South Carolina)

Gourmet Chicken Salad with Fresh Peaches

A delicious luncheon main course.

2 cups chicken, cooked and
  cubed
¾ cup chopped celery
¾ cup white seedless grapes
¾ cup peeled and cubed fresh
  peaches

½ cup mayonnaise
½ cup sour cream
Seasoning salt to taste
Fresh peach slices
Parsley

Lightly toss chicken, celery, grapes and peaches together. Mix mayonnaise and sour cream and pour over salad. Add seasoning salt and mix gently. Store in refrigerator until ready to use. Garnish with fresh peach slices and parsley. Makes 6 servings.

The Peach Sampler (South Carolina)

Exotic Symphonic Chicken Salad

3 cups cooked chicken or turkey,
  cut in large chunks
2 teaspoons grated onion
2 cups diced celery
1 cup slivered almonds
  or chopped pecans
2 (6-ounce) cans water
  chestnuts, drained and
  chopped

2 cups pared and diced apples
2 cups seedless green grapes,
  halved
½ cup mayonnaise
⅓ cup white wine
1 tablespoon salt
⅛ teaspoon pepper
3 avocados
Lemon juice

Combine chicken, onion, celery, almonds, water chestnuts, apples, and grapes. Mix mayonnaise, wine, salt and pepper; toss with chicken mixture. Refrigerate until served. Cut avocados in half, seed and sprinkle with lemon juice just before serving. Serve salad in avocado halves, topped with a few grapes. Serves 6.

Noted Cookery (Texas)

Chicken Salad in a Cream Puff

CHICKEN SALAD:

2 cups cubed, cooked chicken
1 cup seedless green grapes,
  halved
½ cup (2 ounces) shredded
  Swiss cheese
½ cup sliced celery

3 tablespoons sliced green
  onions
½ cup sour cream
¼ cup mayonnaise
¼ cup toasted sliced almonds

Combine chicken, grapes, cheese, celery, onions, sour cream, and mayonnaise. Chill until ready to serve.

CREAM PUFF:

½ cup margarine
1 cup boiling water
1 cup all-purpose flour

¼ teaspoon salt
4 eggs
Leaf lettuce for garnish

Preheat oven to 400°. Add margarine to boiling water and stir until melted; add flour and salt all at once. Stir until well blended and a ball forms. Set aside to cool for 10 minutes. Add eggs to flour mixture, one at a time. Stir after each addition until thoroughly blended. Butter a 9-inch pie pan. Spread batter evenly in bottom and on sides. Bake 30–35 minutes, or until puffed and lightly browned.

When ready to serve, line pastry with lettuce leaves and fill with chicken salad. Sprinkle toasted almonds on top. To serve, cut into wedges. Yields 4–6 servings.

Hints: Cream puff may be made one day ahead and re-crisped in moderate (325°) oven for 5 minutes. Chicken salad may be prepared one to three days ahead.

Even More Special (North Carolina)

Smoked Turkey, Pecan, and Blue Cheese Salad

This surprising meld of flavors will have your guests asking for extra servings—and the recipe, of course!

½ cup vegetable oil
¼ cup white wine vinegar
¼ cup honey
½ cup chopped onion
4 teaspoons Tabasco
Salt and pepper to taste
6 cups assorted salad greens,
  bite-size pieces

2 cups curly endive, bite-size
  pieces
8 ounces smoked turkey, diced
⅔ cup crumbled blue cheese
⅔ cup toasted and chopped
  pecans
1 avocado, peeled, pitted, and
  diced

In a blender, purée oil, vinegar, honey, onion, and Tabasco. Season dressing to taste with salt and pepper. Rinse and dry greens in salad spinner. Greens have to be as dry as possible for dressing to adhere. In a large bowl, combine greens and endive and toss with enough dressing to coat. Add remaining ingredients and drizzle with more dressing. Toss gently. May be made up to 4 hours ahead. Serves 4.

Nutritional values per serving: Calories 880; Carbo. 42.1g; Prot. 22.2g; Fiber 10.3g; Sugar 31.8g; Fat Calories 666; Total Fat 74g; Sat. Fat 14.6g; Chol. 34.6g; Sod. 807.6mg.

LaConner Palates (Washington)

Potato Chip Taco Salad

1 head lettuce, or 1 large
  bowl mixed greens
8 ounces fresh spinach
1 pound ground beef
1 (1¼-ounce) package taco
  seasoning mix
⅔ cup water
1 (15-ounce) can kidney beans

2 large tomatoes, chopped
½ cup finely chopped onion
5 cups crushed rippled potato
  chips
1 cup grated Cheddar cheese
½ cup peppercorn ranch
  dressing
¼ cup salsa

Wash lettuce and spinach. Tear into bite-size pieces and spin dry in a salad spinner. Refrigerate while browning ground beef. Drain fat from ground beef and add taco seasoning, water, and drained kidney beans. Heat to boiling, reduce heat, and simmer for 15 minutes, stirring occasionally. Cool 10 minutes. In a large bowl, mix greens, tomatoes, onion, chips, and cheese. Add ground beef mixture and toss. Combine salad dressing and salsa. Pour over salad and toss gently. Serve immediately.

Red River Valley Potato Growers Auxiliary Cookbook (Great Plains)

Tuna on a Shoestring

1 (6½-ounce) can tuna, drained
1 cup shredded carrots
1 cup sliced celery
¼ cup minced onion
¾–1 cup mayonnaise

1 (14-ounce) can shoestring
  potatoes
Fresh parsley and carrot curls
  for garnish (optional)

In a large bowl, separate tuna into chunks. Add carrots, celery, onion, and mayonnaise. Toss until tuna is well coated. Cover and chill. Just before serving, fold in shoestring potatoes. To add a bright touch, garnish with parsley and carrot curls, if desired. Yields 4–6 servings.

A Century of Recipes (Idaho)

Editor's Extra: Carrot curls are easy to make by running a vegetable peeler down the length of a peeled carrot.

Hot Shrimp-Avocado Salad

Looking for something different and mouthwatering? This is it!

1 tablespoon butter
1½ teaspoons curry powder
1¼ teaspoons salt
1 medium tomato, chopped
1 medium onion, chopped

1½ pounds fresh shrimp,
  cleaned and well-drained
2 tablespoons lemon juice
1 cup sour cream
3 or 4 avocados, peeled

Melt butter and stir in curry powder and salt. Add tomato, onion, and shrimp, and sauté until shrimp are done and seasoning is soft. Add lemon juice. If mixture is a bit watery, drain some of the liquid at this point. Stir in sour cream and heat thoroughly. Serve hot as follows:

   For a salad meal, halve avocados and scoop in shrimp mixture. For a salad accompaniment, spoon onto lettuce and surround with slices of avocado. Serves 6–8.

Louisiana LEGACY (Louisiana)

Bacon, Lettuce and Tomato Salad

1 (7-ounce) box Creamettes
  shells, cooked and drained
1½ pounds bacon, diced,
  fried, and drained
½ head lettuce, shredded
2 or 3 tomatoes, seeded
  and diced

1 tablespoon finely diced
  onion
Pepper to taste
Mayonnaise or Miracle Whip
to coat

In large bowl, mix the first 6 ingredients together. Mix with mayonnaise or Miracle Whip to coat. Refrigerate until ready to serve. Yields 12 servings.

Hint: The shells, bacon, and tomatoes may be prepared the day before and refrigerated.

St. Mary's Family Cookbook (Wisconsin)

Sweet and Sour Pasta Salad

SALAD:

1 (16-ounce) package tricolor
  spiral pasta
1 medium red onion, chopped
1 medium cucumber, peeled,
  seeded, and chopped

1 medium tomato, chopped
1 medium green bell pepper,
  chopped
2 tablespoons minced fresh
  parsley

Cook pasta according to package directions; drain and rinse with cold water. Place in a large serving bowl. Add onion, cucumber, tomato, green bell pepper, and parsley; set aside.

DRESSING:

1½ cups sugar
½ cup vinegar
1 tablespoon ground mustard

1 teaspoon garlic powder
1 teaspoon salt (optional)

In a saucepan, combine sugar, vinegar, mustard, garlic powder, and salt. Cook over medium-low heat for 10 minutes or until sugar is dissolved. Pour over pasta salad and toss to coat. Cover and refrigerate for 2 hours. Makes 16 servings.

Lion House Entertaining (Utah)

Red onions, sometimes called purple onions, tend to be medium to large in size and have a mild to sweet flavor. They are often consumed raw, or added as color to salads. They tend to lose their redness when cooked. Red onions are available throughout the year, and will keep at room temperature for three to four months.

Bow Tie Spinach Salad

Combine the best of pasta and spinach salads with a zesty dressing for a salad that is pretty as well as tasty.

DRESSING:

¾ cup olive oil or vegetable oil

¾ cup white wine vinegar

3 garlic cloves, crushed

2 teaspoons Dijon mustard

½ cup grated Parmesan cheese

1 tablespoon minced fresh oregano, or 1 teaspoon dried oregano

Salt and pepper to taste

Combine the olive oil, vinegar, garlic, mustard, Parmesan cheese, oregano, salt and pepper in a bowl; mix well.

SALAD:

1 (16-ounce) package bow tie pasta, cooked, drained

1 (10-ounce) package fresh spinach, torn

3 tomatoes, chopped

½ cup sliced green onions

½ cup sliced black olives

¾ cup crumbled feta cheese

Combine the pasta, spinach, tomatoes, green onions, olives, and feta cheese in a salad bowl. Add the Dressing; toss to coat well. Chill until serving time. Serves 8–10.

Generations (Illinois)

Everyone knows that spinach is loaded in iron and that's what makes Popeye stronger than the average man. And just look what spinach has done for Popeye's career.

Actually, Popeye was wrong! And that's because a food analyst (in 1957) made an error while calculating the iron in spinach. His decimal point was off by one place, and he reported that spinach contained ten times as much iron content as it really did!

Coleslaw Soufflé Aspic

Southern Foodways Alliance "Coleslaw Award" finalist.

1 (3-ounce) package lemon
  gelatin
1 cup boiling water
½ cup cold water
2 tablespoons vinegar
½ cup mayonnaise
¼ teaspoon salt

Dash of white pepper
2 cups finely chopped cabbage
½ cup finely chopped celery
2 tablespoons minced green
  pepper
1 tablespoon minced onion

Dissolve gelatin in boiling water. Add cold water, vinegar, mayonnaise, salt, and pepper. Beat well until thoroughly blended; chill. When slightly thick, whip until fluffy. Add remaining ingredients. Pour into molds; chill. Serves 6–8.

The South's Legendary Frances Virginia Tea Room Cookbook
(Georgia)

Ritz Cracker Slaw

Try this flavorful slaw stuffed in a tomato.

1 medium cabbage, grated
1 medium onion, chopped finely
⅔ cup chopped celery
⅔ cup chopped bell pepper
2 sleeves Ritz Crackers, crushed
2 tablespoons pickle relish

2 cups mayonnaise
4 tablespoons mustard
Salt and pepper to taste
1 cup grated sharp Cheddar
  cheese

Mix all ingredients together except cheese. Place grated cheese on top of slaw. Chill. Serves 12–15.

When Dinnerbells Ring (Alabama)

Vegetables

GWEN McKEE

When Dr. Ray Turner picks the peas from his well-tended garden behind his house in Shreveport, Louisiana, he solicits a little help from Gwen's husband Barney to shell the peas while Jeanne and Gwen are in the kitchen slicing tomatoes and cucumbers, and cookin' up the squash and onions. Ah, summertime, when the veggies are bountiful and beautiful.

★★★★★★★★★★★★ ★★★★★★★★★★★★

Onion Harvest Medley

2 large onions
  (Idaho-Eastern Oregon)
3 medium tomatoes, quartered
3 medium zucchini, cut in 1-inch
  slices
¼ cup chopped fresh basil, or
  1 teaspoon dried basil
½ teaspoon salt
¼ teaspoon pepper
3 tablespoons vegetable oil

Peel and cut onions into wedges. Arrange in microwave-proof baking dish with tomatoes and zucchini. Sprinkle with seasonings. Drizzle oil over vegetables. Cover with plastic wrap and microwave on HIGH 10–12 minutes, or until onions are tender, rotating dish ¼ turn every 4 minutes. Serves 6.

Onions Make the Meal Cookbook (Idaho)

Vidalia Soufflé

A great alternative to quiche.

6 ounces stale or day-old
  French or Italian loaf (cut
  into chunks)
½ cup butter or margarine
3 large sweet onions, cut into
  thin slices
1 tablespoon fresh thyme, or
  ½ teaspoon dried thyme
1 cup grated Swiss cheese
1 pint light cream
3 eggs, beaten
Salt and pepper to taste

Preheat oven to 350°. Place bread chunks in a 1½-quart buttered soufflé dish. Melt butter in a large skillet. Add onions and cook until slightly limp, or translucent. Pour butter and onions over bread. Scatter thyme and cheese over top. Blend cream into eggs until mixture is light and frothy. Add salt and pepper, if desired. Pour over mixture in soufflé dish. Press down to make sure bread is thoroughly soaked. Bake 45 minutes or until knife inserted in center comes out clean. Serve with a salad. Add ham or bacon for a different flavor, or more onions, if you like! Yields 6–8 servings.

Georgia on My Menu (Georgia)

French-Fried Onion Rings

Onion rings fried in peanut oil taste better than those fried in shortening, and they have less cholesterol.

6 medium Spanish onions,
  thinly sliced
1 cup milk
1 cup buttermilk

1 egg, beaten
1 cup all-purpose flour
2–3 cups peanut oil
Salt to taste

Separate onion slices into rings. Combine milk, buttermilk, and egg in a medium mixing bowl. Add onion rings and refrigerate for 30 minutes. Spread flour on a plate. Heat oil to 375° in a medium saucepan or deep-fat fryer. Remove onion rings from milk mixture and dip one at a time into flour. Fry in hot oil until golden brown. Cook no more than 8–10 rings at one time to prevent oil from cooling below 375°. Remove from oil, drain on paper towels, and sprinkle with salt. Yields 6–8 servings.

More Tastes & Tales (Texas II)

Onion Fries

¾ cup self-rising flour
½ teaspoon baking powder
1 tablespoon cornmeal
½ cup nonfat dry milk

2 teaspoons sugar
½ teaspoon salt
2½ cups chopped onions

Combine all ingredients except onions. Add cold water a little at a time until you have a very thick batter. Add onions and mix well. Make small half-dollar size patties by dripping from spoon into hot shallow oil and flattening slightly with back of spoon. Brown on both sides.

The Farmer's Daughters (Arkansas)

Fresh Corn Casserole

8 slices bacon
8 ears fresh corn, cut from cob
1 cup chopped green bell pepper
½ cup chopped onion

1 teaspoon salt
½ teaspoon pepper
½ teaspoon dry mustard
3 fresh tomatoes, peeled and sliced

Preheat oven to 350°. Fry bacon in large skillet until crisp. Drain on paper towels. In same skillet, pour off all but 2 tablespoons bacon drippings. Add corn, bell pepper, and onion. Sauté 5 minutes.

Combine crumbled bacon, salt, pepper, and mustard in small bowl. In greased 2-quart baking dish, layer ½ corn mixture, ½ bacon mixture, and ½ tomatoes. Repeat layers. Bake uncovered 35 minutes. Serves 8.

Dining by Fireflies (North Carolina)

Skillet Sweet Corn

Cream corn right off the cob.

6 ears corn
6 tablespoons butter
½ cup light cream

½ teaspoon salt
½ teaspoon sugar
Ground pepper to taste

Husk corn and remove silks. Slice off kernels with a long sharp knife or electric knife. Using the back of a dinner knife, scrape the milky substance from the cob into the corn. Heat butter in a skillet, add corn and milky substance, and cook and stir 3–4 minutes or until desired tenderness. Add cream and seasonings. Stir over low heat for 2–3 minutes. Makes 4 servings.

A Cook's Tour of Iowa (Iowa)

In the 1930s, before the machines were available, a farmer could harvest an average of one hundred bushels of corn by hand in a nine-hour day. Today's combines can harvest nine hundred bushels of corn per hour—or one hundred bushels of corn in less than seven minutes!

★★★★★★★★★★★ ★★★★★★★★★★★

Corn Fritters

2 cups fresh, grated corn	¾ teaspoon salt
2 eggs, beaten	¼ teaspoon pepper
¾ cup all-purpose flour	1 teaspoon baking powder

Combine corn and eggs. Add flour that has been sifted with remaining ingredients. Drop corn mixture from tablespoon into 1 inch of melted shortening. Fry until golden brown on both sides, turning once. Sprinkle with additional salt, if desired. Makes about 2 dozen.

From Amish and Mennonite Kitchens (Pennsylvania)

Celery Almondine

Children like it too!

½ cup slivered almonds	Salt, pepper, and seasoned salt
4 tablespoons butter, divided	to taste
4 cups diagonally sliced celery	2 tablespoons dry white wine
1 tablespoon minced onion	

Sauté almonds in 1 tablespoon butter. Remove and reserve almonds. Melt remaining butter; add celery, onion, and seasonings. Cook over low heat, stirring occasionally for about 10 minutes. Add almonds and wine. Cook until almonds are reheated. This can be made ahead, except for adding almonds and wine. Yields 4–6 servings.

Upper Crust: A Slice of the South (Tennessee)

Spinach was the first frozen vegetable brought to market. Its first distribution was in ten retail stores in Springfield, Massachusetts, in 1929.

Basil Carrots

1½ pounds carrots
½ cup firmly packed, minced
   fresh basil leaves

¼ cup olive oil
½ teaspoon salt

Pare carrots; quarter lengthwise and cut into 1½-inch strips. Boil carrots 10 minutes in salted water until barely tender. Drain and rinse under cold water to refresh. Pat dry. Sauté carrots, basil, and salt in oil, stirring until well coated with the mixture and heated through. Serves 6–8. Can partially do ahead.

Standing Room Only (Mississippi)

Carrot Casserole

2 pounds carrots
1 cup crumbled Swiss cheese
   crackers
2 eggs, beaten
½ cup diced green onions

3 tablespoons sugar
½ cup milk
⅔ cup melted butter
1 teaspoon salt

Cut up carrots. Cook until tender; drain and mash. Add all other ingredients. Pour into a 2-quart casserole and bake uncovered at 350° for 45 minutes. Enjoy! Yields 8 servings.

For Crying Out Loud...Let's Eat! (Indiana)

Beignets de Carrottes
(Carrot Fritters)

8 carrots, boiled and mashed
1 egg
½ cup sugar (or artificial
   sweetener)

2–4 tablespoons flour
1 inch cooking oil in skillet

Combine carrots, egg, and sugar; mix well. Add enough flour to reach desired consistency. Drop by spoonful into hot cooking oil to deep-fry to desired brown color. Sprinkle with salt, if desired. Makes about 2 dozen.

Allons Manger (Louisiana II)

Blue Willow Inn's Famous Fried Green Tomatoes

The Blue Willow Inn's Fried Green Tomatoes are legendary, having put the newly opened restaurant on the map shortly after a visit from famed columnist Lewis Grizzard in 1992. Following his visit, Grizzard authored a column in which he raved about the Blue Willow Inn Restaurant and the food it served—especially the Fried Green Tomatoes. Following the national publicity the restaurant received from Grizzard's column, Fried Green Tomatoes became a delicious Blue Willow tradition.

3 green tomatoes
1½ cups buttermilk
2 eggs, lightly beaten
1 teaspoon black pepper, divided

1 teaspoon salt, divided
1 tablespoon plus 1½ cups self-rising flour, divided
2 cups vegetable oil

Wash and slice tomatoes into ¼-inch slices. In medium bowl, mix buttermilk and eggs. Add ½ teaspoon pepper, ½ teaspoon salt, and 1 tablespoon flour; mix well. Place tomato slices in the buttermilk and egg mixture. Set aside to rest.

Preheat oil to 350° in heavy skillet or electric fryer. In medium bowl, mix remaining flour, salt, and pepper. Remove tomato slices from buttermilk/egg mixture and toss, one at a time, in flour mixture, coating thoroughly. Carefully place tomato slices in heated oil and fry until golden brown; turn 2–3 times. Be careful not to crowd tomatoes during frying. Do not allow them to overlap or they will stick together. Cook until crisp. Drain on paper towels. Serve immediately. Makes 6 servings.

The Blue Willow Inn Bible of Southern Cooking (Georgia)

Okra Fritters

1 cup sliced okra
½ cup chopped onion
¼ cup all-purpose flour
½ cup chopped tomatoes

¼ cup cornmeal
1 egg
Salt and pepper to taste

Mix all ingredients together. Salt and pepper to taste. Drop by spoonful into hot oil to fry.

Cooking with Watkinsville First Christian Church (Georgia)

Old-Time Fried Okra

½ cup all-purpose flour
½ cup cornmeal
½ teaspoon salt
⅛ teaspoon pepper

1 quart okra, sliced crosswise, ¼ inch or less
1 egg, beaten
1 cup shortening

Combine flour, cornmeal, salt, and pepper; mix well. In separate bowl, stir beaten egg into okra. Dredge in flour mixture. Heat shortening in large skillet until hot. Add okra and fry until brown and crisp. Remove from pan and drain well on paper towels.

Encore (Georgia)

Fun Lady's Tomato Pie

Rich and delicious.

CRUST:

1 (9- or 10-inch) deep-dish pie crust, baked

Bake in preheated 350° oven for 10 minutes. Cool completely.

FILLING:

3 cups (12 ounces) shredded mozzarella cheese
1 pound cooked, crumbled bacon
1½ cups chopped green bell pepper
2 avocados, sliced
2 large or 4 medium tomatoes, sliced and seeded

Oregano
Basil
1 cup mayonnaise
1 cup freshly grated Parmesan cheese
⅛ teaspoon bottled hot pepper sauce
½ teaspoon Worcestershire
¼ cup chopped fresh parsley

In prebaked, cooled crust, layer in order, 1 cup mozzarella cheese and ½ each of the bacon, green bell pepper, avocados, and tomatoes. Sprinkle with oregano and basil. Repeat. Put the third cup of mozzarella cheese over the second layer.

Mix mayonnaise, Parmesan, hot pepper sauce, and Worcestershire; spread over the top. Sprinkle with chopped parsley. Bake at 350° for 30 minutes or until golden. Let stand 10–15 minutes. Serve warm or cool. Store in refrigerator. Serves 6.

Presentations (Great Plains)

★★★★★★★★★★★★ ★★★★★★★★★★★★

Smithfield Inn Stewed Tomatoes

One of the renowned dishes of the Smithfield Inn.

1 pint tomatoes, slightly mashed
2 (day-old) biscuits
¼ cup or less sugar
½ teaspoon vanilla

½ teaspoon lemon extract
1 teaspoon flour
1 tablespoon butter

Combine ingredients. Pour into greased casserole dish and bake at 350° for 30–40 minutes.

The Smithfield Cookbook (Virginia II)

Peas and Cheese Stuffed Tomatoes

2 cups English peas, cooked
1 cup shredded Cheddar cheese
2 hard-boiled eggs, chopped
¼ cup chopped celery
2 tablespoons chopped onion
2 tablespoons chopped pimento

⅓ cup mayonnaise
½ teaspoon salt
⅛ teaspoon pepper
¼–½ teaspoon Tabasco
6 medium tomatoes
6 large lettuce leaves

In a large bowl, combine peas, cheese, eggs, celery, onion, and pimento. In another bowl, combine mayonnaise, salt, pepper, and Tabasco. Add to pea mixture and toss to coat. Cover and chill several hours or overnight. Cut each tomato into wedges, being careful not to cut all the way through. Spoon mixture on top and serve on lettuce leaves. Serves 6.

It's Our Serve (New York)

New Peas and Potatoes

This is a good way to stretch the first peas from the garden.

3 cups shelled fresh peas
12 small new potatoes, washed
1½ teaspoons salt

1½ cups milk
1½ teaspoons flour
2 tablespoons butter, melted

Cook peas and potatoes separately in salted water until soft and almost dry. Add peas to potatoes and pour milk over them. Bring milk to boiling point, then add paste of butter and flour. Cook until slightly thickened, and serve.

An Amish Kitchen (Pennsylvania)

Asparagus and Tomatoes

3 slices bacon
½ cup sliced green onions
3 tablespoons vinegar
1 tablespoon water
2 teaspoons sugar
¼ teaspoon seasoned salt

Pepper to taste
1½ pounds asparagus, cut in
   1½-inch pieces
2 medium tomatoes, cut in
   eighths

Cook and crumble bacon. To the drippings, add onions and cook until tender. Add vinegar, water, sugar, seasonings, and bacon. Bring to a boil; add asparagus, cover, and cook until just crispy. Toss in tomato wedges and heat through, about 3 minutes. As pretty as it is tasty! Serves 6.

The Cooking Book (Kentucky)

Sautéed Asparagus

2 pounds fresh asparagus
½ medium–size onion,
   finely chopped
1 garlic clove, chopped

2 tablespoons vegetable oil
2 tablespoons butter
Salt and pepper to taste

Wash the asparagus thoroughly in cold water to eliminate any sand. Snap off the tough bottom portion of the asparagus stalks and discard. Parboil (partially cook by boiling briefly) the asparagus in a small amount of lightly salted boiling water for 5 minutes. Drain.

In a skillet, sauté the onion and garlic in the oil and butter for 3–5 minutes over medium heat. Add the asparagus. Cover and cook to the desired tenderness (5–10 minutes). Turn once, being careful not to break the stalks. Add salt and pepper to taste, and serve at once.

Caring is Sharing (Illinois)

Asparagus au Gratin

1 pound fresh mushrooms,
  sliced
3 tablespoons butter

2 pounds fresh asparagus,
  cooked to tender-crisp (few
  minutes in microwave)

Brown mushrooms in butter until tender. Drain. Grease a 2-quart casserole dish. Carefully combine mushrooms and asparagus (cut into ½-inch pieces) and place in casserole dish.

SAUCE:

3 tablespoons butter
3 tablespoons flour
1½ cups milk or light cream
1 cup finely grated Cheddar
  cheese

1 teaspoon Worcestershire
1 teaspoon salt
¼ teaspoon pepper
Bread crumbs and paprika

Melt butter; add flour and slowly stir in milk. Add cheese, Worcestershire, salt, and pepper. Heat slowly, stirring often, until cheese melts. Pour over asparagus mixture. Edge casserole with bread crumbs and sprinkle center generously with paprika. Bake at 350° for 20 minutes or until bubbly. Serves 6–8.

Red Flannel Town Recipes (Michigan)

Did you know…
• that the small "scales" at the tip of an asparagus spear are actually the leaves?
• that all asparagus grown commercially must be harvested by hand?

Gourmet Cabbage Casserole

1 medium cabbage	½ teaspoon salt
4 tablespoons butter	½ teaspoon pepper
4 tablespoons flour	2 cups milk

Cut cabbage into small wedges and cook until tender; drain and place in a 9x13-inch casserole. Melt butter in saucepan; blend in flour, salt, and pepper. Cook over low heat, stirring, until smooth and bubbly. Stir in milk and continue cooking, stirring constantly, until mixture comes to a boil. Continue cooking one additional minute. Spread sauce over cabbage. Bake at 375°for 20 minutes.

TOPPING:

½ green bell pepper, chopped	½ cup mayonnaise
½ onion, chopped	3 tablespoons chili sauce
⅔ cup shredded Cheddar cheese	

Mix green bell pepper, onion, cheese, mayonnaise, and chili sauce. Spread over top of casserole and bake at 400° an additional 20 minutes. Serves 8.

More Hoosier Cooking (Indiana)

Sweet-Sour Red Cabbage

½ medium head red cabbage, shredded	¼ cup vinegar
¼ cup butter	¼ cup sugar
½ medium onion, diced	1 apple, sliced
1 tablespoon soy sauce	¼ cup water
	1 tablespoon flour

Place all ingredients, except flour, in a covered kettle and let simmer for at least an hour. Then stir and sift in the flour to thicken.

Family Fare (Wisconsin)

★★★★★★★★★★★   ★★★★★★★★★★★

Boiled Butter Beans—Lima Beans

Butter beans and lima beans are cooked in the same manner. The lima bean is larger and more mealy. They may be seasoned with butter, ham, or salt meat.

**2 cups fresh butter beans or
  lima beans
4 cups water
1 teaspoon salt
1 teaspoon sugar**

**2 tablespoons butter*
½ cup milk or cream
  (optional)
Pepper to taste**

Wash and pick over the beans; cover with water in a saucepan with lid. Add salt and sugar. Boil for about 10 minutes, then add the butter.* Boil slowly until beans are tender, about 45 minutes to 1 hour. If pan becomes too dry, add a little warm water. There should be a little broth left with the beans. If desired, just before serving, add the milk or cream and season to taste with pepper; reheat. Serves 4–6.

*May substitute a piece of boiling meat about 2 inches square, 1-inch thick for the butter, if desired.

Marion Brown's Southern Cook Book (North Carolina)

The fewer beans in the pan, the quicker they cook and the better they taste. If cooking more than one pound at a time, use separate pans.

★★★★★★★★★★★★   ★★★★★★★★★★★★

Green Beans and Stewed Potatoes

3 slices bacon
3 cups snapped fresh green
  beans
4 cups water
1 teaspoon salt
½ teaspoon pepper

4 small fresh potatoes,
  scraped
3 tablespoons margarine,
  melted
2 tablespoons flour

Brown bacon in large saucepan. Add green beans, water, salt, pepper, and potatoes. Cover and simmer 40–50 minutes or until potatoes are tender. (Gently stir at 10-minute intervals to prevent sticking. Additional water may be added, if needed.)

After potatoes are cooked, remove ½ cup hot liquid from beans and potatoes. Combine with margarine and flour to make creamy paste. Stir paste into beans and potatoes while still cooking. Simmer 10 minutes, or long enough to thicken liquid. Serves 4.

Dinner on the Ground (Louisiana II)

Greek-Style Green Beans

4 medium white onions, chopped
3 garlic cloves, crushed
1 tablespoon olive oil
4 large tomatoes, peeled, sliced

Pepper to taste
2 pounds fresh green beans,
  trimmed
Salt to taste

Sauté onions and garlic in olive oil in skillet until light brown. Add tomatoes and season with pepper.

Cook beans in salted water in a saucepan for 5 minutes; drain. Add tomato mixture and cover. Simmer 30–60 minutes or until done to taste, removing cover toward end of cooking time. Adjust seasonings. Serves 6.

Wild Thyme and Other Temptations (Arizona)

★★★★★★★★★★★ ★★★★★★★★★★★

Emmitt Smith's
Sour Cream Green Beans

2 pounds green beans
1 medium onion, thinly sliced
1 tablespoon chopped parsley
2 tablespoons melted butter
  or margarine
2 tablespoons flour

2 tablespoons grated lemon
  rind
1 teaspoon salt
¼ teaspoon pepper
1 cup lite sour cream
1 cup buttered bread crumbs

Prepare beans as usual; cook in slightly-salted water until tender. Drain; set aside. Sauté onions and parsley in butter. Reduce heat; add flour, lemon rind, salt, and pepper. Stir until bubbly. Combine sour cream and beans; stir well. Pour into a greased baking dish; sprinkle with bread crumbs. Bake at 350° for 20 minutes.

Dallas Cowboys Wives' Family Cookbook (Texas II)

Herbed Broccoli Sandwich

This quickly became a lunchtime favorite. Simple, easy, and delicious.

2 cups finely chopped broccoli
½ cup finely chopped onion
2 tablespoons oil
A few dashes each: dried basil,
  thyme, and pepper

½ teaspoon salt
4–6 slices French bread
¾ cup shredded Cheddar
  cheese

In large frying pan, sauté broccoli and onion in oil until broccoli is bright green. Mix in basil, thyme, pepper, and salt.

Top French bread slices with vegetable mixture. Sprinkle cheese on top and broil until melted. Serve immediately.

Simply in Season (Pennsylvania)

★★★★★★★★★★★ ★★★★★★★★★★★

Fried Cauliflower with Cheese Sauce

1 large head cauliflower
1 (12-ounce) can beer, at room temperature

1¼ cups all-purpose flour
Vegetable oil for deep-frying

Wash cauliflower; cut into small florets. Cook, covered, in a small amount of water in saucepan for 8–10 minutes or until tender–crisp; drain.

Combine beer and flour in bowl; mix well. Dip cauliflower in batter. Deep-fry in 375° oil until golden brown; drain. Serve Cheese Sauce with cauliflower. Yields 6 servings.

CHEESE SAUCE:
2 tablespoons butter
2 tablespoons all-purpose flour
1 cup milk

1½ cups shredded Cheddar cheese

Melt butter in heavy skillet. Add flour, stirring until smooth. Cook for 1 minute, stirring constantly. Add milk gradually. Cook over medium heat until thickened, stirring constantly. Remove from heat. Add cheese, stirring until melted.

Approx Per Serving: Cal 316; T Fat 15g; 44% Calories from Fat; Prot 13g; Carbo 29g; Fiber 3g; Chol 46g; Sod 237mg. Nutritional information does not include oil for deep-frying.

Pioneer Pantry (Illinois)

Squash Puppies

5 medium yellow squash
1 egg, beaten
½ cup buttermilk

1 onion, chopped
¾ cup self-rising cornmeal
¼ cup all-purpose flour

Slice squash and cook in small amount of water until tender. Drain squash and mash. Combine squash and remaining ingredients. Drop mixture by tablespoon into hot oil. Fry 5 minutes or until golden brown. Makes about 2½ dozen puppies.

Third Wednesday Homemakers Volume II (West Virginia)

★★★★★★★★★★★   ★★★★★★★★★★★

Country Club Squash

6 or 8 tender, small squash
Salt and pepper to taste
2 tablespoons butter
1 chicken or beef bouillon cube
  (or 1 teaspoon granules)
1 tablespoon grated onion

1 egg, well beaten
1 cup sour cream
¾ cup bread crumbs
½ cup grated cheese
Dash of paprika

Cut and cook squash until tender; drain and mash. Add salt, pepper, butter, bouillon cube, and onion. Add well beaten egg, and sour cream. Pour into a 1-quart casserole dish. Combine bread crumbs, grated cheese, and paprika, and sprinkle on top of squash. Bake at 350° for 30 minutes. Serves 6.

The Mississippi Cookbook (Mississippi)

Pecan Squash

We serve it at Chickadee Cottage in the fall when we can get locally grown squash.

4 cups baked winter squash,
  mashed and beaten smooth
¼ teaspoon white pepper
2 tablespoons brown sugar
⅓ cup butter or margarine,
  melted

⅓ cup evaporated milk
½ teaspoon nutmeg
1 teaspoon salt
½ cup broken pecans
2 tablespoons light or dark
  corn syrup

Combine all ingredients except pecans and corn syrup. Turn into sprayed 1½-quart casserole. Sprinkle pecans on top and drizzle on corn syrup. Bake at 375° about 30 minutes. Makes 6–8 servings.

Chickadee Cottage Cookbook (Minnesota)

Zucchinis are tender and tasty when young, but most varieties are tasteless when large and overgrown. Most people don't realize that the flowers of the zucchini plant may also be eaten, as long as the stamens and pistils are removed. Choose flowers that are only slightly open, as they are fresher.

Creole Eggplant

1 large eggplant, peeled and
    sliced
2 fresh tomatoes, chopped
½ onion, chopped
½ bell pepper, chopped
Salt and pepper to taste
2 tablespoons dried parsley
1 egg, beaten
1 teaspoon oregano
½ cup Pepperidge Farm herb
    stuffing
1 tablespoon butter, softened
2 tablespoons grated Parmesan
    cheese

Soak eggplant in cold salted water for 10–15 minutes. Simmer tomatoes, onion, and bell pepper in a little water until tender. Drain eggplant and cook in boiling salted water until tender (about 10 minutes). Drain and separate eggplant into chunks, but don't mash. Add egg, sautéed vegetables, and seasonings. Put into buttered casserole dish and top with crushed stuffing that has been mixed with softened butter and Parmesan cheese. Bake in 325° oven until brown and bubbly.

Without a Doubt (Alabama)

Zucchini Lover's Casserole

6 medium zucchini, sliced
1 medium brown onion,
    chopped
3 medium carrots, grated
2 sticks butter (or less),
    divided
1 pint sour cream
2 (10¾-ounce) cans cream of
    mushroom soup, undiluted
8 ounces herbed croutons,
    crumbled, divided

Steam zucchini until tender and drain. Sauté onion and carrots in one stick of butter until soft. Mix sour cream with undiluted soup, and add zucchini, carrots, and onions. Stir in ½ of the croutons. Put into a buttered 9x13-inch baking dish. Cover with remaining croutons and dot with butter. Preheat oven to 375°. Bake 45 minutes or until golden on top.

Shaloha Cookbook (Hawaii)

Fried Zucchini Rounds

⅓ cup biscuit mix
¼ cup grated Parmesan cheese
⅛ teaspoon pepper
2 eggs, slightly beaten

2 cups shredded, unpeeled
zucchini (2 medium)
2 tablespoons butter or
margarine

Combine biscuit mix, cheese, and pepper. Stir in eggs just till mixture is moistened. Fold in zucchini. In 10-inch skillet, melt margarine over medium heat. Using 2 tablespoons for each round, cook 2–3 minutes on each side or until brown. Makes 12 rounds.

The Dinner Bell Rings Again! (Pennsylvania)

Greek Spinach

A great combination of flavors!

2 pounds fresh spinach
1 tablespoon olive oil
½ cup pine nuts (or walnuts)
3 tablespoons chopped basil
2 tablespoons chopped Italian
parsley

1 garlic clove, minced
1 small onion, finely chopped
2 tablespoons cider vinegar
Dash of salt

Wash and tear the spinach, removing heavy stems. Heat a large skillet. Add the oil and nuts and sauté until golden. Add remaining ingredients. Stir, cover, and cook 2 minutes, until the spinach is barely tender.

Herbs in a Minnesota Kitchen (Minnesota)

Turnip and Collard Greens

1 pound ham hocks (or
  smoked turkey)
7 cups water
1 bunch fresh collard greens
  (about 5 pounds)
1 bunch fresh turnip greens
  (about 5 pounds)

1 teaspoon salt
Pepper to taste
1 small whole red bell pepper
  (optional)

Combine ham hocks and water in a large pot. Bring to a boil. Cover and reduce heat to simmer for about one hour or until meat is tender. In the meantime, wash greens thoroughly and drain. Cut into bite-size pieces. Add greens, salt, and pepper (and bell pepper, if desired) to boiled meat. Bring to a boil. Cover; reduce heat and simmer for 1–1½ hours or until greens are tender.

The Best of Down-Home Cooking (Nevada)

Southern-Style Greens

3½–4 pounds collard, turnip or
  mustard greens, or a mixture
½ pound lean salt pork or
  smoked ham hock
1 tablespoon sugar

3 beef bouillon cubes
8 cups water
1 tablespoon margarine
Salt and pepper to taste

Wash greens in a sink full of water. Swish greens to remove any grit. Drain and rinse sink. Repeat washing. Lift greens out of water. Remove and discard all large stems. Combine pork, sugar, bouillon cubes, water, and margarine in a large soup pot. Bring to a boil over medium-high heat. Boil for 5–10 minutes. Add greens. Reduce heat and simmer, covered, for 1½ hours or until greens are tender. Add salt and pepper to taste. You may peel and quarter turnip roots and add to the soup pot for the last 30 minutes of cooking. Makes 8–10 servings.

Cooking Wild Game & Fish Southern Style (Mississippi)

★★★★★★★★★★★   ★★★★★★★★★★★

Natalie's Potatoes

6 medium red potatoes
⅓ cup chopped onion
¼ cup margarine plus
** 2 tablespoons, divided**
1½ cups sour cream*

2 cups shredded Cheddar
** cheese**
1 teaspoon salt
½ teaspoon black pepper

Boil potatoes, then drain, cool, and peel. Grate potatoes, placing them in buttered 9x13-inch casserole. To make the sauce, sauté onions in ¼ cup margarine. Add sour cream and shredded cheese to melt. Add other ingredients. Heat thoroughly and pour over cooked and grated potatoes. Dot with remaining 2 tablespoons margarine. Bake 35 minutes in 350° oven. Makes 8–10 servings. May be frozen prior to baking.

*If I have only one carton of sour cream (8 ounces) on hand, I rinse the carton with ½ carton of milk which works very well.

Turnip Greens in the Bathtub (Louisiana)

Potato Facts:

• The potato is the fourth most important crop in the world after wheat, rice, and corn.
• The potato produces more food per acre than any other crop (39,100 pounds per acre).
• The average American eats about 140 pounds of potatoes per year.

Crusty Baked Potatoes

4 tablespoons butter
4 medium baking potatoes
1 cup fine dry bread crumbs
1 teaspoon salt
1 teaspoon paprika

Preheat oven to 350°. Melt butter in saucepan. Wash and peel potatoes; pat dry. Mix bread crumbs, salt, and paprika together. Roll potatoes in butter; coat evenly with bread crumb mixture. Place potatoes in buttered 2-quart casserole. Cover and bake for 45–50 minutes. Remove cover; turn potatoes. Bake another 15–20 minutes, until potatoes are tender. Serve with butter and sour cream, if desired. Yields 4 servings.

Guess Who's Coming to Dinner (Georgia)

Swiss Scalloped Potatoes

1½ cups shredded Swiss cheese, divided
½ cup sliced green onions
2 tablespoons butter
2 tablespoons flour
1 teaspoon salt
Pepper to taste
1 cup milk
1 cup sour cream
6–7 cups, cooked, peeled, thinly sliced potatoes (about 4 large)
¼ cup fine bread crumbs
¼ cup butter, melted

In a small bowl, toss together 1 cup Swiss cheese and onions; set aside. In quart saucepan, melt 2 tablespoons butter; stir in flour, salt, and pepper. Gradually stir in milk. Cook over medium heat, stirring constantly, until thickened. Remove from heat; stir in sour cream.

In a shallow, buttered baking dish, layer ⅓ of potatoes, ½ Swiss cheese mixture, and ½ of sour cream mixture. Repeat, making the top layer with last ⅓ of potatoes.

Combine remaining ½ cup Swiss cheese with bread crumbs and melted butter. Sprinkle over top of casserole. Bake at 350° for 30–35 minutes.

Simply the Best Recipes (Alaska)

Vegetable Loaf

5 tablespoons butter (a little
  bacon grease is good)
3 tablespoons flour
1 small onion, chopped
2 cups milk or vegetable
  water
1 teaspoon salt
1 teaspoon pepper
1 cup grated Cheddar cheese
2 eggs, beaten
2 cups cooked sliced string
  beans
2 cups cooked sliced carrots
2 cups cooked sliced potatoes
1 cup bread crumbs

Melt butter in pan. Add flour, onion, milk, and seasonings. Cook
until thick, then add cheese. Remove from heat; add a little to the
eggs, then add eggs to sauce. Arrange beans, carrots, and potatoes
in layers in greased pan. Pour white sauce over and put buttered
crumbs on top. Bake at 350° for 30 minutes.

Armstrong Centennial (Iowa)

Cheddar Harvest Pie

This is a great success served with fresh salad.

1 cup finely shredded Cheddar
  cheese
2 pie crusts
¼ cup butter
2 cups broccoli florets (or ½
  cauliflower and ½ broccoli)
1 large carrot, sliced
½ cup chopped onion
3 garlic cloves, minced
2 cubes chicken bouillon,
  dissolved in 2 cups boiling
  water
1 tablespoon lemon juice
1 teaspoon poultry seasoning
¼ cup all-purpose flour
Salt and pepper to taste

Press cheese into top and bottom crusts. In large skillet, melt butter; add broccoli, carrot, onion, and garlic, and cook till veggies are
tender-crisp. To dissolved bouillon, add lemon juice and poultry
seasoning; gradually add flour to thicken. Fold into vegetables.
Season to taste. Place mixture into prepared crust in 9-inch pie
pan. Cover with top crust and cut slits in top. Place on baking
sheet and bake at 375° for 35 minutes; cool slightly before serving.
Serves 6–8.

Soul Food (Michigan)

Vegetable Pot Pie

SAUCE:

½ cup butter or margarine,
  melted*
¼ cup all-purpose flour

2 cups chicken broth
½ cup whole milk

Melt butter in saucepan. Add flour and stir until paste becomes almond-colored. Stir in chicken broth. After sauce thickens, add milk. More milk may be needed. (This should be a medium sauce.)

2 carrots, cooked and diced
2 medium new potatoes, cooked
  and diced
½ cup field peas or butter
  beans, cooked

½ cup corn, cut from cob,
  cooked
¼ teaspoon black pepper
1 teaspoon salt
Pastry crust

Add vegetables and seasoning to Sauce, folding in gently. Place in greased casserole. Cover with pastry crust, brush with melted butter or margarine, and bake in preheated 425° oven until crust has lightly browned.

*Fresh fat skimmed from boiling a baking hen is preferred to butter, but not absolutely necessary.

Southern Vegetable Cooking (South Carolina)

Sweet Potato St. Cecilia

4 sweet potatoes
½ cup butter
½ cup sugar
2 teaspoons cinnamon

½ cup orange juice
4 oranges
Miniature marshmallows

Boil sweet potatoes until soft (30 minutes). Cool and peel. Mash potatoes and add butter, sugar, cinnamon, and orange juice. Mix well. Halve the oranges, remove the meat and juice. Stuff each half with sweet potato mixture. Top with marshmallow. Bake at 350° for 15–20 minutes. Makes 8 servings.

The Junior League of Grand Rapids Cookbook I (Michigan)

★★★★★★★★★★★ ★★★★★★★★★★★

Sweet Potato Casserole

3 cups cooked sweet potatoes
½ cup brown sugar
2 eggs, beaten
½ teaspoon salt

½ stick margarine, melted
½ cup evaporated milk
1½ teaspoons vanilla

TOPPING:
½ cup brown sugar
⅓ cup plain flour

1 cup chopped pecans
⅓ stick margarine, melted

Mash sweet potatoes. Add sugar, eggs, salt, margarine, milk, and vanilla. Put mixture into buttered casserole dish. Mix Topping ingredients and spread over sweet potato mixture. Bake at 325° for 30 minutes. Serves 6.

Sample West Kentucky (Kentucky)

Mrs. Collier's Candied Yams

A marvelous, southern treat!

4 medium-size sweet potatoes
1 cup sugar
Dash of salt
1 teaspoon cinnamon or
    nutmeg

¾ stick butter
2 slices lemon
1 tablespoon flour
¼ cup water

Peel and cut potatoes as for thick french fries. Place in a 9x13-inch baking dish. Combine sugar and salt; cover potatoes. Sprinkle with cinnamon or nutmeg. Cover with pieces of butter. Squeeze lemon slices then place slices in with potatoes. Sift flour evenly over potatoes. Add water to mixture so it may be barely seen. Bake in 400° oven for one hour, or until potatoes are done and sugar and butter have made a thick syrup, about the consistency of molasses. Baste potatoes frequently with syrup. Serves 4–6.

Calling All Cooks, Two (Alabama)

Despite a physical similarity and a frequent confusion with their names, yams and sweet potatoes are not even distantly related. They are in two different botanical families. Yams are actually related to grasses and lilies.

Buttered Red Radishes

One of spring's earliest crops. If you cook red radishes quickly, they will not lose their color.

1 bunch red radishes   **Salt to taste**
1 tablespoon butter,
 margarine, or Butter Buds

Clean radishes and slice into thin rounds. Melt butter in skillet and sauté radishes briefly. Salt lightly and serve. Yields 4 servings.

Favorite New England Recipes (New England)

Watermelon Rind Pickles

The time and effort you put into making watermelon pickles is well worth it when the accolades are heaped on the cook. Wonderful with fried chicken or baked turkey, and you'll love them mixed into ham or chicken salad.

4 pounds watermelon rind   **2 quarts vinegar**
2 quarts plus 1 pint water,   **4½ pounds sugar**
 divided   **2 tablespoons whole cloves**
4 tablespoons coarse salt   **10 (2-inch) cinnamon sticks**

Use rind of a firm (not overripe) watermelon and, before weighing it, trim off outer green skin and pink flesh. Cut rind into 1-inch cubes, and soak 12 hours in 2 quarts of water mixed with salt. Drain, then cover with fresh water and cook for 10 minutes. Let stand overnight in cooking water. Drain.

Combine vinegar, remaining 1 pint water, sugar, and spices tied loosely in cheesecloth. Add drained watermelon, and boil gently for 2 hours, or until syrup is fairly thick. Remove spice bag and pack rind into hot, sterilized jars; cover with spiced vinegar to within ¼ inch of top. Seal immediately. Makes about 3 quarts.

Let's Talk Food from A to Z (Florida)

★★★★★★★★★★★ ★★★★★★★★★★★

Green Tomato Pickles

2 gallons green tomatoes
4 large onions
4 bell peppers, green or red
Hot peppers to taste

3 cups sugar
2 cups vinegar
2 tablespoons salt
1 jar pickling spice

Wash and remove stems from tomatoes. Chop tomatoes and place in container to cook. Chop onions and peppers, and add other ingredients, except pickling spice to tomatoes. Place pickling spice in cloth bag with mixture. Cook until tomatoes change color, approximately 25 minutes—no more than 30 minutes. Place, while hot, in sterilized jars and seal.

Tastes from the Country (Tennessee)

Bread and Butter Pickles

1 gallon medium cucumbers
6–12 large onions
2 green bell peppers, chopped
½ cup coarse salt
5 cups vinegar
5 cups sugar

1½ teaspoons turmeric or
   allspice
2 teaspoons mustard seed
1½ teaspoons celery seed
½ teaspoon ground cloves

Slice unpeeled cucumbers very thinly. Slice onions very thinly. Combine cucumbers, onions, and green peppers in large bowl. Sprinkle with salt. Chill, covered with weighted lid, in refrigerator 3 hours.

Drain well. Rinse with cold water; drain well. Combine vinegar, sugar, turmeric, mustard seed, celery seed, and cloves in very large saucepan. Bring to a boil; reduce heat. Add vegetables gradually, stirring very little. Scald vegetables in liquid; do not boil. Pack pickles into hot sterilized jars. Add hot liquid, leaving ½-inch headspace; seal with 2-piece lids. Chill before serving. Yields 10–12 quarts.

Kentucky Kitchens Volume II (Kentucky)

Sweet Pickled Okra

3 pounds fresh small okra pods
6 garlic cloves
Hot pepper pods as you wish
   (6 pods for fanatic, 4 for
   convinced, 2–3 for undecided)

6 teaspoons dill seed
6 teaspoons celery seed
1 quart white wine vinegar
½ cup salt (not iodized)
1 cup sugar

Pack washed okra into 6 pint jars (leave stem ends). Divide garlic, dill, celery seed, and pepper among jars. Put vinegar, water, salt, and sugar into big saucepan; bring to boil. Pour into jars, to within ½ inch of top. Seal jars; place in hot water bath (jars must be covered) 7–8 minutes. Remove to wire racks to cool. Makes 6–8 pints.

Suggestion: Chopped peeled baby turnips and celery, with some of these okra pods sliced on a bed of lettuce hearts, with lemony mayonnaise make a delicious and unforgettable salad in mid-winter.

Delectable Dishes from Termite Hall (Alabama)

Tomato Chutney

2 pounds tomatoes, peeled,
   coarsely chopped
1 pound tart apples, peeled,
   cored, chopped
2 medium onions, chopped
1 cup cider vinegar
1 tablespoon salt
1 cup packed brown sugar

1 cup golden raisins
1 garlic clove, minced
½ teaspoon ground cinnamon
½ teaspoon dry mustard
¼ teaspoon cayenne pepper
⅛ teaspoon ground allspice
⅛ teaspoon ground ginger
⅛ teaspoon ground cloves

Combine all the ingredients in a large saucepan or Dutch oven; bring to a boil. Reduce heat and simmer, uncovered, for about 1½–2 hours or until mixture thickens, stirring frequently. Pack hot chutney into hot sterilized jars, leaving ¼-inch head space. Adjust caps. Process for 10 minutes in a boiling water bath. Yields 3 pints.

Dutch Pantry Cookin' Volume II (West Virginia)

Most pasta and pizza sauces are made with tomatoes, and according to the U.S. Department of Agriculture, the key ingredient in 78% of American's favorite recipes is tomatoes. Americans eat 22 to 24 pounds of tomatoes per person per year, and more than half of the quantity eaten is tomato sauce and ketchup.

WWW.WIKIPEDIA.ORG

★ ★ ★ ★ ★ ★ ★ ★ ★ ★ ★ ★　　　★ ★ ★ ★ ★ ★ ★ ★ ★ ★ ★ ★

Bow Ties with Gorgonzola

1 pound bow tie pasta, cooked
1 pound fresh spinach
3 large garlic cloves, minced
1 tablespoon olive oil
8 large plum tomatoes, cut into
  wedges
1 cup wine or chicken broth
Salt and pepper to taste
2–3 fresh basil leaves, chopped
8 ounces Gorgonzola cheese
  (broken into chunks)

Cook pasta according to package directions (al dente). Wash and take stems off spinach. Sauté garlic in olive oil. Add tomato wedges; simmer for 20 minutes. Add spinach, wine, salt, pepper, and basil. Simmer for 5 minutes. Add Gorgonzola and stir. When cheese melts, mix with pasta and serve. Serves 4.

Savor the Flavor (New York)

Macaroni Mousse

1 cup elbow macaroni, uncooked
1 pimento, chopped
1 green bell pepper, chopped
1 tablespoon chopped parsley
1 tablespoon chopped onion
½ teaspoon salt
Dash of red pepper
½ cup margarine
3 eggs
2 slices loaf bread, cut into
  small cubes
1½ cups grated sharp
  Cheddar cheese, divided
1½ cups milk

Heat oven to 350°. Butter a 1½-quart baking dish. Cook macaroni according to directions on package. Mix pimento, pepper, parsley, onion, salt, red pepper, and margarine together with macaroni. Beat eggs slightly; pour over bread cubes. Add 1¼ cups cheese. Combine with macaroni mixture. Place in prepared dish. Pour milk over, and top with remaining ¼ cup cheese. Bake 45 minutes, until top is golden brown. Serves 6–8.

Note: May be prepared several hours in advance or day before and refrigerated until an hour before cooking time.

Palate Pleasers (Tennessee)

Country Pasta with Mozzarella

8 ounces uncooked rigatoni
8 slices bacon, cut into 1-inch
  pieces
2 cups broccoli florets
½ teaspoon minced fresh garlic

2 cups (8 ounces) shredded
  mozzarella cheese
¼ cup grated Parmesan cheese
Pinch of cayenne pepper
¼ cup chopped fresh parsley

Cook rigatoni according to package directions; drain. Meanwhile, in 10-inch skillet, cook bacon over medium-high heat, stirring occasionally, until bacon is browned (6–8 minutes). Reduce heat to medium. Add broccoli and garlic. Cook, stirring occasionally, until broccoli is tender-crisp (4–5 minutes). Add rigatoni and remaining ingredients except parsley. Continue cooking, stirring occasionally, until cheese is melted (3–5 minutes). Sprinkle with parsley.

Cooking with Cops, Too (Idaho)

Lemon Asparagus Pasta

1 (8-ounce) package angel hair
  pasta
2½ cups cut fresh asparagus
  (1-inch pieces)
1 tablespoon butter
½ cup chopped green onions
1½ teaspoons grated lemon peel

3 tablespoons lemon juice
¾ cup milk
2 eggs
1 tablespoon chopped fresh dill
¼ teaspoon salt
⅛ teaspoon ground nutmeg

Cook pasta in boiling water 4 minutes. Add asparagus and cook 2 minutes longer or until tender. Drain.

While pasta cooks, melt butter in large frying pan over medium heat. Add green onions and lemon peel and sauté 1 minute. Add lemon juice and cook until liquid is almost evaporated.

Beat together milk and eggs. Add milk mixture, pasta, and asparagus to pan with green onions. Cook over low heat until milk mixture is slightly thick, about 4 minutes. Do not boil. Stir in dill, salt, and nutmeg. Serve immediately. Serves 4–6.

Simply in Season (Pennsylvania)

Summer Linguine

This is a crowd pleaser. The fresh basil makes all the difference.

4 large tomatoes, chopped
1 pound Brie cheese, coarsely
  chopped
5 garlic cloves, peeled, minced
1 cup chopped fresh basil
1 cup olive oil
½ teaspoon salt
½ teaspoon pepper

6 quarts water
⅛ teaspoon olive oil
1 tablespoon salt
1½ pounds uncooked linguine
¼ cup freshly grated Parmesan
  cheese
Freshly ground pepper to taste

Combine tomatoes, Brie cheese, garlic, basil, 1 cup olive oil, ½ teaspoon salt, and ½ teaspoon pepper in bowl; mix well. Let stand, covered, for 1 hour or longer.

Bring water to a boil in large saucepan. Stir in ⅛ teaspoon olive oil and 1 tablespoon salt. Add linguine. Cook for 8–10 minutes or until firm; drain. Toss hot linguine with tomato mixture in bowl. Brie will melt into pasta. Sprinkle with Parmesan cheese and fresh pepper. Yields 6 servings.

The Best of Wheeling (West Virginia)

Seafood Giovanni

2 large onions, chopped
2 bell peppers, chopped
3 cups sliced fresh mushrooms
Butter
3 cups chopped tomatoes
1 (8-ounce) package vermicelli
  pasta, cooked

3 cups flaked crabmeat,
  shrimp, or prawns (small)
2 cups sour cream
1 cup grated sharp Cheddar
  cheese

Sauté onions, bell peppers, and mushrooms in butter. Add tomatoes, cooked vermicelli pasta, and crabmeat. Mix well. Add sour cream. Mix well again. Turn into greased 9x13-inch casserole. Sprinkle with grated cheese. Bake in moderate oven, 300°–350° for 30 minutes. Makes 12 servings.

Recipe from Time After Time B&B, Victor, Montana
Recipes from Big Sky Country (Big Sky)

Crab Après la Chasse

1 small head broccoli
2 cups chopped onions
½ pound fresh mushrooms
2 garlic cloves or shallots,
   minced or mashed
½ cup butter, melted
½ pound vermicelli, cooked
2–3 cups fresh crabmeat, picked
¼ cup chopped stuffed green
   or black olives

½ pound shredded sharp
   Cheddar cheese
½ cup sour cream
1 (1-pound, 12-ounce) can
   tomatoes, drained and
   chopped
2 teaspoons salt
½ teaspoon basil
Seasoned bread crumbs
Butter, melted

Break broccoli into smallest florets; discard all stems; boil 2 minutes and drain. In large frying pan, sauté onions, mushrooms, and garlic in butter until tender. Combine with remaining ingredients, except bread crumbs and butter, stirring until well mixed. Pour mixture into greased 3-quart casserole or baking dish. Sprinkle with seasoned bread crumbs and drizzle with melted butter. Bake, uncovered, in 350° oven for 35–45 minutes or until hot and bubbly. Can double easily. Serves 12.

The Philadelphia Orchestra Cookbook (Pennsylvania)

Why should you eat your broccoli?

Because broccoli is a proven cancer fighter. And because it is a good source of iron for those who don't eat meat. It is also free of saturated fat, low in sodium, cholesterol free, low in calories, high in vitamin C, and a good source of folate, which helps prevent birth defects. *That's* why!

Vegetable Pasta Pie

2⅔ cups cooked spaghetti
   (small box)
1½ ounces grated Parmesan
   cheese (¾ cup)

1 tablespoon plus 1 teaspoon
   margarine
1 teaspoon parsley

Combine the above 4 ingredients in a medium bowl; mix well. Press spaghetti mixture into the bottom and up the sides of a 9-inch pie pan to form a crust; set aside.

FILLING:

1 cup chopped zucchini
½ cup chopped green bell
   pepper
3 ounces onion, chopped
   (⅔ cup)
½ cup sliced mushrooms
2 tablespoons water

1 garlic clove, minced
1 cup tomato sauce
½ teaspoon oregano
½ teaspoon marjoram
½ cup tomato paste
¼ teaspoon salt
½ teaspoon basil

In a large nonstick skillet combine vegetables, water, and garlic; cook over medium heat, stirring often, about 10 minutes or until vegetables are tender-crisp. Stir in remaining ingredients and simmer 5 minutes. Place over spaghetti pie crust.

TOPPING:

2½ ounces grated Cheddar
   cheese (⅔ cup)

1⅓ cups cottage cheese

Combine Cheddar cheese and cottage cheese and top vegetable mixture. Bake at 350° for 30 minutes or until heated throughout and cheese is melted.

Enjoy (Iowa)

Zucchinis are low in calories, with only sixteen calories for each one-cup serving.

★★★★★★★★★★★   ★★★★★★★★★★★

Chicken Melanzana with Spaghetti

2 whole large chicken breasts
  (1½ pounds total), split
Garlic salt and freshly
  ground pepper to taste
1 small eggplant (¾ pound),
  peeled and cubed

½ cup chopped onion
1 (6-ounce) can tomato paste
1 cup water
½ teaspoon Italian seasoning
3 cups tender-cooked spaghetti

Season chicken pieces with garlic salt and pepper, and place them skin-side-up in a shallow roasting pan. Quick-bake at 450° for 15–20 minutes until well-browned. Pour off all the fat.

In medium bowl, combine eggplant, onion, tomato paste, water, and Italian seasoning, then pour it around the chicken. Cover roaster loosely with foil, and bake at 350° for 40–50 minutes, stirring occasionally, until chicken is tender and liquid is reduced to a thick sauce. Serve with ¾ cup spaghetti per person. Serves 4.

Recipe submitted by Bernadette and Terry Bradshaw
The Southern Gospel Music Cookbook (Tennessee)

Susan's White Spaghetti

2 whole large chicken breasts,
  boned and skinned
1 tablespoon cooking sherry
2 teaspoons cornstarch
½ teaspoon salt, divided
4 tablespoons oil, divided
2 medium zucchini, thinly sliced
1 (8-ounce) package angel hair
  pasta

1 (4-ounce) package sliced ham,
  cut into ¼-inch strips
⅓ cup half-and-half
3 tablespoons butter
¼ teaspoon pepper
2 tablespoons grated Parmesan
  cheese

Mix chicken, cut into bite-sized pieces, in mixture of sherry, cornstarch, and ¼ teaspoon salt. Set aside. In 1 tablespoon oil over medium heat, cook zucchini with remaining ¼ teaspoon salt until tender-crisp. Remove with slotted spoon. Add remaining 3 tablespoons oil to pan and sauté chicken. Mix chicken with zucchini. Cook pasta, drain, then add chicken mixture, ham, half-and-half, butter, pepper, and cheese. Toss and serve.

St. Francis in the Foothills 30th Anniversary Cookbook (Arizona)

Herbed Chicken Pasta

1 teaspoon vegetable oil
1½ cups sliced mushrooms
½ cup chopped onion
1 garlic clove, minced
1 pound skinned, boned
   chicken breasts, cut into
   1-inch pieces, divided
½ teaspoon salt

½ teaspoon dried basil
¼ teaspoon pepper
2 cups coarsely chopped
   tomatoes
4 cups cooked fettuccine
¼ cup grated Parmesan
   cheese

Heat oil in a large skillet over medium-high heat. Add mushrooms, onion, and garlic; sauté 2 minutes. Add chicken, salt, basil, and pepper; sauté 6 minutes or until chicken is done. Add tomatoes; sauté 2 minutes. Serve over pasta; sprinkle with cheese. Makes 4 servings.

Recipes from the Heart (Nevada)

Spinach Lasagne

½ pound fresh spinach
½ onion, chopped
1 garlic clove, minced
1 tablespoon olive oil
1 cup low-fat cottage cheese
1 egg, beaten
Salt and pepper to taste

1 teaspoon basil
½ teaspoon oregano
2 tablespoons chopped parsley
½ pound lasagne noodles
½ pound mozzarella cheese
3 cups tomato sauce

Wash spinach carefully, tearing out stems, and chop coarsely. Sauté chopped onion and minced garlic in oil. Combine sautéed onion and garlic with spinach, cottage cheese, and beaten egg. Mix well. Season with salt, pepper, basil, oregano, and parsley.

Cook lasagne noodles until tender. Coarsely grate mozzarella cheese. In a buttered oblong baking dish, layer noodles, cottage cheese mixture, mozzarella cheese, and tomato sauce, in order listed. Repeat layering 3 times, making sure tomato sauce is on top. Cover with aluminum foil. Bake at 350° for 40 minutes. Remove foil and bake 10 minutes more. Serve with garlic bread and green salad. Serves 4.

In Good Taste (North Carolina)

★★★★★★★★★★★   ★★★★★★★★★★★

Pasta Primavera

¼ cup butter
1 small onion, chopped
1 garlic clove, minced
3 ounces cauliflower, in pieces
½ carrot, sliced
½ zucchini, sliced
½ pound fresh asparagus, cut in
  ¼-inch pieces
¼ pound fresh mushrooms,
  sliced

½ cup heavy cream
¼ cup chicken stock
1 teaspoon dried basil
Salt and pepper to taste
½ cup frozen peas, thawed
2 scallions, thinly sliced
12 ounces vermicelli or
  linguine, cooked al dente
Freshly grated Parmesan
  cheese

In large skillet, melt butter and sauté onion and garlic. Add cauliflower and carrot; cook 3 minutes. Add zucchini, asparagus, and mushrooms to skillet and cook 2 minutes more. Add cream, stock, and seasonings, and cook until liquid is slightly reduced. Add peas and scallions and cook briefly. Serve sauce over cooked and drained noodles. Sprinkle with lots of fresh Parmesan cheese. Yields 4 servings.

Even More Special (North Carolina)

Pasta with Chicken

Different and very easy.

1 pound green spinach noodles
4 tablespoons olive oil
8 tablespoons butter, divided
1 cup finely chopped onion
1 teaspoon minced garlic
4 whole chicken breasts, cubed
1½ cups cubed zucchini

4 cups cherry tomatoes, halved
2 teaspoons salt
Few grindings pepper
1 teaspoon basil
1 teaspoon oregano
2 cups shredded Swiss cheese

While pasta is cooking, heat oil and 4 tablespoons butter in skillet over high heat. Add onion and garlic and cook until onion is golden. Turn down heat and add chicken. Cook until chicken is white, about 5 minutes. Add zucchini, tomatoes, salt, pepper, basil, and oregano. Mix hot, drained pasta with remaining 4 tablespoons butter. Add chicken mixture and toss gently. Sprinkle with cheese and serve. Makes 6 servings.

Soupçon II (Illinois)

★★★★★★★★★★★   ★★★★★★★★★★★

Spicy Crawfish Pasta

Great dish served with garlic bread and salad.

1 package rotini (spiral) pasta	1 pint half-and-half
1 stick butter or margarine	6–8 ounces jalapeño-Jack
1 bunch green onions, chopped	cheese
1 medium yellow onion,	Salt, black pepper, and red
chopped	pepper to taste
1 teaspoon minced garlic	Parmesan cheese (optional)
1 (1-pound) package crawfish	
tails	

Prepare pasta according to package directions. Drain and set aside to cool. In a large nonstick skillet, melt butter. Add onions and garlic; sauté approximately 3 minutes. Add crawfish and sauté another 3 minutes. Reduce heat to medium and add half-and-half. Reduce heat to low and add slices of jalapeño-Jack cheese to the sauce. Stir sauce frequently until the cheese is thoroughly melted (sauce will be slightly lumpy). Season to taste, but go lightly with the red pepper; the jalapeños in the cheese make the sauce very spicy.

In a large casserole dish, combine drained, cooked pasta and crawfish sauce. Sprinkle with Parmesan cheese, if desired, and serve while hot. (Can be prepared ahead and reheated in oven at 350°.) Serves 4–5 adults.

Fiftieth Anniversary Cookbook (Louisiana II)

The world's heaviest onion weighed 16.52 pounds and was grown by John Sifford of Halesowen, West Midlands, UK, and recorded on September 16, 2005. Sifford beat the ten-year-old record of 15 pounds 15½ ounces at the Harrogate Autumn Flower Show.

Greek-Style Shrimp with Pasta

1 teaspoon finely chopped garlic
5 tablespoons olive oil, divided
2 cups cubed peeled tomatoes
½ cup dry white wine
Salt and black pepper to taste
¾ cup finely chopped fresh
  basil
1 teaspoon dried crumbled
  oregano

1½ pounds medium shrimp,
  peeled, deveined
⅛ teaspoon hot red pepper
  flakes
8 ounces crumbled feta cheese
6 ounces rigatoni, cooked,
  drained

Sauté garlic in 2 tablespoons olive oil in a skillet. Add tomatoes. Cook 1 minute. Add wine, salt, pepper, basil, and oregano. Cook over medium heat 10 minutes. Season shrimp with salt and pepper. Heat remaining 3 tablespoons olive oil in large skillet. Add shrimp. Sauté 1 minute or until shrimp turn pink. Sprinkle with red pepper flakes. Spoon into a small, greased baking dish. Sprinkle with feta cheese. Spoon tomato sauce over top. Bake at 400° for 10 minutes or until bubbly. Spoon over hot pasta on a serving platter. Yields 4 servings.

America Celebrates Columbus (Ohio)

Tomatoes are one of the most common garden fruits in the United States, and along with zucchini, have a reputation for out-producing the needs of the grower.

John Wayne Cheese Casserole

2 (4-ounce) cans whole green
  chiles, drained, seeded
4 cups shredded Monterey Jack
  cheese
4 cups shredded Cheddar cheese
4 eggs, separated

1 (5-ounce) can evaporated
  milk
1 tablespoon flour
½ teaspoon salt
⅛ teaspoon pepper
2 medium tomatoes, sliced

Chop the green chiles and place them in a large bowl. Add the
Monterey Jack cheese and Cheddar cheese and mix lightly. Spoon
into a greased shallow 2-quart casserole.

Beat the egg whites in a mixer bowl until stiff peaks form.
Whisk the egg yolks and evaporated milk in a bowl until well
blended. Stir in the flour, salt, and pepper. Fold the egg whites
into the egg yolk mixture. Pour over the cheese mixture in the
casserole.

Pierce the layers with a fork to allow the cheese mixture to
absorb some of the egg mixture.

Bake at 325° for 30 minutes. Remove from the oven. Arrange
the tomato slices around the edge of the casserole. Bake for 30
minutes longer or until a knife inserted in the center comes out
clean. Serves 8.

Tucson Treasures (Arizona)

Carrot Brown Rice

A flavorful and colorful rice.

2⅓ cups chicken broth
1 cup brown rice
½ pound carrots, peeled and
  chopped or julienned

2 medium onions, sliced
1 tablespoon butter
½ teaspoon salt

Bring broth to a boil. Add rice, carrots, onions, butter, and salt; stir.
Cover tightly and cook over low heat until all liquid is absorbed,
about 50 minutes.

Of Tide & Thyme (Mid-Atlantic)

Bring Home the Bacon

1 cup grated Cheddar cheese
1 cup cottage cheese
3 cups cooked rice
12 strips bacon, fried crisp
   and crumbled
1 cup sliced fresh mushrooms,
   or 1 (8-ounce) can, drained

1 pound fresh asparagus spears,
   or 1 (16-ounce) can, drained
½ teaspoon salt, or to taste
Pepper to taste
½ cup butter or margarine
1 cup milk

In small bowl, blend cheeses and set aside. Mix together rice and bacon; place in greased 9x13x2-inch casserole dish. Spread mushrooms over rice. Arrange asparagus spears on top of mushrooms. Sprinkle on salt and pepper. Top with cheese mixture, dot with butter, and pour milk over top. Bake 45 minutes at 350°. Serves 6–8.

The VIP Cookbook: A Potpourri of Virginia Cooking (Virginia)

Rice with Ham and Shrimp

½ cup Spanish olive oil
¼ pound chorizo, thinly sliced
2 medium onions, finely chopped
4 garlic cloves, minced
3 cups chicken broth
3 medium tomatoes, finely
   chopped
2 medium green bell peppers,
   seeded and cut into strips
3 tablespoons chopped Italian
   parsley

2 teaspoons sugar
½ teaspoon salt
1 teaspoon ground cumin
½ teaspoon freshly ground
   pepper
2 cups uncooked short-grain
   white rice
1 pound medium shrimp,
   cleaned
½ pound lean ham, cut into
   1½-inch cubes

Heat oil in Dutch oven until light haze forms. Add chorizo, onion, and garlic, and cook until chorizo is browned and onions are soft (approximately 5 minutes). Stir in remaining ingredients except rice, shrimp, and ham. Cook, covered, over medium heat until almost tender (approximately 12 minutes). Stir in rice, shrimp, and ham. Cook for 8–10 minutes, or until all liquid has been absorbed. Serve as an entrée with a hearty loaf of bread. Serves 6.

Basque Cooking and Lore (Idaho)

Skillet Chicken Risotta

1 (3-pound) chicken, cut up
2 tablespoons oil
½ cup rice
½ cup onion, chopped
2 teaspoons salt (to taste)
½ teaspoon poultry seasoning

1 (4-ounce) can mushroom
  pieces
3 carrots, peeled and sliced
  on bias
1 cup chopped tomatoes
1½ cups water

Brown chicken in oil. Remove chicken pieces from skillet. Drain all but 2 tablespoons fat from skillet. To skillet add rice, onion, salt, and poultry seasoning. Cook and stir until rice is lightly browned. Add mushrooms, carrots, tomatoes, and water. Place chicken atop rice mixture. Cover and simmer 45 minutes or until chicken and rice are done.

Herrin's Favorite Italian Recipes Cookbook (Illinois)

Brown Rice Pilaf with Kiwi Fruit

Even kids will enjoy this high-fiber, low-fat, low-sodium side dish with its hint of sweetness.

1⅓ cups water
1⅓ cups unsweetened apple
  juice
1 cup uncooked long-grain
  brown rice
2 tablespoons currants or
  raisins

¼ teaspoon ground cinnamon
⅔ cup peeled, coarsely chopped
  kiwi fruit (about 2)
¼ cup diced unpeeled red
  apple
¼ teaspoon grated orange rind

Combine first 3 ingredients in a large saucepan. Bring to a boil; add currants and cinnamon, stirring well. Reduce heat; cover and cook rice 45 minutes without lifting cover (or according to package directions, omitting salt). Remove from heat, and add remaining ingredients; toss gently. Yields 4 cups.

Per Serving: Cal 125 (6.0% from fat); Fat 0.8g (Sat 0.2g); Chol 0mg; Fiber 1.8g; Sod 4mg. Diabetic Exchange: 1 starch + ½ fruit.

Here's To Your Heart: Cooking Smart (Wisconsin)

Mississippi Dirty Rice

6 tablespoons cooking oil
Finely chopped giblets from
   3 chickens
2 large onions, diced
1 cup diced celery
2 dozen oysters, chopped
¼ cup oyster liquid

½ cup chopped parsley
½ cup chopped green onions
2 garlic cloves, minced
1 cup rice, cooked
Salt, black pepper, and cayenne
   pepper to taste

Pour oil into heavy skillet or Dutch oven and add chopped giblets, onions, and celery. Cook on medium heat, stirring as needed, until giblets are browned and onions and celery are soft. Add oysters and liquid, parsley, green onions, and garlic; cover and simmer for 10 minutes. Stir in cooked rice, salt and pepper and heat to steaming. Makes 8–10 servings.

Note: May substitute 1½ cups of ground beef, veal, or pork for the giblets. The flavor is better if the oysters, giblets, and vegetables are ground and not just chopped. Seasonings may be varied according to personal preference. Worcestershire may be added. Tabasco may be used instead of cayenne pepper.

   This may be used as a stuffing in a turkey or large hen. It may also be put in a greased casserole dish and baked in a 350° oven for 20 minutes.

The Mississippi Cookbook (Mississippi)

Jambalaya Grits

2 tablespoons bacon grease
2 tablespoons flour
½ cup chopped onion
1 green bell pepper, chopped
½ cup chopped celery

1 cup quick grits
3 fresh tomatoes, peeled and
   chopped (about 1 cup)
1 cup ground ham
Bacon, cooked and crumbled

In a heavy skillet, heat bacon grease and gradually add flour, stirring constantly, until roux becomes light brown. Add onion, green bell pepper, and celery; cook 5 minutes. Cook grits according to package directions and add to roux. Add tomatoes and ham. Sprinkle with bacon and serve immediately. Serves 6.

Jambalaya (Louisiana)

★★★★★★★★★★★ ★★★★★★★★★★★

Lane's Landing Jambalaya

4 slices bacon, chopped
1 pound fresh Italian sausage
1 large yellow onion, chopped
2 garlic cloves, chopped,
  mashed
3 potatoes, peeled, quartered
1 green bell pepper, chopped
1 cup Donax (bean clams)
  broth
4 medium tomatoes, skinned

1 tablespoon sweet basil
1 (6-ounce) can tomato paste
2 tablespoons Worcestershire
½ teaspoon chili powder
2 large bay leaves
3 cups water
1 cup rice, uncooked
Salt and pepper to taste
2 cups raw shrimp, peeled
1 cup blue crabmeat, picked

Fry bacon in large heavy skillet. Remove bacon, and wipe pan clean before browning thick slices of sausage. Add onion, garlic, potatoes, and green bell pepper; lightly sauté. Return bacon to pan, and add remaining ingredients except shrimp and crabmeat. Simmer until potatoes are tender. Add shrimp and crabmeat. Continue to cook until shrimp are fully pink. Serve in bowls along with hot French bread. Serves 6.

A Taste of Archaeology (South Carolina)

Potato Trivia:

• In October 1995, the potato became the first vegetable to be grown in space.
• You can treat aches and pains by rubbing boiled potato water (cooled) to the affected area.
• You can treat facial blemishes by washing your face daily with cool potato juice.

Poultry

Known as the sweetest onion in the world, Vidalias can only be grown in the fields around Vidalia and Glennville, Georgia. The Vidalia onion was officially designated the state vegetable of Georgia in 1990.

Touch of Italy Chicken

4 chicken breasts, skinned
  and boned
Italian seasoning, salt, and
  pepper to taste
½ (10-ounce) package fresh
  spinach, cooked and drained
Provolone cheese

4 teaspoons plus ½ cup
  (1 stick) butter, divided
2 eggs
2½ cups bread crumbs
1 teaspoon Italian seasoning
1 teaspoon paprika

Wash chicken breasts; place between wax paper and pound thin.
Sprinkle breasts with Italian seasoning, salt and pepper. Place ¼
of spinach down the center of each breast. Top with a finger of
provolone cheese. Top with one teaspoon butter. Fold chicken like
an envelope, encasing spinach, cheese, and butter.

Beat eggs. Combine bread crumbs, Italian seasoning, and paprika and mix well. Dip chicken in egg, then in bread crumbs, hold-
ing so envelopes don't unfold. Let dry in refrigerator for 15 minutes then re-dip in egg and crumbs. (You can bake at this time or
hold them in the refrigerator for several hours.) When ready to
bake, melt the stick of butter and roll the chicken in the butter, turning to coat. Place in a shallow baking dish and pour any remaining butter over the chicken. Bake at 375° for 25–30 minutes, turning once. Make a small cut in the chicken to check for doneness.
(No pink!) Makes 4 servings.

Apples, Brie & Chocolate (Wisconsin)

Did you know that spinach is healthy in different ways in both its cooked and raw
form? When cooked, it makes the carotenoids, including beta-carotene, more available. When raw, the vitamin C and folate content is stronger.

50 Clove Garlic Chicken

Slow roasting the garlic mellows and sweetens it.

2 whole chickens
50 whole garlic cloves, unpeeled
1 pound carrots

2 stalks celery
2 tablespoons cooking sherry
½ teaspoon nutmeg

Cut up, skin, and trim fat from chicken. Separate garlic cloves. Cut carrots lengthwise and then into 3-inch pieces. In a 3-quart casserole, lay celery stalks followed by alternating layers of chicken, garlic, and carrots. Drizzle on sherry. Sprinkle with nutmeg. Cover tightly with heavy foil. Bake at 375° for 90 minutes. Spoon garlic cloves into a side dish, and spread on warm sourdough French bread. Serve with a tossed salad to 8 people.

Be Our Guest (Alaska)

Breast of Chicken in Cream and Apples

8 chicken breasts
3 tablespoons flour
8 tablespoons butter
4 tablespoons minced onion
8 fresh apple rings, peeled and
   cut ½-inch thick

1½ cups cider
½ cup brandy
2 cups whipping cream
Salt and pepper to taste

Dust chicken breasts with flour and sauté in butter with onion over low heat. Poach apple rings in cider until soft. When chicken is nicely browned, add the brandy and ignite. Drain the apple rings and add the cider used for poaching to the chicken. Cook at low heat until chicken is tender, about 10 minutes. Add cream and continue cooking until the sauce is thickened. Season to taste. Place chicken on a serving platter, put a slice of apple on each piece, and pour sauce over all. Run under the broiler to brown. Serves 8.

Bravo, Chef! (Texas)

Chicken Broccoli Vegetable Sauté

2 tablespoons margarine, divided
4 skinless, boneless chicken breast halves (about 1 pound)
1 cup cut-up broccoli
½ cup thinly sliced carrots
1 cup sliced mushrooms
1 (10¾-ounce) can cream of broccoli soup
⅓ cup milk
⅛ teaspoon pepper

In skillet over medium heat, in one tablespoon hot margarine, cook chicken 10 minutes or until browned on both sides. Remove chicken; keep warm.

In same skillet, in remaining margarine, cook broccoli, carrots, and mushrooms 5 minutes, stirring often. Stir in soup, milk, and pepper. Heat to boiling. Return chicken to skillet. Reduce heat to low; simmer 5 minutes or until chicken is fork-tender. Makes 4 servings. Good served with rice.

Home Cooking with the Cummer Family (Iowa)

Raspberry Chicken

1 (12-ounce) jar pure raspberry jam
1 cup unsweetened pineapple juice concentrate
1 cup low-sodium soy sauce
2 tablespoons rice vinegar
1 teaspoon chili powder
1 teaspoon curry powder
1 teaspoon garlic powder
1 cup fresh raspberries, mashed, divided
4 (4-ounce) skinless, boneless chicken breasts
1 cup chopped fresh basil, for topping

Mix jam, pineapple juice, soy sauce, vinegar, chili powder, curry powder, garlic powder, and ¼ cup mashed raspberries; pour over chicken breasts in baking dish. Marinate in refrigerator for one hour. Top with remaining raspberries and basil. Bake at 350° for 30–40 minutes.

Let Freedom Ring (Nevada)

★★★★★★★★★★★ ★★★★★★★★★★★

Coq a Vin Simplified

A great dish to take to a convention for a first night dinner.

3 medium potatoes, peeled, cut
  in chunks
3 carrots, peeled, cut into pieces
  same size as potatoes
2 medium onions, also cut into
  same size chunks

4 chicken breasts or thighs
2 cups red wine (preferably
  Pinot Noir)
Salt and pepper to taste
Water to cover

Place all ingredients in a crockpot. Use enough water to cover.
Cook on HIGH overnight or about 8 hours.

Taste Trek! (Virginia II)

Tomato Cheese Chicken

½ cup flavored bread crumbs
2 whole chicken breasts,
  skinned, boned, halved and
  flattened, with excess fat
  removed
2 teaspoons olive oil

2 tomatoes, sliced
¼ teaspoon dried basil (or
  chopped fresh basil leaves)
4 slices provolone cheese
Sprig of fresh parsley,
  chopped

In a flat dish, press crumbs into chicken on both sides; reserve.
Grease a large oven-proof casserole dish. Lay chicken in casserole. Top chicken with tomato slices. Sprinkle tomato slices with
basil or basil leaves. Top with provolone cheese and garnish with
chopped parsley. Bake in a preheated 400° oven for 20 minutes.
Remove from oven with a spatula. Serve on heated plates.

Chicken Expressions (New England)

Vegetables that are boiled actually lose some of their water content. They will
weigh less after boiling in water than they did before. This is caused by the heat,
which breaks down the cell walls and allows some of the water to leak from the
plants cells.

★★★★★★★★★★★ ★★★★★★★★★★★

Chicken with Apple Pecan Stuffing

The wonderful aroma this dish creates will call your family to the table before the table is set.

2 Granny Smith apples, chopped
1 cup chopped onion
⅓ cup raisins
3 tablespoons chopped pecans
1 (8-ounce) package cornbread stuffing mix

¾ teaspoon sage
½ teaspoon salt
¼ teaspoon pepper
1 cup chicken broth
6 skinless chicken breast halves with bone

Place all ingredients, except chicken, into a large slow-cooker; stir to combine. Place chicken on top and cook, covered, on LOW for 6 hours. Remove chicken breasts carefully, using a large spoon or spatula so that bones are not left in the stuffing. Place on a plate and serve with stuffing. Yields 6 servings.

Per serving: Cal 379; Fat 8g; Prot 32g; Carb 43g; Chol 72mg; Sod 704mg; Dietary fiber 4g.

More of What's Cooking (Texas II)

Chicken with Purple Onions

2 large purple onions
2 pounds boneless, skinless chicken breasts
6 tablespoons Parmesan cheese dressing

1 (8-ounce) jar grated Parmesan cheese
Cayenne pepper to taste
Parsley, chopped

Peel onions. Cut into 6 (½-inch-thick) slices. Place on ungreased baking sheet. Trim chicken of any visible fat and cut breasts lengthwise into ½-inch strips. Lay chicken strips on onion rounds to solidly cover onion slice. Drizzle 1 tablespoon dressing over each serving. Generously sprinkle Parmesan cheese and add cayenne pepper to taste. Sprinkle with parsley. Bake at 425° for 25–30 minutes. Serves 6.

A Treasury of Recipes for Mind, Body & Soul (Ohio)

Weekender Party Pleaser

2 cups diced cooked chicken
½ cup shredded carrots
½ cup chopped fresh broccoli
½ cup chopped sweet red bell
  pepper
1 cup shredded sharp Cheddar
  cheese
½ cup mayonnaise

2 garlic cloves, chopped
¼ teaspoon salt
Pepper to taste
2 (8-ounce) tubes refrigerated
  crescent rolls
1 egg white, beaten
2 tablespoons slivered almonds

In a bowl, mix chicken, carrots, broccoli, red bell pepper, cheese, mayonnaise, garlic, salt, and pepper; mix well. Unroll crescent roll dough and place on cookie sheet, side by side, pressing out perforations and making a 15x12-inch rectangle (dough will hang over pan). Spread filling down center of dough. On each side, cut 1-inch wide strips. Start at one end and alternate strips from each side, twisting the ends across the filling and pinching to seal (it will look like it's braided). Brush with egg white and top with almonds. Bake at 375° for 30–35 minutes. Makes 12 servings.

Kingman Welcome Wagon Club Cookbook (Arizona)

Chicken with Tri-Color Peppers

1 medium onion, finely chopped
Olive oil
2 boneless, skinless chicken
  breasts, cut into chunks
1 garlic clove, peeled and
  chopped

½ each: red, yellow, and green
  bell peppers, seeded and cut
  into chunks
½ cup white wine

Sauté onion in olive oil until soft, then add chicken pieces and garlic. Cook until chicken is cooked through. Add peppers and wine and cook until peppers are cooked, but still firm, and liquid is slightly reduced. Serve with pasta of your choice.

Dishing It Out (New York)

Chicken Waikiki

2–3 pounds chicken pieces
Flour
Salt and pepper to taste

2 cups fresh pineapple chunks
1 large green bell pepper, cut
  crosswise (in circles)

Shake the chicken in a paper bag with flour, salt and pepper. Brown in a skillet, then place uncovered in glass baking dish. Bake in 350° oven for 1–1¼ hours. While chicken is baking, make the Sauce. Place pineapple and green bell pepper over chicken during last half hour of baking time. Serve with rice and a tossed salad or cooked vegetables.

SAUCE:
½ cup sugar
2 tablespoons cornstarch
⅜ cup cider vinegar
⅜ cup pineapple juice

1 tablespoon soy sauce
½ teaspoon ginger
1 chicken bouillon cube

Combine ingredients in a saucepan; cook, stirring constantly, and boil 2 minutes until Sauce thickens. Pour immediately over chicken while it is baking.

Friends and Celebrities Cookbook II (Hawaii)

In 1493, Christopher Columbus brought a pineapple back to Europe from his voyage through the Carib Islands. To the Carib, the pineapple symbolized hospitality, and the Spaniards soon learned they were welcome if a pineapple was placed by the entrance to a village. This symbolism spread quickly throughout Europe and North America. Families often put a fresh pineapple in the center of the table when they had visitors. This was not only a colorful centerpiece but symbolized the greatest welcome and hospitality to the visitor. The fruit would then be served after the meal as a special dessert.

Chicken Curry

Katzinger's Deli's traditional house recipe. A simply fabulous lunch idea!

½ pound raisins
½ cup flaked coconut
¼ Spanish onion, cut into julienne strips
3 pounds chicken, cooked, skinned and cut into ½-inch cubes
1 green apple (Granny Smith if available), cut into ½-inch cubes

1 red apple, cut into ½-inch cubes
1 pear, cut into ½-inch cubes
4 stalks celery, bias cut
7 ounces pineapple chunks, drained
1½ cups mayonnaise
¼ cup honey
2 tablespoons curry powder

Place raisins in hot water for 5 minutes to plump. Drain well. Spread coconut on a cookie sheet and broil until golden brown. Deep-fry onion until golden brown. Drain on paper towel.

Toss together raisins, coconut, and onion with all but last 3 ingredients. Combine mayonnaise, honey, and curry powder. Mix thoroughly with rest of ingredients. Refrigerate until chilled. Serves 8–10.

A Taste of Columbus Vol III (Ohio)

Chicken and Asparagus Casserole

1 pound fresh asparagus
1½ cups cooked cubed chicken
1 (10½-ounce) can cream of asparagus or cream of mushroom soup
⅓ cup milk

¾ cup shredded Cheddar cheese
2 tablespoons butter or margarine, melted
5 tablespoons bread crumbs

In a shallow casserole dish, arrange asparagus on bottom. Spread chicken cubes over asparagus. Combine soup and milk. Pour over chicken. Sprinkle cheese over top. In small bowl melt margarine. Add bread crumbs and stir. Sprinkle over cheese. Bake at 450° for 15 minutes or until hot throughout and lightly browned. Yields 4 servings.

Irene's Country Cooking (Big Sky)

Lincoln Logs

WHITE SAUCE:

½ cup chicken stock   ½ cup heavy cream

Combine well.

1½ cups diced, cooked   ¼ cup finely chopped celery
  chicken   ¼ cup finely chopped onion
1½ cups bread crumbs   ½ teaspoon salt
1 cup finely chopped   ¼ teaspoon paprika
  walnuts   Bread crumbs

Mix chicken, bread crumbs, walnuts, celery, onion, salt and paprika. Moisten with a little White Sauce. Form mixture into logs 3-inches long. Roll in bread crumbs and fry in oil. Drain and serve with remaining White Sauce.

Cook Book: Favorite Recipes from Our Best Cooks (Illinois)

Chicken Pot Pie

3 chicken breasts   1 (10¾-ounce) can cream of
2 cups sliced carrots   celery soup
2 cups diced potatoes   ½ cup chicken broth
2 cups diced onions   1 stick margarine, melted
1 (8-ounce) can Le Sueur peas, 1 cup self-rising flour
  drained   1 cup milk
1 (10¾-ounce) can cream of
  chicken soup

Cook chicken breasts, carrots, potatoes, and onions in water to cover. Cut chicken into bite-size pieces. Line the bottom of a 9x13-inch dish with chicken. Layer vegetables plus can of peas over chicken. Pour mixture of soups and broth over chicken layers. Mix margarine, flour, and milk. Pour over mixture. Bake at 350° for 30 minutes; increase temperature to 375° and bake for 15 minutes.

Centennial Cookbook (Florida)

★★★★★★★★★★★ ★★★★★★★★★★★

Chicken and Dumplings

1 (3½-pound) chicken, cut up
1½ quarts water
Salt and freshly ground pepper
  to taste
1 small onion, quartered
1 small carrot, cut into chunks
2 celery stalks with leaves, cut
  into chunks

3 tablespoons butter or chicken
  fat
¼ cup all-purpose flour
⅛ teaspoon paprika
½ cup half-and-half
White pepper to taste
Parsley for garnish

Wash chicken and pat dry with paper towels. Place chicken in large pot. Add water, salt, pepper, onion, carrot, and celery, and simmer, covered, 45 minutes to 1 hour or until chicken is tender. Remove from broth; strain and reserve broth. Cool chicken until able to handle, then discard skin and bones; dice meat; refrigerate.

In a large, heavy saucepan, heat butter or chicken fat. Stir in flour and paprika. Gradually add 3 cups reserved chicken broth, stirring until thickened and smooth. Cook 2 minutes. Add half-and-half and white pepper. Taste and adjust seasonings. Return diced chicken to broth. Prepare Dumplings.

DUMPLINGS:
1½ cups all-purpose flour
½ teaspoon salt
3 teaspoons baking powder

1 tablespoon shortening, melted
⅓ cup milk

In a medium bowl, combine flour, salt, and baking powder. Blend in shortening and milk; mix well.

Dip a teaspoon into cold water; spoon teaspoonfuls of batter on top of simmering chicken mixture. Cook, covered, 15 minutes, without lifting lid. Sprinkle with parsley and serve immediately. Makes 6 servings.

More than Beans and Cornbread (West Virginia)

Carrots are high in sugar and fiber and are an excellent source of carotene, which gives the carrots their bright orange color.

Turkey Cranberry Sandwiches

6 ounces smoked turkey
  breast, thinly sliced
4 slices low-fat cheese (Swiss,
  mozzarella, Cheddar)

8 tomato slices
4 lettuce leaves
8 slices whole-wheat bread

DRESSING:

½ cup whole berry
  cranberry sauce
1 tablespoon Kraft Free
  Nonfat Miracle Whip

⅓ cup diced celery
1 tablespoon lemon juice

Mix together dressing ingredients and set aside. Assemble sandwiches, dividing turkey and cheese evenly among the 4 sandwiches. Spread bread with Dressing and serve.

Amount per serving: Calories 361; Grams of fat 10.7; Cholesterol 20mg; Sodium 746mg; % of Fat 28%.

Eat To Your Heart's Content, Too! (Arkansas)

Turkey and Spinach Burgers

The spinach, herbs, and apricot preserves add a special flavor to these turkey burgers. They are delicious topped with grilled onions or a combination of fresh pineapple slices, onion, and green bell pepper slices.

1½ pounds ground turkey
1½ cups packed fresh
  spinach, washed, dried, and
  cut into small pieces
1 cup minced onions
½ cup whole-wheat bread
  crumbs

¼ cup chopped parsley
2 tablespoons apricot
  preserves
1 teaspoon freshly ground
  pepper
¼ teaspoon salt

Combine turkey, spinach, onions, bread crumbs, parsley, apricot preserves, pepper, and salt in a large bowl and blend well. Cover bowl and refrigerate several hours.

Form turkey mixture into 6 patties. Over hot coals, place burgers on a grilling grid coated with nonstick vegetable spray. Cover grill and cook 9–11 minutes, turning burgers every 3 minutes.

Per serving: 255 Cal; 22.1g Prot; 13.6g Carbo; 12.0g Fat; 42% Cal. from Fat; 1.1g Fiber; 230mg Sod; 58mg Chol.

The Lowfat Grill (Iowa)

Hood River Turkey

4 apples
4 onions
1 fresh (10-pound) turkey

1 cup water
1 cup soy sauce
1 cup white wine

Cut up apples and onions. Stuff turkey with apples and onions. Secure legs and wings. Put turkey in large pan. Mix water, soy sauce, and wine. Cook on low setting of gas grill with lid closed. Baste the turkey with the soy mixture every 20–30 minutes. If the turkey becomes too brown, cover it with aluminum foil. The entire cooking time will be 1½–2 hours, depending upon the exact size of the turkey. Serves 4–6.

Savor the Flavor of Oregon (Oregon)

Citrus Duck

1 (4- to 6-pound) duck
½ teaspoon salt
Rind of 1 lime, cut into pieces
Rind of 1 lemon, cut into pieces
Rind of 1 orange, cut into pieces
½ cup orange liqueur, divided
1 onion, quartered

2 chicken bouillon cubes
1 cup boiling water
2 tablespoons fresh orange juice
1 tablespoon fresh lemon juice
1 tablespoon fresh lime juice
1 tablespoon honey
2 teaspoons cornstarch

Rub inside of duck cavity with salt. Preheat oven to 350°. Soak citrus rinds in ¼ cup orange liqueur for at least 30 minutes. Place citrus rinds and onion and some of liqueur into cavity. Roast about 2½ hours or until tender.

In the meantime, dissolve bouillon in 1 cup boiling water in a saucepan. Add remaining ¼ cup orange liqueur and remaining ingredients. Heat mixture over low heat until thickened. Brush duck with mixture during last half hour of roasting. Heat extra sauce; serve with duck. Makes 4 servings.

Duck Soup & Other Fowl Recipes (Washington)

Stuffed Carolina Quail

1 cup fresh spinach, wilted in
  butter
4 ounces smoked Gouda cheese
6 shallots, roasted in oven

4 semi-boneless quail
2 tablespoons extra virgin olive
  oil
½ cup seasoned flour

Combine first 3 ingredients. Divide mixture into 4 portions, and stuff into body cavity of quail. Brush each bird liberally with extra virgin olive oil, then lightly dredge in flour. In a hot pan, sear quail on both sides to achieve a golden crust. Transfer to a 425° oven and roast 8–10 minutes, or until firm to touch. Yields 2 servings.

Recipe from Poogan's Porch, Charleston
Lowcountry Delights II (South Carolina)

Spiced Cranberry Sauce

Spicy and not too sweet.

1½ cups sugar
¾ cup water
¼ cup lemon juice
½ teaspoon grated lemon
  rind

½ teaspoon ginger
½ teaspoon nutmeg
3 cloves
1 stick cinnamon
1 pound cranberries

In saucepan, combine sugar, water, lemon juice, rind, and spices. Boil for 5 minutes. Remove cinnamon and cloves. Add cranberries. Boil 5 minutes or until skins pop open. Cool. Refrigerate until served. Yields 1 quart.

The Cookbook II (New England)

Do you know which state produces more cranberries than any other state in the nation? Wisconsin! It produces a whopping 300 million pounds a year.

★★★★★★★★★★★★ ★★★★★★★★★★★★

My Old-Fashioned Dressing

1 medium onion, diced
1 cup diced celery (include some tops)
1 large apple, cored and chopped
Liver from chicken or turkey, cooked
10 cups (2- or 3-day-old) bread, cubed or broken
½ pound pork sausage, cooked
1 (10-ounce) can cream of celery soup
2 eggs, beaten
½ cup raisins
Dash of garlic powder
Salt and pepper to taste
⅓ cup margarine, melted
1–2 teaspoons rubbed sage
1 cup milk or broth

Dice or chop onion, celery, apple, and cooked chicken liver. Break or cube bread. Mix all ingredients in large bowl. (I use a large Tupperware salad bowl. If I do not have pork sausage, or for a change, we like oysters in place of the sausage.) More moisture may be needed; the secret of good dressing is to have it very moist, but not soupy. Stuff turkey or chicken, if that's the way you like it. More often than not, I bake it in a greased 9x13-inch pan at 350° for 35–40 minutes; either way, my son-in-law thinks it is great.

Apples, Apples, Apples (Missouri)

If you grew 100 apple trees from the seeds of the same tree, the new apple trees would all be different.

Apple-Walnut Stuffing

1 pound day-old loaf bread,
  cut into large croutons
3 large onions, chopped
4 tablespoons butter
5 stalks celery, chopped
2 cups sliced leeks
4 large Granny Smith apples,
  diced

2 cups toasted chopped walnuts
2 tablespoons celery seed
2 tablespoons chopped fresh
  sage
1 tablespoon poultry seasoning
2 eggs, beaten
4 cups dark turkey stock
Salt and black pepper to taste

Place croutons in a large bowl. In a saucepan, sauté onions in butter until translucent. Add celery, leeks, and apples. Continue to cook a few minutes more. Pour mixture over croutons and cool to room temperature. Add walnuts, celery seed, sage, and poultry seasoning to cooled mixture; combine thoroughly. Mix in eggs and enough stock to moisten. Season with salt and pepper.

Transfer stuffing to lightly greased 9x13-inch baking dish. Cover with aluminum foil. Bake at 350° until stuffing is heated through, about 30 minutes. Uncover stuffing and bake until top is crisp, about 20 minutes. The dressing may also be stuffed into the turkey cavity. Serves 8.

An Apple a Day (California)

The old saying, "An apple a day keeps the doctor away," comes from an old English adage, "To eat an apple before going to bed will make the doctor beg his bread."

★★★★★★★ ★★★★★★★

© KEITH LAZELLE NATURE PHOTOGRAPHY.

More than half of all apples grown in the United States for fresh eating come from orchards in Washington state.

Baked Fish and Vegetables

A tasty, healthful way to serve baked fish.

1 teaspoon cooking oil
1 pound fish fillets, cut into
  5 or 6 serving pieces
⅛ teaspoon pepper
⅛ teaspoon paprika
⅛ teaspoon oregano
⅛ teaspoon thyme
½ cup shredded or finely cut
  carrots

¾ cup finely chopped celery
⅓ cup finely chopped green
  onions
½ cup finely chopped fresh
  mushrooms
½ cup snipped parsley
1 tablespoon lemon juice

Preheat oven to 350°. Pour teaspoon of oil into 8x8x2-inch baking dish. Rinse fillets under cold water; dry with paper towels and arrange in baking dish. Sprinkle pepper, paprika, oregano, and thyme over fish. Spoon carrots, celery, green onions, mushrooms, and snipped parsley over fish.

  Sprinkle with lemon juice. Cover tightly with foil and bake 45 minutes to one hour.

Singing in the Kitchen (Iowa)

Minnesota Lobster

3 quarts water
1 medium-size onion, quartered
Salt to taste
½ cup lemon juice
3 stalks celery, chopped

3–4 pounds fish fillets, cut into
  2-inch pieces
1 cup butter, melted, divided
Paprika

Place water, onion, salt, lemon juice, and celery in a 4-quart pot; bring to a boil. Add fish and boil for 5 minutes. Drain fish and place on a baking sheet. Brush with melted butter and sprinkle with paprika. Broil fish for 2 minutes. Sprinkle with paprika and serve with remaining melted butter. Serves 8.

Note: Northern Pike, Lake Trout, Coho Salmon, Steelhead, or any other firm deep-water fish may be used.

License to Cook Minnesota Style (Minnesota)

Georgia Mountain Trout in Wine

6 pieces trout
Salt and pepper to taste
Juice of 2 fresh lemons
3 large tomatoes, peeled and
   sliced

2 medium onions, thinly sliced
½ cup chopped parsley
½ cup dry white wine
¼ cup chicken broth

Oil shallow baking dish; place trout in dish; season with salt, pepper, and lemon juice (sprinkle outside and rub inside cavity). Cover trout with sliced tomatoes, then cover tomatoes with sliced onions. Sprinkle with chopped parsley. Pour wine and chicken broth over all. Bake uncovered 30 minutes at 400°. Garnish with lemon slices and parsley. Serve with brown rice. Serves 6.

Flavors of the Gardens (Georgia)

Chile Trout

Having a trout farm just down the road, we've come up with some great ways to prepare this wonderful, delicate fish. This is probably the most popular.

1 onion, chopped
1 tablespoon oil
1 red bell pepper, roasted
2 dried Ancho chiles, soaked in
   water till soft
4 garlic cloves

1 bunch fresh cilantro
3 tablespoons fresh lime juice
¼ teaspoon salt
6 whole trout, filleted
2 limes, cut into wedges

Purée onion, oil, pepper, chiles, garlic, and cilantro in a food processor; add lime juice and salt. Rub paste over fish. Bake at 450° for 10–15 minutes, or until fish is flaky. Don't overbake. Serve with lime wedges.

Note: This chile paste works well with catfish, or any other white fish and can also be made ahead of time and stored in the fridge or freezer.

White Grass Cafe Cross Country Cooking (West Virginia)

Baked Orange Roughy

Butter	Cayenne pepper to taste
6 orange roughy fillets	Tarragon leaves, crushed

Butter a large baking sheet. Lay fillets in a single layer on sheet. Sprinkle with pepper and crushed tarragon. Bake at 425° for 10–12 minutes. Melon Salsa dressing is served on the side. Serves 6.

MELON SALSA:

½ honeydew, finely chopped	2 tablespoons olive oil
½ cantaloupe, finely chopped	2 tablespoons minced fresh
1 jalapeño pepper, seeded,	mint
2 tablespoons fresh lime juice	

Combine all ingredients. Let stand 15 minutes to allow flavors to blend. You may want to drain off some of the liquid before serving. Serves 6.

A Treasury of Recipes for Mind, Body & Soul (Ohio)

Halibut à la Orange

1 orange	3 green onions, chopped
Zest from orange	1 teaspoon chicken bouillon
1 cup orange juice	1½–2 pounds halibut, thawed
4 teaspoons cornstarch	

Zest orange, then peel, section, and chop. Place all ingredients, except fish, in Dutch oven. Cook, stirring often, until thickened and bubbly. Remove from heat. Remove most of sauce and place fish in pot. Pour sauce over fish and bake at 350° for 15–25 minutes or until fish is flaky. (Use 10–12 coals under, 18–22 on lid if cooking outdoors.) Serve with sauce spooned on fish.

Dutch Oven Delites (Utah)

The orange was the first fresh fruit to bear a trademark. In 1919 the California Fruit Growers Exchange burned "Sunkist" on their oranges.

★★★★★★★★★★★ ★★★★★★★★★★★

Grouper with Dilled Cucumber Sauce

DILLED CUCUMBER SAUCE:

1 cup peeled, seeded, and
  diced cucumber
¼ cup sliced green onions
¼ cup oil
1 tablespoon lemon juice

2 sprigs fresh dill, or 1
  teaspoon dried dill weed
½ teaspoon salt
Freshly ground pepper to
  taste

In an electric blender or food processor, combine all sauce ingredients and purée. Refrigerate.

3 tablespoons butter
1 tablespoon lemon juice

2 (6-ounce) grouper fillets
2 sprigs fresh dill

Melt butter in a small saucepan and add lemon juice. Set aside.

Grill fillets over hot coals for 5 minutes per side. Baste while cooking, using sprigs of dill to brush on lemon butter. Serve with Dilled Cucumber Sauce. Serves 2.

Note: The Dilled Cucumber Sauce is also an excellent accompaniment to grilled or steamed vegetables.

Hooked on Fish on the Grill (Missouri)

Molly Morgan's Tuna Casserole Sandwich

1 (6½-ounce) can tuna fish
3 tablespoons mayonnaise
3 tablespoons sliced mushrooms
5 coarsely chopped black olives
2 hoagie rolls

Commercial Thousand Island
  dressing
6 tablespoons grated Cheddar
  cheese
4 asparagus spears

Drain tuna well and put in a small bowl. Add mayonnaise, mushrooms, and black olives, mixing until well combined. Split hoagie rolls in half, and spread each with Thousand Island dressing. Distribute tuna mixture evenly over each roll. Divide cheese over each half and top with asparagus. Place hoagie rolls on a baking sheet and bake 4–5 minutes in a 500° oven until the hoagies brown. Serves 4.

South Carolina's Historic Restaurants (South Carolina)

★★★★★★★★★★★ ★★★★★★★★★★★

Grilled Mahi Mahi with Mango Salsa

MANGO SALSA:

3 tablespoons lime juice
1 tablespoon fish sauce or fish extract
1 teaspoon sugar
2 tablespoons sliced green onions
1½ cups chopped tomatoes
2 ripe but firm mangos, peeled and diced

1 cup chopped Walla Walla or other sweet onions
2 tablespoons chopped fresh cilantro
1 or 2 jalapeño peppers, chopped, or 1 teaspoon crushed red pepper
1 teaspoon minced garlic

Combine lime juice, fish sauce, and sugar in a large bowl. Stir until sugar dissolves. Add remaining salsa ingredients; mix, cover and refrigerate for 30 minutes. Stir well before serving.

2 pounds Mahi Mahi (or halibut, cod, or red snapper)

Grill Mahi Mahi over medium-hot coals until fish flakes easily, about 15 minutes. Serve Mango Salsa over fish. Serves 4.

Note: Fish sauce can be found in the International section of many supermarkets.

Gold'n Delicious (Washington)

Broccoli Salmon Quiche

1 (9-inch) pie crust
2 cups fresh broccoli florets
1 (16-ounce) can salmon (or leftover cooked salmon, if available)
1 cup shredded Swiss cheese

¼ cup chopped, fresh chives
5 eggs, beaten
1 cup heavy whipping cream
¼ teaspoon cayenne red pepper
1 teaspoon dried dill weed

Preheat oven to 350°. Spray nonstick cooking spray in bottom of 9-inch deep pie dish. Line with pie pastry. Cover bottom of dish with broccoli florets, chunks of salmon, and sprinkle with cheese and chives. Set aside. In medium bowl, beat eggs, whipping cream, cayenne, and dill until thoroughly combined. Pour over all. Bake in preheated oven for 1 hour, or until crust and eggs are lightly browned, and quiche is puffy in center. Yields 6 servings.

Alaska's Gourmet Breakfasts (Alaska)

★★★★★★★★★★★ ★★★★★★★★★★★

Grilled Salmon
with Warm Pineapple Sauce

A delicious and healthful dish with very little cholesterol.

2 tablespoons fresh lemon or
  lime juice
2 teaspoons minced garlic
½ teaspoon freshly ground
  black pepper
6 (6-ounce) salmon fillets
2 tablespoons butter
2 tablespoons minced shallots
2 teaspoons seeded, minced
  jalapeño peppers

3 tablespoons peeled, minced
  fresh ginger root
1¼ cups fresh orange juice
½ teaspoon curry powder
2 cups chopped fresh
  pineapple
2 tablespoons chopped fresh
  mint

In shallow glass dish, combine lemon juice, garlic, and pepper. Add salmon and marinate at room temperature 30 minutes. Preheat grill to medium-high. In medium skillet, heat butter over medium heat. Add shallots, jalapeño, and ginger; cook 2 minutes. Add orange juice and curry powder and cook until reduced by half, about 10 minutes. Add pineapple and mint, reduce heat to low, and cook until thoroughly heated. Grill salmon 4–5 minutes per side. Place salmon on individual servings plates and spoon warm pineapple sauce on top. Makes 6 servings.

Colorado Collage (Colorado)

★★★★★★★★★★★★ ★★★★★★★★★★★★

Grilled Salmon
with Roasted Pepper Salsa

The Omega–3 fatty acids in salmon have received praise from the scientific community for their possible role in the reduction of cholesterol. Teamed here with an easy-to-prepare, low-fat, very colorful salsa, the result is a healthy meal.

4 (6-ounce) salmon fillets
Olive oil vegetable spray
1 (6-ounce) red bell pepper
1 (6-ounce) yellow bell pepper
1 (6-ounce) green bell pepper
2 tablespoons chopped red
  onion

1 tablespoon chopped opal basil
1 teaspoon extra virgin olive oil
  (or V8 juice)
1 shallot, chopped
Juice of 1 lime
Salt and cracked black pepper
  to taste

Grill salmon over hot coals using nonstick olive oil vegetable spray on grill. Roast peppers until black on all sides. Cover with plastic wrap for 5 minutes. Rinse off charred skin and remove seeds. Dice. Mix with remaining ingredients, and season salsa to taste. Yields 4 servings.

Chef's Note: Salmon should be removed from the grill when the middle is still reddish. It will continue to cook somewhat and will remain moist.

Recipe by Jim Makinson, Kingsmill Resort, Williamsburg
Culinary Secrets of Great Virginia Chefs (Virginia II)

A pineapple will never become any riper than it was when harvested. A fully ripe pineapple can bruise and rot quickly.

Shrimp and Crab Étouffée

Excellent Cajun cuisine, this is one of our most special dishes at White Grass. It looks involved, but is definitely worth it.

1 large onion
6 green onions
1 large green bell pepper
1 large red bell pepper
3 ribs celery
¾ cup chopped parsley
6 garlic cloves
½ stick butter
3 tablespoons flour
1½ pounds large raw shrimp, shells on

6 cups water
1 tablespoon seafood seasoning
½ teaspoon cayenne pepper
2 teaspoons salt
½ teaspoon ground black pepper
½ teaspoon ground white pepper
1 tablespoon vegetable bouillon
1 pound crabmeat

In a food processor, finely chop onion, peppers, celery, parsley, and garlic.

Melt butter in a large pot over medium-high heat. Add flour to make a roux, and stir constantly until it becomes peanut butter colored. (Be careful not to burn the roux.) Add the chopped vegetables and let them cook until soft, about 30 minutes. Remember to stir occasionally so they don't stick.

In the meantime, peel and devein shrimp. Save shells and make a stock by boiling them in water and seafood seasoning for 8–10 minutes, then strain.

When the veggies are done, add stock and stir. Simmer, then add remaining seasonings. You may want to adjust them to your own taste. About 15 minutes before you are ready to eat, add crab and shrimp. Cook until shrimp are pink and tender; don't overcook—they will get tough. This dish goes best over hot fluffy rice. Serves 6.

White Grass Cafe Cross Country Cooking (West Virginia)

The variety of the pepper plant and the stage of the ripeness determine the flavor and color of each pepper. For example, a red bell pepper is simply a mature green bell pepper. It is sweeter than an orange pepper, which is sweeter than yellow, which is sweeter than green.

★★★★★★★★★★★ ★★★★★★★★★★★

Shrimp Stuffed Peppers

6 bell peppers
2 cups shrimp, cooked, cleaned
2 eggs, beaten
1 cup bread crumbs
½ cup milk
3 tablespoons butter or margarine

3 tablespoons chopped celery
1 tablespoon chopped onion
1 teaspoon salt
⅛ teaspoon pepper
1 tablespoon Worcestershire

Cut off tops and remove seeds from peppers. Cook pepper shells in boiling water for 5 minutes, then plunge into cold water. Chop shrimp slightly. Combine with eggs, crumbs, and milk. Melt butter; sauté onion and celery for about 3 minutes, then add to shrimp mixture with remaining ingredients. Stuff mixture into peppers. Dot tops with butter. Bake in 350° oven for 30 minutes. Makes 6 servings.

Historic Kentucky Recipes (Kentucky)

Cantonese Shrimp with Rice

2 cups sliced celery (sliced
  diagonally)
2 cups sliced onions
2 tablespoons vegetable oil
1 quart fresh spinach leaves
3 (6-ounce) cans shrimp,
  drained

1 (16-ounce) can mixed Chinese
  vegetables, rinsed, drained
¼ teaspoon lemon pepper
¼ cup soy sauce
1¼ cups chicken broth
2 tablespoons cornstarch

Sauté celery and onions in vegetable oil about 2 minutes, stirring often. Add spinach, shrimp, and vegetables. Cover and cook 1 minute. Blend lemon pepper, soy sauce, chicken broth, and cornstarch. Stir into shrimp-vegetable mixture. Cook, stirring until sauce is clear and thickened, about 2 minutes. Serve over hot fluffy rice. Serves 6.

"Cate"ring to Shrimp (Oregon)

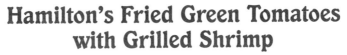

Hamilton's Fried Green Tomatoes with Grilled Shrimp

2½ cups rice flour, divided
1 egg
1½ cups ice water
1 large green tomato
1 cup vegetable oil

3 jumbo shrimp, peeled, deveined
½ cup white balsamic vinegar
3 tablespoons butter

In medium bowl combine 2 cups rice flour, egg, and ice water; whisk until smooth. Set aside. Core and slice tomato, using 4 middle slices and dusting them in remaining rice flour. In medium-size frying pan, bring oil up to high temperature then turn down to medium. Dip tomato slices in flour, egg, and water mixture, then gently place in hot oil. Fry on one side for 2–3 minutes (depending on thickness), then flip over to other side for 2 minutes or so. Remove and place tomato slices on paper towels. Grill shrimp and set aside.

In small saucepan, take balsamic vinegar and reduce it by three-fourths. Slowly stir in butter. When finished, add salt and pepper to taste. Arrange tomatoes and shrimp on plate and drizzle with sauce. Yields 1 serving.

Recipe from Hamilton's, Auburn
Alabama's Historic Restaurants and Their Recipes (Alabama)

Most tomatoes need temperatures above 60 degrees to finish ripening, so if you have some green tomatoes left on the vine, try slicing, breading, and frying them. I think you'll agree, they're absolutely delicious!

Eggplant Lynette

2 medium eggplants
1 medium onion, chopped
1 bell pepper, chopped
1 stalk celery, chopped
½ pound shrimp, deveined
  and chopped
3 tablespoons margarine
3 tablespoons olive oil
Salt and pepper to taste
1 cup oyster juice (optional)
4 tablespoons butter
1 cup fresh lump crabmeat

Steam eggplant until tender. Let cool, then slice in half lengthwise. Remove pulp, leaving ¼ inch around skin of the eggplant. Reserve pulp. Sauté chopped onion, bell pepper, and celery in margarine and olive oil. Add salt, pepper, oyster juice, and pulp. Stuff all ingredients in eggplant shell and bake at 450° until brown crust appears. In separate skillet, melt butter and add crabmeat. Top on eggplant just before serving.

Recipe from Jerry Psanos, The Fisherman's Wharf
Hospitality Heirlooms (Mississippi)

Ice House's Shrimp Scampi

4 teaspoons butter
2 ounces oil (olive or peanut)
2–3 garlic cloves, sliced
1 pound medium shrimp,
  shelled
½ teaspoon lemon juice
½ medium onion, chopped
1 tomato, chopped
½ green bell pepper, chopped
1 teaspoon black pepper
1 teaspoon salt
1 tablespoon chopped fresh
  parsley
¼ cup white wine

In skillet, melt butter; add oil, and sauté garlic lightly. Add shrimp, cooking until it turns pink and begins to curl. Add lemon juice, onion, tomato, green bell pepper, black pepper, salt, parsley, and wine. Cook only a minute or so until tender. Remove shrimp and pour sauce from skillet over top. Serves 4.

Virginia's Historic Restaurants and Their Recipes (Virginia)

Feta Shrimp

2 large onions, thinly sliced
⅓ cup olive oil
4 large tomatoes, peeled and
  coarsely chopped
3 tablespoons finely chopped
  parsley
½ teaspoon dried dill weed
¼–½ teaspoon freshly ground
  black pepper

¼ teaspoon sugar
1 garlic clove, minced or
  mashed
2 pounds large raw shrimp,
  peeled and deveined
¾ pound Greek feta cheese
1 large whole tomato, peeled
  (optional)
Parsley or dill sprigs

In an oven-proof skillet or Dutch oven, sauté onions in oil until
tender. Add chopped tomatoes, chopped parsley, dill, pepper,
sugar, and garlic. Cover and simmer 30 minutes, stirring occasionally. Add shrimp, dipping them down into the sauce and
arranging in a circle. Crumble feta cheese over shrimp. Place
whole tomato in center, if desired. Bake, uncovered, in 450° oven
for 10–15 minutes or until shrimp are done and cheese is melted.
Garnish with parsley or fresh dill sprigs.

Recipes and Remembrances (Florida)

According to the U.S. Department of Agriculture, Americans eat 22 to 24 pounds of
tomatoes per person, per year. (More than half of the quantity eaten is ketchup and
tomato sauce.)

Pan-Seared Scallops

1 pound fresh or frozen sea
  scallops (thawed)
2 tablespoons all-purpose
  flour
1–2 teaspoons blackened
  steak seasoning or Cajun
  seasoning

1 tablespoon cooking oil
1 (10-ounce) package fresh
  spinach, washed
1 tablespoon water
2 tablespoons balsamic
  vinegar
¼ cup cooked bacon pieces

Rinse scallops; pat dry with paper towels. In a plastic bag, combine flour and seasoning. Add scallops; toss to coat. In a large skillet, heat oil. Cook scallops in hot oil over medium heat about 6 minutes or until browned and opaque, turning to brown evenly. Remove scallops. Add spinach to skillet; sprinkle with water. Cover and cook over medium-high heat about 2 minutes or just until spinach is wilted. Add vinegar; toss to coat evenly. Return scallops to skillet; heat through. Sprinkle with bacon pieces.

Recipes for the House that Love Built (North Carolina)

The United States is only the world's second largest producer of spinach, producing a mere 3% of global production. China is the world's largest spinach producer with 85% of global production

Sea Scallops
with Fresh Pineapple Salsa

Scallops are best if cooked very quickly over high heat. They should have a rich golden brown crust and be moist and tender inside.

1½ pounds sea scallops
1 tablespoon olive oil
2 garlic cloves, minced

2 tablespoons Sauterne wine
Salt and pepper to taste

Discard tough, crescent-shaped membrane at side of each scallop. Rinse scallops with cold water; drain and pat dry. Heat olive oil in large sauté pan to very hot. Add scallops, garlic, Sauterne, salt and pepper to taste. Sauté until golden brown on each side, 3–4 minutes. Serve with Fresh Pineapple Salsa.

FRESH PINEAPPLE SALSA:

2 cups chopped fresh, ripe
  pineapple
⅓ cup chopped sweet onion
⅓ cup chopped fresh cilantro
1 tablespoon seeded, chopped
  jalapeño pepper

1 tablespoon lemon juice
1 tablespoon tarragon vinegar
½ teaspoon salt

Place all ingredients in food processor fitted with metal blade. Process until chopped, but not puréed. Salsa may be made several hours before serving. Serves 4.

Note: Pineapple should be very ripe, or it may make the salsa bitter.

Northern Lites: Contemporary Cooking with a Twist (Idaho)

Since about 2000, the most common fresh pineapple fruit found in U.S. and European supermarkets is a low acid hybrid that was developed in Hawaii in the early 1970s.

Oysters Michelina

8 medium-size oysters in shell

FILLING:

1½ cups chopped fresh spinach
1 egg
½ tablespoon chopped fresh
   garlic

¼ cup grated Parmesan cheese
½ cup grated mozzarella
   cheese

In a small bowl combine all ingredients.

SAUCE:

1½ cups heavy cream
⅓ cup bay shrimp
1 teaspoon chopped fresh
   parsley
1 tablespoon butter

¼ teaspoon chopped fresh
   garlic
¼ cup grated Parmesan cheese
Paprika

Combine all ingredients except paprika.

   Clean oysters and open shell. Divide filling between each oyster and stuff. Place oysters in a sauté pan and add sauce. Sprinkle with paprika and cook over medium heat 7–8 minutes. Sauce will thicken. Serve warm. (Oysters and filling may be prepared a day ahead and cooked in sauce when needed.)

Contributed by Michelina's, Phoenix
Arizona Chefs: Dine-In Dine-Out Cookbook (Arizona)

Meats

© TRAVEL MICHIGAN

Cherry blossoms abound in Michigan each spring. Michigan produces about 75 percent of the tart cherries grown in the United States. That makes Michigan the nation's number one cherry-producing state.

Burrito Bake

1 (16-ounce) can refried beans
1 cup Bisquick
¼ cup water
1 pound ground beef
1 small jar Pace Picante Sauce

1 tomato, chopped
1 avocado, sliced
1–2 cups shredded Cheddar
 cheese
Sour cream

Combine refried beans, Bisquick, and water and spread on a greased pie pan. Brown meat and spread on bean mixture; layer picante, tomato, avocado, and cheese on top of meat. Bake at 350° for 30 minutes. Remove from oven and spread sour cream on top.

M. D. Anderson Volunteers Cooking for Fun (Texas II)

Zucchini Beef Skillet

1 pound ground beef
1 cup chopped onion
¾ cup chopped green bell
 pepper
1½ teaspoons salt
¼ teaspoon pepper
1 teaspoon chili powder

5 cups sliced zucchini
2 large tomatoes, chopped
½ cup water
2 cups fresh corn kernels
2 tablespoons chopped pimento
¼ cup chopped parsley

Sauté beef, onion, and bell pepper in large skillet until browned. Drain. Add remaining ingredients. Cover and simmer 15 minutes or until vegetables are tender.

River Brethren Recipes (Pennsylvania)

Biggest is not always best: the most flavorful zucchinis are small to medium in size.

Ground Meat with Green Beans
(Fasolakia Me Kima)

1 pound ground beef
1 large onion, chopped
1 garlic clove, minced
1 tablespoon oil

1 (8-ounce) can tomato sauce
1 cup water
½ pound fresh string beans
Salt and pepper to taste

In a large skillet, sauté meat, onions, and garlic in oil till brown; drain. Combine tomato sauce with water and add to mixture. Bring to a boil. Add string beans, salt and pepper. Cover. Reduce heat and cook over medium heat about 45 minutes or until beans are cooked.

Treasured Greek Recipes (New York)

Cabbage-Potato Meatloaf

8 potatoes
Salt and pepper to taste
1 head cabbage, sliced
1½–2 pounds ground round

2 eggs
10–15 saltine crackers
½ cup chopped onion
1½–2 cups water

Spray Dutch oven with vegetable cooking spray. Peel and slice half the potatoes and layer on bottom of Dutch oven. Sprinkle with salt and pepper. Add a layer of sliced cabbage. Mix ground round, eggs, saltine crackers, and chopped onion. Make a large patty and place on top of cabbage. Cover with another layer of cabbage and then another layer of remaining potatoes. Sprinkle with more salt and pepper. Add water; bring to a boil, then cover and simmer 45–50 minutes.

Heavenly Delights (Arizona)

The most popular type of green bean is the string bean.

Meatloaf Stuffed Tomato

3 teaspoons minced garlic
½ cup diced red onions
½ cup diced white onions
2 tablespoons oil
2½ pounds ground beef
   tenderloin
¾ cup toasted bread crumbs

1 cup shredded Parmesan
   cheese, divided
Salt and pepper to taste
½ cup Maytag blue cheese
   (crumbled)
6 large tomatoes (cored and
   insides removed)

Sauté vegetables in oil. Add meat and bread crumbs and brown to medium. Once cooked, add ½ the Parmesan cheese and blend until melted. Season with salt and pepper. Cool in large container covered with perforated plastic wrap to allow steam to escape. When cool, add blue cheese. Place 3-ounce portion into tomato. Bake at 350° for 10 minutes. Garnish with remaining Parmesan and top with Brown Gravy. Yields 6 servings.

BROWN GRAVY:

¾ cup ketchup
½ cup red wine

4 teaspoons Worcestershire

Combine ingredients in saucepan and heat over medium heat. Serve over baked tomatoes.

Recipe from Julep Restaurant and Bar, Jackson
Fine Dining Mississippi Style (Mississippi)

Storing ripe tomatoes in the refrigerator will cause them to lose some of their flavor.

Meal-In-One

2 pounds ground round
1 cup chopped onion
½ cup chopped red bell
    pepper
½ cup chopped green bell
    pepper
Dashes of pepper, oregano,
    marjoram, and garlic salt
1 (10¾-ounce) can cream of
    mushroom soup, undiluted

1 (10¾-ounce) can tomato
    soup, undiluted
¾ cup water
2 cups cooked cut green
    beans, drained
2 cups cooked sliced carrots,
    drained
4 cups mashed potatoes
1½ cups shredded sharp
    Cheddar cheese

In a saucepan, brown beef and cook onion and peppers until tender. Drain. Add seasonings, soups, water, beans, and carrots. Stir and simmer 3–4 minutes. Pour into greased 9x13x2-inch casserole. Spoon mashed potatoes over top. Sprinkle with cheese. Bake at 350° for 30 minutes. Serves 8.

Without a Doubt (Alabama)

Calf's Liver and Apples

This is a German recipe and very, very excellent!

2 pounds calf's liver
½ cup bread crumbs
Salt to taste
1 teaspoon white pepper
½ pound butter

2½ cups thinly sliced onions
3 apples, peeled and sliced
    ½ inch thick
4 tablespoons sugar

Rinse liver; cut into pencil-thin 2-inch pieces and dry on paper towels. Toss the meat with a mixture of bread crumbs, salt, and pepper. Melt 3 tablespoons butter in a skillet and sauté the liver 3 minutes until just browned. Remove and keep warm. Now sauté the onions until brown. In another pan, sauté the apples until golden, sprinkling with sugar. Arrange the apples and onions over the liver. Serves 6.

Mushrooms, Turnip Greens & Pickled Eggs (North Carolina)

Southwestern Beef Brisket

1 (3-pound) fresh beef brisket
1¼ teaspoons salt, divided
½ teaspoon pepper, divided
2 tablespoons cooking oil
1½ cups water
1 (8-ounce) can tomato sauce
1 small onion, chopped
2 tablespoons red wine vinegar
1 tablespoon chili powder
1 teaspoon dried oregano
¾ teaspoon ground cumin
½ teaspoon garlic powder
⅛ teaspoon ground red pepper
3 sweet red bell peppers, cut
  into strips
1½ cups sliced carrots

Season beef with 1 teaspoon salt and ¼ teaspoon pepper. In a Dutch oven, heat oil; brown the beef on both sides. Combine water, tomato sauce, onion, vinegar, chili powder, oregano, cumin, garlic powder, red pepper, and remaining salt and pepper. Pour over meat. Cover and bake at 325° for 2 hours. Add red bell peppers and carrots; bake 1 hour longer or until meat is tender. Remove meat; let stand 15 minutes before cutting. Thicken juices with a little flour, or cook over high heat to reduce and thicken.

Feeding the Herd (Big Sky)

Roast Beef Barcelona

3–4 pounds pot roast
1 (8-ounce) bottle French
  dressing
½ cup water
1 cup sliced stuffed olives
8 small onions
8 whole potatoes

Brown roast in ¼ cup dressing. Add remaining dressing and water. Cover and cook slowly 2–2½ hours on low heat. Add olives, onions, and potatoes. Cook 45 minutes longer, or until vegetables are tender. Serves 6–8.

Cookin' in the Spa (Arkansas)

★★★★★★★★★★ ★★★★★★★★★★★

Mustard Roast Beef & Vegetables

1 (4-pound) boneless rump
  roast
1½ teaspoons salt
Pepper to taste
1 tablespoon prepared mustard

3 large carrots
4 small potatoes
4 small onions
2 large ribs celery

Season beef with ¾ teaspoon salt and pepper. Spread top and sides of roast with mustard. Place on small rack in lightly greased roasting pan. Peel and cut vegetables in chunks and place around rack in pan. Season with remaining salt and pepper. Roast in preheated 325° oven 1½ hours or until meat thermometer registers desired doneness (rare 140°, medium 160°, well done 170°)—approximately 25 minutes per pound. Remove from oven; let stand about 10 minutes.

Taste the Good Life! Nebraska Cookbook (Great Plains)

Sweet and Sour Pot Roast

Outstanding—this one will catch your fancy.

1 tablespoon oil
1 (4-pound) chuck roast
1 (10½-ounce) can beef
  bouillon
1 (16-ounce) can jellied
  cranberry sauce

1 (5-ounce) bottle prepared
  horseradish
8 carrots, peeled and cut
  into 2-inch pieces
2 onions, quartered

Preheat oven to 350°. Heat oil in Dutch oven and brown roast. Add bouillon, cranberry sauce, and horseradish. Cover and bake at 350° for 1½ hours. Add carrots and onions to roast. Bake an additional 1½ hours.

Reserve pan juices and pour over meat. Serve with buttered noodles, if desired. Serves 6–8.

Winners (Indiana)

★★★★★★★★★★★ ★★★★★★★★★★★

Glazed Country Steak

The 1990 Iowa Beef Cook-Off winning recipe.

¼ cup all-purpose flour
½ teaspoon salt
¼ teaspoon pepper
1½ pounds boneless beef
  chuck shoulder steak, cut
  into serving-size pieces
2 tablespoons vegetable oil
¼ cup dry white wine
1 garlic clove, finely chopped

¼ cup tomato juice
1 teaspoon parsley flakes
½ cup beef broth
1 small onion, chopped
2 cups cubed raw potatoes
1 cup carrot chunks
2 tablespoons brown sugar
1 cup raisins

Combine flour, salt, and pepper; pound into steak. In skillet, brown steak pieces on both sides in oil. Pour off drippings. Add wine, garlic, tomato juice, parsley flakes, beef broth, and onion. Cook, covered, over low heat for 30 minutes. Add potatoes and carrots; cook 30 minutes more. Sprinkle with brown sugar and raisins; simmer 15 minutes, or until meat is tender. Serve on platter encircled with vegetables. Makes 4–6 servings.

Lehigh Public Library Cookbook (Iowa)

Onion Marmalade

Good with roasted meat or poultry.

½ cup butter
6 medium red onions (about
  2½ pounds), sliced
1 bunch scallions, white
  parts only

3 tablespoons sugar
¼ cup red wine vinegar or
  balsamic vinegar
1 cup dry red wine

In a medium skillet, melt butter. Add onions and scallions; cook over medium high heat, stirring, 15 minutes or until tender. Add sugar and cook 1 minute, stirring constantly. Add remaining ingredients and continue cooking, stirring until liquid is absorbed, about 15 minutes. Easy. Can do ahead—may freeze. Yields 2½ cups.

Cooking in Clover II (Missouri)

Braised Beef Short Ribs

5 pounds beef short ribs,
  cut into 1-rib pieces
All-purpose flour, seasoned
  with salt and pepper
¼ cup rendered bacon fat
4 garlic cloves, chopped
3 onions, chopped

6 carrots, sliced
½ teaspoon crumbled dried
  rosemary
Salt and pepper to taste
Mushrooms (optional)
1 cup red wine
3 cups beef broth

Dredge ribs in flour, knocking off excess. Heat bacon fat in a 6-quart Dutch oven over moderately high heat until hot but not smoking. Brown the short ribs. Transfer ribs to a large plate. Pour off all but about 2 tablespoons bacon fat remaining in Dutch oven, and in it, cook garlic, onions, carrots, and rosemary with salt and pepper to taste over moderate heat, stirring until browned lightly; add mushrooms, if desired. Cook mixture about 6 more minutes.

    Preheat oven to 350°. Deglaze the pot with red wine. Add beef broth to the vegetable mixture and bring to a boil, stirring. Return ribs to the pot and cover. Cook (braise) in the oven until tender, about 2 hours.

The Best of Down-Home Cooking (Nevada)

Ancient Egyptians worshipped the onion, believing that its spherical shape and concentric rings symbolized eternity.

Oven Ribs

5 pounds baby back ribs
Seasoned salt
Black pepper
6 garlic cloves, finely chopped
Jalapeño pepper, chopped
  (optional)
2 green bell peppers, thinly
  sliced
2 yellow bell peppers, thinly
  sliced
2 red bell peppers, thinly sliced
2 onions, thinly sliced

Season ribs with seasoned salt and pepper. Rub chopped garlic and jalapeño pepper, if desired, into ribs. Cut ribs into serving-size pieces. Layer sliced peppers and onions on top of ribs. Wrap individual servings in heavy-duty foil, and place in refrigerator for up to 48 hours.

When ready to prepare, unwrap ribs and let come to room temperature, about an hour. Rewrap the foil and bake (on cookie sheet to catch drips) in 300° oven for 8 hours.

Offerings for Your Plate (Mississippi)

Blueberry Backstrap

2 tablespoons plus ¼ cup
  butter, divided
4 venison loin steaks, cut
  ½ inch thick
Juice and zest of 1 large lemon
1 cup chicken broth
1 cup fresh blueberries
Several dashes ground
  cinnamon
Several dashes ground ginger
Salt and freshly ground pepper
  to taste

Melt 2 tablespoons butter in a large skillet, and cook steaks until brown on both sides and cooked medium-rare. Remove to platter and keep warm. Pour lemon juice, zest, and chicken broth into skillet and bring to a boil. Cook until mixture is reduced to about ½ cup. Lower heat to medium, and whisk in remaining ¼ cup butter, 1 tablespoon at a time. Stir in blueberries, cinnamon, ginger, salt and pepper. Serve sauce over steaks. Makes 4 servings.

Wild Fare & Wise Words (South Carolina)

★ ★ ★ ★ ★ ★ ★ ★ ★ ★ ★   ★ ★ ★ ★ ★ ★ ★ ★ ★ ★ ★

Pork Steak - Vegetable Bake

4 medium potatoes, peeled and
  cut into ¼ inch slices
4 carrots, peeled and sliced
4 pork steaks

½ cup water
½ envelope dry onion soup
  mix
2 tablespoons soy sauce

Place potatoes and carrots in bottom of a 9x13-inch (or larger) baking dish. Brown steaks well on both sides. In small saucepan, combine water, onion soup mix, and soy sauce; bring to a boil. Spoon half of the soup mixture over the potatoes and carrots; top with steaks. Spoon remaining soup mixture over meat. Cover; bake at 350° for 1 hour. Uncover and bake 10 additional minutes. Serves 4.

Sharing Our Best–Franklin (Tennessee)

Pork Chops with Apples, Onions, and Raisins

4 pork chops, center cut
  (1½ inches thick)
Salt and pepper to taste
1 tablespoon cooking oil
1 large yellow onion, sliced

¼ cup raisins
1 large sweet apple, cut in
  wedges
1 ounce port wine
⅓ stick butter

Use a 10- or 12-inch skillet that can be covered. Season chops with salt and pepper. Oil skillet and brown chops well on both sides. Place sliced onion over chops, and cover skillet. Cook slowly for 15 minutes. Remove cover. Place pork chops over the onions. Sprinkle raisins around pan bottom. Place apple wedges around chops; add wine and butter, cover, and simmer 15 minutes. Turn apple wedges during cooking to assure even cooking. Remove skillet top and simmer an additional 5 minutes to thicken sauce. Serve chops with sauce, apples, onions, and raisins. Serves 4.

Paul Naquin's French Collection II: Meats & Poultry (Louisiana)

Company Pork Chops

6 Ida Red apples, peeled,
  thickly sliced
6 pork chops
2 teaspoons butter or
  margarine

6 tablespoons brown sugar
6 tablespoons catsup

Preheat the oven to 375°. Line a large baking dish with enough foil to overlap the casserole and seal. Arrange the apple slices in a single layer in the prepared dish. Brown the pork chops in the butter in a skillet. Arrange over the apples. Sprinkle with the brown sugar and spread with the catsup. Fold the foil over the pork chops, sealing with a double fold. Bake at 375° for one hour or until the pork chops and apples are tender. Serve immediately. Serves 6.

The Dexter Cider Mill Apple Cookbook (Michigan)

Pork Chop Casserole

6 pork chops
½ cup all-purpose flour
Salt and pepper to taste
4 sweet potatoes, peeled, sliced,
  divided

½ cup brown sugar, divided
1½ cups sliced apples, divided
½ cup apple juice

Coat chops with mixture of flour, salt, and pepper. Brown in small amount of oil in heavy skillet. Arrange in greased 2-quart casserole. Arrange ½ the sweet potato slices over top. Sprinkle with ½ the brown sugar. Top with ½ the sliced apples. Sprinkle with remaining brown sugar. Top with remaining potatoes and apples, and pour juice over all. Cover. Bake at 350° for 1½ hours. Remove cover for last 15 minutes.

Cooking with 257 (Florida)

Pork Chops and Cheesy Potatoes

A simple meat and potato dish, but oh so good.

8 potatoes, sliced
1 onion, chopped
6 slices Cheddar cheese
2 (10¾-ounce) cans cream of
  mushroom soup

1 soup can milk
Salt and pepper to taste
6 pork chops, browned

In a 1½-quart buttered dish, place alternate layers of potatoes, onions, and cheese. Combine soup, milk, and seasonings; pour over all (do not stir). Top with browned pork chops; cover and bake at 350° for 1½ hours. Serves 6.

Holiday Treats (Virginia)

Spiced Pork Chops

A make-ahead recipe.

¼ cup all-purpose flour
½ teaspoon dry mustard
¼ teaspoon pepper
⅛ teaspoon ground allspice
4 pork chops, cut 1 inch thick

2 tablespoons oil
1½ cups apple juice
2 tablespoons brown sugar
½ teaspoon cinnamon
2 apples, peeled and sliced

Combine flour, dry mustard, pepper, and allspice. Dredge pork chops in mixture, reserving remaining flour mixture. In skillet, brown chops in oil; remove and keep warm. To drippings, add apple juice, brown sugar, and remaining flour mixture. Cook and stir until bubbly. Return pork chops to skillet, and sprinkle with cinnamon. Cover and simmer for about 60 minutes until pork is no longer pink. Add apples during the last 20 minutes of cooking. Cool and place in Ziploc bag to freeze.

Thaw. Arrange in baking dish sprayed with nonstick spray. Bake covered at 350° until fully heated and bubbly. Serves 4.

Note: Ham slices can be a yummy replacement for the pork chops.

Per serving: Calories 421; Fat 22g; Calories from Fat 47%.

What's for Dinner? (Oregon)

★★★★★★★★★★★ ★★★★★★★★★★★

Grilled Pork Tenderloin
with Fresh Peach and Ginger Sauce

1 tablespoon vegetable oil
1 cup chopped onion
5 tablespoons sugar
1½ cups dry red wine
¼ cup balsamic vinegar
2½ tablespoons, peeled, finely chopped fresh ginger
1½ teaspoons ground cinnamon
3 (14- to 16-ounce) pork tenderloins

3 medium peaches, blanched in boiling water, peeled, pitted, and chopped
2 tablespoons chopped fresh chives
½ teaspoon coarsely ground black pepper

Heat oil in heavy saucepan over medium-high heat. Add onion and sugar. Sauté until onion is golden brown, about 6 minutes. Mix in wine, vinegar, ginger, and cinnamon. Cook 1 minute longer. Remove from heat. Cool sauce completely. Place pork in large resealable plastic bag. Pour 1 cup sauce over pork. Seal and refrigerate at least 6 hours, or overnight (turning to coat). Cover remaining sauce separately and refrigerate.

Prepare barbecue (medium heat). Remove pork from marinade; discard marinade. Grill pork until meat thermometer inserted into center registers 155°, turning often, about 35 minutes. Meanwhile, boil remaining sauce in heavy medium saucepan until reduced by half. Add peaches, stir until heated through, about 1 minute. Slice pork and arrange on platter. Spoon sauce over top; sprinkle with chives. Season with pepper. Pass remaining sauce separately.

The Cookbook AAUW (New York)

Peaches can be ripened by placing them in a brown paper bag for two to three days. Ripe peaches freeze well for later use.

Glorified Boston Butt

1 (3½- to 4-pound) Boston
  butt roast
2 tablespoons vegetable oil
1 (10¾-ounce) can cream of
  mushroom soup
½ cup water
1 cup chopped onions
1 teaspoon salt

¼ teaspoon pepper
⅛ teaspoon red pepper
1 bay leaf
1 tablespoon paprika
1½ pounds potatoes, peeled,
  quartered
4 medium carrots, peeled, sliced
1 tablespoon Worcestershire

Brown roast in hot oil in large Dutch oven. Pour off fat. Combine soup and next 7 ingredients. Pour over roast. Cover and simmer 1½ hours, stirring occasionally.

Add potatoes, carrots, and Worcestershire. Cover and simmer 30 minutes or until vegetables are done. Remove bay leaf. Remove pot roast and vegetables to a serving platter, reserving drippings. Cook pan drippings over medium heat until slightly reduced. Serve gravy over rice.

Bountiful Blessings from the Bauknight Table (South Carolina)

Baked Ham and Sweet Potatoes

2 medium-thick slices cured
  ham
4 or 5 medium sweet potatoes,
  peeled, sliced 1 inch thick

1 large orange, divided
Brown sugar to taste
Butter

In a large greased baking dish, lay one slice of ham. Place layer of potatoes. Cover potatoes with thin slices of ½ the orange, leaving 3 or 4 slices with peeling on them. Sprinkle with sugar and dot with butter. Lay second slice of ham on this and slice remaining ½ of orange over this. Sprinkle again with brown sugar and dot with butter. Arrange remaining potatoes around edges of pan. Add small amount of water. Cover and bake in 350° oven 1½ hours. Uncover last half hour. Serves 6–8.

Ohio State Grange Cookbook - Gold (Ohio)

Ham 'n' Apple Cheese Pie

I love the mix of the tastes. It seems traditional and novel at the same instant. And scrumptious!

1½ pounds ham slices,
  ½–¾ inch thick
	2 tablespoons margarine,
	  melted

2–3 tart apples, pared and sliced	6 slices mild cheese
⅓ cup all-purpose flour	1 cup cultured sour cream
½ cup brown sugar	

Cut ham slices into serving pieces and arrange them to cover the bottom of a greased shallow casserole or pie plate. Arrange apple slices to cover ham.

Mix together the flour, brown sugar, and margarine, then crumble over apples. Top with cheese slices. Drop dollops of sour cream over cheese. Bake at 350° for 1 hour. Makes 8 servings.

The Festive Cookbook (Pennsylvania)

Ham and Cauliflower Brooks

1 head cauliflower	2 egg yolks, slightly beaten
2 cups chopped, cooked country ham	⅛ teaspoon nutmeg
	⅛ teaspoon mace
2 tablespoons butter	1½ teaspoons paprika
1½ cups sour cream	¼ teaspoon pepper
¼ cup chopped onion	¾ cup grated Cheddar cheese

Cook cauliflower in salted boiling water to cover until almost done, about 15 minutes. Drain, run cold water on cauliflower, then break into florets. In bottom of a greased casserole, alternate layers of florets with layers of ham. Dot top with butter.

Preheat oven to 375°. Combine sour cream, onion, eggs, and spices; mix well, and pour over casserole. Cover and bake 25–30 minutes. Remove cover; top with cheese. Brown slightly and serve. Serves 6.

Note: Fresh mushrooms may be added to this recipe. Sauté them in butter first, then add between layers of cauliflower and ham. This casserole can be made the day before and baked just before serving.

The Ham Book (Virginia II)

Sausage-Squash-Pecan Casserole

2 pounds yellow squash or
  zucchini, sliced ½ inch thick
4 tablespoons butter
2 medium onions, sliced
1 garlic clove, finely chopped
1 cup milk
1 cup bread crumbs
1 pound sausage, cooked,
  crumbled

4 eggs, lightly beaten
1½ cups grated sharp Cheddar
  cheese
1 cup chopped pecans
1 tablespoon salt
Freshly ground pepper to taste

Grease a 2-quart casserole and set aside. Put sliced squash in a heavy pan and add enough water to cover. Bring to a boil, uncovered; then reduce heat and simmer for ½ hour or until squash is soft enough to mash. Drain and mash. Melt butter in a separate pan; add onions and garlic and cook until soft. Add this to the squash. Heat milk in same pan; stir in bread crumbs and add this mixture to the onions and squash. Stir in sausage, eggs, cheese, pecans, salt, and pepper. Pour combined mixture into buttered casserole.

TOPPING:
4 tablespoons butter, melted   ½ cup chopped pecans
½ cup bread crumbs

Preheat oven to 350°. Combine the butter, bread crumbs, and pecans and sprinkle over top of casserole. Bake for 30 minutes. Serves 4.

A Samford Celebration Cookbook (Alabama)

Even though most people identify squash with vegetables, from a botanical standpoint, they are considered fruits, because they contain the seeds of the plant.

Smoked Sausage Delight

4–5 large potatoes	**1 medium head cabbage**
1 large onion, sliced	**2 pounds smoked sausage**
1 medium bell pepper, sliced	**¾–1 cup water**
Salt, pepper, and Cavender's	
Greek Seasoning to taste	

Slice potatoes ¼–½ inch thick in bottom of large roasting pan. Put onion and bell pepper slices on top of potatoes. Season at this time to taste. Chop cabbage, and put on top of potatoes, onion, and bell pepper. Season a little more, if desired. Slice smoked sausage into rounds ¼–½ inch thick, and scatter over top of cabbage, covering completely. Pour water over all. Cover with foil or lid and bake in 350° oven 1–1½ hours or until potatoes are done.

Cooking with My Friends (Kentucky)

Because cabbage only requires three months of growing time, one acre of cabbage will yield more edible vegetables than any other plant. There are many different varieties of cabbage, although green and red cabbages are the most common.

Cakes

Berries signify summer, and rightfully so, as the warmer months are the peak harvest for these fruits. Berries have traditionally included blueberries, strawberries, raspberries, and blackberries. However, there are other varieties that have since flooded the markets.

Butterscotch Apple Cake

2½ cups plain flour
2 cups sugar
1 teaspoon baking soda
1 teaspoon salt
1 teaspoon cinnamon
1 teaspoon baking powder
1 cup corn oil (no substitute)

1 teaspoon vanilla
3 eggs, beaten
3 cups cored, peeled, chopped
  apples
1 cup chopped nuts
1 (12-ounce) package
  butterscotch morsels

Mix all dry ingredients well, then add oil, vanilla, and eggs. Fold in apples and nuts. Pour into greased 9x11-inch baking pan. Sprinkle with butterscotch morsels. Bake at 350° for 45 minutes, or until toothpick comes out clean.

Recipes & Memories (South Carolina)

Crockpot Apple Cake

2 cups sugar
1 cup oil
2 eggs
2 teaspoons vanilla
2 cups all-purpose flour
1 teaspoon salt (or less)

1 teaspoon baking soda
1 teaspoon nutmeg
2 cups finely chopped, unpeeled
  Delicious apples
1 cup chopped walnuts

Beat sugar, oil, and eggs together well; add vanilla. Sift flour, salt, soda, and nutmeg together. Add apples to sugar mixture; mix well. Stir in flour mixture and nuts; mix well. Pour batter into greased and floured 2-pound can. Fill can no more than ⅔ full. Place in crockpot; cover top of can with 4–6 paper towels. Cover and cook on HIGH about 3½ hours. Crockpot lid should not be tightly closed—slightly raise lid to allow release of excess moisture. Add no water and do not peek until last hour.

Oregon: The Other Side (Oregon)

★★★★★★★★★★★ ★★★★★★★★★★★

Cake That Doesn't Last

3 cups all-purpose flour
2 cups sugar
1 teaspoon baking soda
1 teaspoon salt
1 teaspoon cinnamon
1½ teaspoons vanilla
3 eggs
1½ cups oil
2 cups mashed bananas
1 (15-ounce) can crushed
   pineapple, with juice
1 cup nuts

Combine all ingredients by hand until well blended. Pour into a large greased and floured Bundt pan. Bake at 350° for 1 hour and 20 minutes.

High Cotton Cookin' (Arkansas)

Banana Cake

½ cup shortening
1½ cups sugar
2 egg whites, beaten until fluffy
2 egg yolks
2 cups all-purpose flour
¼ teaspoon baking powder
¾ teaspoon baking soda
½ teaspoon salt
¼ cup buttermilk
1 cup mashed bananas (about 3
   medium)
1 teaspoon vanilla
½ cup chopped nuts

Cream shortening and sugar. Add egg whites and beat well, then add egg yolks. Sift flour, baking powder, baking soda, and salt together and then add to egg mixture. Mix in buttermilk, bananas, and vanilla. Add nuts and mix well. Pour into greased and floured cake pan. Bake at 350° for 30–35 minutes.

West Virginia Country Cooking (West Virginia)

Bananas are loaded with potassium. Potassium is important in keeping your blood pressure at a healthy level.

★★★★★★★★★★★   ★★★★★★★★★★★

Strawberry Meringue Cake

1 (2-layer) package yellow
  cake mix
1 cup orange juice
⅓ cup water
4 eggs, separated
1 teaspoon grated orange rind

¼ teaspoon cream of tartar
1¼ cups sugar, divided
2 cups whipping cream
1 quart fresh strawberries,
  hulled, sliced

Combine cake mix, orange juice, water, egg yolks, and orange rind in mixer bowl. Beat for 4 minutes. Pour into 2 greased and wax paper-lined round cake pans. Beat egg whites with cream of tartar in mixer bowl until soft peaks form. Add 1 cup sugar gradually, beating constantly until stiff peaks form. Spread gently over batter. Bake at 350° for 35–40 minutes or until layers test done. Cool completely in pans.

Remove from pans, keeping meringue side up. Beat whipping cream and remaining ¼ cup sugar in mixer bowl until stiff peaks form. Spread ⅔ of the whipped cream over bottom layer. Arrange sliced berries over whipped cream. Add top layer. Spread with remaining whipped cream. Garnish with whole strawberries. Yields 12 servings.

Approximately per serving: Cal 450; Prot 5g; Carbo 63g; Fiber 1g; Total Fat 20g; 40% Calories from Fat; Chol 125mg; Sod 297mg.

Best Bets (Nevada)

Tips on How to Make a Perfect Meringue:

• Meringues should have no less than 2 tablespoons of sugar per egg white.
• The tiniest bit of egg yolk will wreck a meringue.
• After separating, bring egg whites to room temperature to ensure volume when beating, as warmer eggs whip faster than cold eggs.
• Copper, stainless-steel, or glass bowls work best for making meringues.
• Make sure that all your utensils are immaculately clean, completely grease-free, and completely dry.
• For soft peaks, beat egg whites on medium speed until egg whites form peaks with tips that curl over when the beaters are lifted.
• For stiff peaks, continue beating egg whites on high speed until they form peaks with tips that stand straight when the beaters are lifted.
• Once you start whipping the egg whites, don't stop until finished.

Homemade Strawberry Shortcake

The contrast of hot and cold makes this simple dessert outstanding.

1 quart strawberries, hulled and cut in half	½ teaspoon salt
2 tablespoons orange liqueur (optional)	1½ sticks unsalted butter
½ cup sugar, divided	1 cup light cream or milk
3 cups sifted all-purpose flour	Additional sugar for sprinkling over shortcakes
4 teaspoons baking powder	1 cup heavy cream
	¼ cup confectioners' sugar
	1 teaspoon vanilla

Mix halved berries with liqueur and ¼ cup sugar. Chill several hours. Sift flour with baking powder, salt, and remaining ¼ cup sugar. Cut in butter until particles are size of small peas. Add light cream or milk all at once. Stir just enough to moisten dry particles. Turn dough out on lightly floured board and knead just a few times to shape into smooth ball.

With rolling pin or with fingers, shape dough into a rectangle about 6x9 inches. With sharp knife, cut oblong into 6 (3-inch) or 12 (1½-inch) squares. Put biscuits on a lightly greased cookie sheet. Sprinkle additional granulated sugar over top of shortcakes, and bake in preheated 425° oven 15–20 minutes or until biscuits are deeply browned.

While biscuits are baking, whip heavy cream with confectioners' sugar and vanilla until stiff. When biscuits are ready, split them while hot into halves. Spoon berries over bottom half. Top with second half of biscuit. Add more berries and top with whipped cream. Serve immediately.

Someone's in the Kitchen with Melanie (North Carolina)

★★★★★★★★★★★ ★★★★★★★★★★★

Strawberry Cream Cake

Light and refreshing.

1 (18¼-ounce) box angel food cake mix	⅓ cup lemon juice
1 (8-ounce) package cream cheese	1 teaspoon almond extract
1 (14-ounce) can sweetened condensed milk	2 cups sliced strawberries
	1 (8-ounce) carton Cool Whip or whipped cream
	Additional strawberries

Bake cake according to package directions and cool completely. Cut a 1-inch slice from top of cake and set aside. Cut one inch from center hole and outer edge and remove center of cake, pulling with fingers. Leave 1 inch at bottom.

Beat cream cheese. Add sweetened condensed milk, lemon juice, and almond extract. Fold in cake pieces and strawberries. Spoon into center of cake. Top with the reserved top slice. Chill 8 hours or overnight. Frost with Cool Whip and garnish with additional strawberries.

Note: Can use fat-free cream cheese and fat-free sweetened condensed milk for a very low-fat dessert. It is just as delicious. May use store-bought angel food cake.

Shared Treasures (Louisiana II)

Fresh Peach Cake

1 package yellow or white cake mix	½ cup water
1½ cups sugar	1 (8-ounce) carton sour cream
4 tablespoons flour	2 whipping cream
4 cups chopped fresh peaches	3 tablespoons powdered sugar

Bake cake according to package directions using 2 (9-inch) cake pans; split into 4 layers when cool. Combine sugar, flour, peaches, and water. Cook over low heat until thick; remove from heat and cool completely. Assemble cake by placing first layer on a platter, top with ⅓ the peach mixture, then ⅓ the sour cream; repeat layers and finish with fourth cake layer. Whip cream with powdered sugar. Frost cake and refrigerate.

The Junior Welfare League 50th Anniversary Cookbook (Kentucky)

★★★★★★★★★★ ★★★★★★★★★★★

Bobbie's Blackberry Cake

Fresh blackberries make the difference with this one. A richly flavored cake with a frosting that's out of this world. (In fact, the icing would "make" any cake!)

1 cup butter or margarine	2 teaspoons baking soda
2 cups sugar	1 teaspoon cinnamon
3 eggs	1 teaspoon ground cloves
3 cups all-purpose flour	2 cups blackberries with juice

Preheat oven to 350°. Grease and flour 3 round cake pans. Cream butter and sugar. Add eggs. Combine flour, soda, cinnamon, and cloves and add to creamed mixture. Blend in blackberries. Pour into cake pans and bake for 25–30 minutes. Allow to cool in pans 10 minutes, then invert onto racks to cool completely. Ice when cool.

ICING:

1½ cups brown sugar	1 tablespoon shortening
1½ cups sugar	2 tablespoons butter or
1½ cups milk	margarine

To prepare Icing, combine sugars and milk in a saucepan. Cook, stirring constantly, until mixture forms a very soft ball in cold water. Remove from heat; add shortening and butter. Cool to lukewarm, then beat until thick and creamy. Spread Icing between layers, and on top and sides of cake. Serves 12–16.

Louisiana LEGACY (Louisiana)

Blackberries Facts:
- According to the USDA, 1 cup of blackberries contains about 62 calories.
- Researchers have known for quite some time that berries contain antioxidants that help to fight cancer-causing free radicals. A study at the University of Ohio has found that blackberries are the most potent cancer fighting berries of them all, by nearly 40 percent!
- A quart of blackberries weighs about 1½ pounds.
- Blackberries only keep for one to two days in the refrigerator, so if you need them to keep longer, they should be frozen.
- Blackberries are one of the few fruits that contain vitamin E. Berries also strengthen blood vessels, protect eyesight, and reduce the risk of heart disease.

★★★★★★★★★★★★ ★★★★★★★★★★★★

Luella's Blueberry Cake with Lemon Butter Sauce

This old-timey (sauce) recipe originally called for one cup butter and vinegar instead of lemon juice. If you're watching your fat intake, the cake tastes good by itself.

CAKE:

1 tablespoon butter	2 teaspoons baking powder
1 cup sugar	½ teaspoon salt
1 egg	1 cup milk
2 cups all-purpose flour	2 cups fresh blueberries

Grease and flour a 9-inch-square cake pan. Cream butter and sugar. Add beaten egg into creamed mixture. Combine dry ingredients and add to egg mixture alternately with milk. Coat berries with a small amount of flour, then add to mixture. Bake at 375° for about 30 minutes.

LEMON BUTTER SAUCE:

2–4 tablespoons butter	Grated lemon rind
¾ cup sugar	3 tablespoons cornstarch
1 cup water, divided	1 teaspoon vanilla
Juice of 2 lemons	

Melt butter and stir in sugar. Add ½ cup water, lemon juice, and rind to melted butter mixture. Mix cornstarch with remaining water until dissolved. Add to melted butter mixture. Boil until clear. Take off heat and add vanilla. Pour over cake as you serve.

Take Two & Butter 'Em While They're Hot! (West Virginia)

Forty to fifty percent of blueberries grown commercially are harvested by hand, to gather the best of the early fruit. Hand-harvesting blueberries has been estimated to require up to 550 worker-hours per acre, which works out to be about $1.00 per pound.

★ ★ ★ ★ ★ ★ ★ ★ ★ ★ ★   ★ ★ ★ ★ ★ ★ ★ ★ ★ ★ ★

Esther's Blueberry Sour Cream Cake

½ cup butter or margarine
1 cup sugar
3 eggs
1 cup sour cream
1 teaspoon vanilla
2 cups sifted all-purpose flour
1 teaspoon baking soda

1 teaspoon salt
2 cups fresh blueberries
⅓ cup packed brown sugar
½ cup chopped nuts
½ teaspoon cinnamon
Powdered sugar

Cream butter and sugar together until fluffy. Add eggs, one at a time, beating well after each addition. Blend in sour cream and vanilla. Sift together flour, soda, and salt; add to creamed mixture, beating until smooth. Fold in blueberries. Spread one-third of batter into greased and floured Bundt pan. In a small bowl combine brown sugar, nuts, and cinnamon; spread half evenly over top of batter in the pan. Spread another third of batter evenly over nut mixture, top with remaining nut mixture, and then top with remaining batter. Bake at 350° for 1 hour or until done. Cool cake in pan on wire rack. Sprinkle with powdered sugar before serving. Makes 12–16 servings.

The Blueberry Lover's Cookbook (Texas II)

Blueberries are the fruits of a shrub that belong to the heath (Ericaceae) family, whose other members include the cranberry and bilberry, as well as the azalea, mountain laurel, and rhododendron.

★★★★★★★★★★★   ★★★★★★★★★★★

Blueberry-Raspberry Upside-Down Cake

I bake this wonderfully moist cake in my 9-inch cast-iron frying pan—the heavy pan keeps the butter from burning and the handle makes it easy to flip the cake upside down when it is done. It can be served warm from the oven for dessert or as a coffee cake for a brunch, but once it has cooled, the cake needs to be tightly wrapped in plastic wrap—it will get more moist the longer it sits.

7 tablespoons butter, divided	1 teaspoon baking powder
1 cup brown sugar	1 pint fresh raspberries
2 eggs	1 pint fresh blueberries
1 cup sugar	1 pint (2 cups) heavy cream
½ cup milk	¼ cup powdered sugar
¼ teaspoon salt	1 teaspoon vanilla
1 cup all-purpose flour	

Preheat oven to 375°. Melt 5 tablespoons butter in a heavy cast-iron skillet and stir in brown sugar. Cook over medium heat until sugar dissolves. Keep warm over low heat. Beat eggs and sugar together until light, about 4 minutes. Melt remaining 2 tablespoons butter in milk over low heat, or in microwave on HIGH for 1 minute. Sift together salt, flour, and baking powder. Add dry ingredients and warm milk to beaten eggs and sugar. Sprinkle raspberries and blueberries over mixture in skillet. Pour batter over berries, and bake for 45 minutes, or until a toothpick inserted in center of cake comes out clean.

As soon as it is done, carefully turn cake upside down onto a large platter with a lip, to catch the juices. Whip cream with powdered sugar and vanilla. Serve cake warm with a dollop of whipped cream. Makes 8 servings.

Dungeness Crabs and Blackberry Cobblers (Oregon)

Cranberry Cake

FROSTING:

5 tablespoons flour
1 cup sugar
1 cup milk

½ cup butter, softened
½ cup cream cheese, softened
1 teaspoon vanilla

Mix flour and sugar in saucepan. Whisk in milk and cook until thickened. Cool. Cream butter and cream cheese until smooth. Beat in flour mixture and vanilla. Chill until cake is cool. Beat occasionally until thick enough to spread.

1½ cups cranberries
¼ cup chopped walnuts
¼ cup water
½ cup butter, softened, or
  shortening
1½ cups sugar
2 eggs, beaten
1 teaspoon red food coloring

Grated rind from 1 orange
2½ cups sifted all-purpose flour
1 teaspoon baking soda
1 teaspoon salt
3 tablespoons cocoa
1 teaspoon vinegar
1 cup buttermilk

Grease and flour 2 (8-inch) cake pans. Cook cranberries with walnuts in water until skins pop and berries are soft. Cool. Cream butter and sugar; add eggs, food coloring, and orange rind. Sift together flour, baking soda, salt, and cocoa. Add vinegar to buttermilk. Mix sifted ingredients alternately with buttermilk mixture into the egg mixture. Fold in cranberries and walnuts mixture. Bake at 325° for 25–30 minutes. Cool and frost. Serves 10–12.

Cape May Fare (Mid-Atlantic)

Sunshine Lemon Cake

The intense lemon flavor in this two-layer cake with a luscious lemony frosting is sure to please lemon fans!

LEMON CAKE:

2 cups bread flour	**1 teaspoon vanilla**
1 cup sugar, divided	**1 tablespoon finely grated**
1 tablespoon baking powder	**lemon peel**
¼ teaspoon salt	**⅛ teaspoon lemon oil**
1 (6-ounce) jar pear baby food	**4 egg whites, at room**
1 cup skim milk	**temperature**

Preheat oven to 350°. Combine flour, ¾ cup sugar, baking powder, and salt in a large mixing bowl.

Combine pears, milk, vanilla, lemon peel, and lemon oil in a small bowl and blend well.

In mixing bowl of electric mixer, beat egg whites on moderate speed until they are foamy. Gradually add remaining ¼ cup granulated sugar, one tablespoon at a time, beating well after each addition. Increase speed to high and beat until stiff peaks form but are not dry. Add lemon mixture to egg whites and beat on moderate speed to lightly blend. Add lemon and egg white mixture to dry ingredients and quickly mix with a fork to blend. Pour batter into 2 (8-inch) round cake pans that have been coated with vegetable spray. Bake for 25 minutes, or until cake tester inserted into center of cakes comes out clean. Cover cakes with wax paper and cool on cake racks for 10 minutes. Remove cakes from pans, re-cover with wax paper, and cool completely.

LEMON FROSTING:

2 tablespoons each: fat-free	**2 tablespoons fresh lemon**
and light margarine, at	**juice**
room temperature	**1 tablespoon finely grated**
3 cups powdered sugar, divided	**lemon peel**

In mixing bowl of electric mixer, beat margarines until smooth. Add 2 cups powdered sugar , lemon juice, and lemon peel, and beat until blended. Add remaining 1 cup powdered sugar and beat until light and fluffy. Makes 16 servings.

Nutritional analysis per serving: 202 Cal; 4% Cal from Fat; 3g Prot; 46g Carbo; 1g Fat; 0g Fiber; 128mg Sod; 0mg Chol.

101 Great Lowfat Desserts (Iowa)

Key Lime Coconut Angel Cake

No baking! Looks elegant under a glass-domed cake dish.

1 (10-inch) round angel food
  cake
1 (14-ounce) can sweetened
  condensed milk
⅓ cup freshly squeezed Key
  lime juice

1 tablespoon grated Key lime
  peel
1 (12-ounce) carton frozen
  Cool Whip, thawed
1 cup flaked coconut
Sliced kiwi and strawberries

Cut angel food cake horizontally into 3 layers. Place bottom layer, cut side up, on cake plate. Beat milk, lime juice, and peel in large bowl with wire whisk until smooth and thickened. Fold in Cool Whip. Spread 1 cup lime mixture evenly over top of first layer of cake. Place second layer of cake carefully on bottom layer; spread evenly with 1 cup lime mixture. Top with remaining layer of cake. Frost top and sides of cake with remaining lime mixture. Sprinkle with coconut. Garnish cake with kiwi and strawberries. Serves 15.

Cooking with Classmates, Teachers, Family & Friends
(North Carolina)

The large, green, seedless limes found in your supermarket are either the Persian limes (Citrus latifolia), a hybrid developed in the early 20th century. The fruit is larger than the Key lime, more resistant to disease and pests, and has a thicker rind. They are picked slightly immature, while they are still green in color (they turn yellow when fully ripe, and might be confused with lemons). Key limes are smaller, yellower in color, seedy, more sour, and grow on thorny trees that are sensitive to cold weather.

Mother's Rich Orange Cake

No worries about this cake drying out when cut; it doesn't last that long.

Juice of 1 orange	1 cup chopped walnuts
1⅔ cups sugar, divided	1¾ cups all-purpose flour
½ cup shortening	½ teaspoon baking soda
2 eggs, unbeaten	1 teaspoon baking powder
1 cup ground raisins	¾ teaspoon salt
Grated peel of 1 orange	⅔ cup milk

Mix orange juice and ⅔ cups sugar; set aside. Mix remaining 1 cup sugar, shortening, and eggs; add raisins, orange peel, and walnuts. Blend dry ingredients and mix with milk; add to sugar mixture. Beat well; pour into greased, floured tube or Bundt pan. Bake 50–60 minutes at 350°. Remove from oven. Turn hot cake out onto deep plate and immediately pour and spread the orange juice mixture over it. Set cake plate on rack to cool. Serve warm or cold.

Begged, Borrowed and Stöllen Recipes (Oregon)

Rhubarb Upside-Down Cake

5 cups chopped rhubarb stalks	3 cups mini marshmallows
1 cup sugar	1 white or yellow cake mix,
1 (3-ounce) package raspberry	prepared according to
Jell-O	package directions

Spread rhubarb in a greased 9x13-inch cake pan. Sprinkle with mixture of sugar and Jell-O. Top with marshmallows. Mix the cake mix as directed, then pour over the rhubarb. Bake at 350° for 45–55 minutes. Let sit for 5 minutes; when done, turn upside-down into a cookie sheet.

Cookin' in Paradise (Idaho)

Watermelon Cake

Make several cakes when you have a watermelon. Freeze on a cardboard base; cover well with several layers of plastic wrap and then wrap in foil.

1 (18¼-ounce) box white or
  yellow cake mix
1 tablespoon flour
1 (3-ounce) package
  watermelon Jell-O

¾ cup oil
4 eggs
1 cup watermelon pieces

Preheat oven to 325°. Mix cake mix, flour, Jell-O, oil, and eggs. Add watermelon; beat, leaving a few little bits of watermelon showing in batter. Pour batter into greased and floured Bundt pan. Bake 45 minutes to 1 hour, until toothpick inserted comes out clean. Invert onto wire rack; cool completely before frosting.

FROSTING:
⅓ stick margarine, softened
1 (1-pound) box powdered
  sugar

¼ cup (or a little more)
  watermelon pieces

Beat margarine and powdered sugar together, adding watermelon a little at a time to keep the Frosting rather thick so it will spread over the cake without running down. Adjust thickness with more powdered sugar or watermelon.

Sharing Our Best (Alabama)

A few little-known watermelon facts:
• Watermelons are vegetables related to cucumbers, pumpkins, and squash.
• The first recorded watermelon harvest occurred nearly 5,000 years ago in Egypt.
• Early explorers used watermelons as canteens.
• The word "watermelon" first appeared in the English dictionary in 1615.
• Watermelons are grown in over 96 countries worldwide.
• Watermelons don't contain any fat or cholesterol, are high in fiber and vitamins A and C, and are a good source of potassium, making it an ideal health food.
• Over 1,200 varieties of watermelon are grown worldwide.
• Every part of a watermelon is edible, even the seeds and rinds.
• Watermelons are 92% water.

★★★★★★★★★★★   ★★★★★★★★★★★

Pumpkin Cake

½ cup shortening
1 cup sugar
1 cup firmly packed brown
  sugar
2 eggs, beaten
1 cup cooked, mashed pumpkin
  or winter squash

3 cups sifted cake flour
4 teaspoons baking powder
¼ teaspoon baking soda
½ cup milk
1 cup chopped walnuts
1 teaspoon maple extract

Cream shortening and slowly add sugars, eggs, and pumpkin. Sift together flour, baking powder, and soda; add alternately with milk to pumpkin mixture. Fold in walnuts and extract. Pour into 3 greased 8-inch layer cake pans. Bake at 350° for 30 minutes. Cool and frost with Harvest Moon Frosting.

HARVEST MOON FROSTING:

3 egg whites, unbeaten
1½ cups firmly packed brown
  sugar

Dash of salt
6 tablespoons water
1 teaspoon vanilla

Combine in double boiler the eggs, sugar, salt, and water. Beat well; place over rapidly boiling water. Cook 7 minutes, beating constantly, or until frosting will stand in peaks. Remove from boiling water; add vanilla. Beat until thick enough to spread. Put cake layers together with frosting. Frost sides, bringing frosting slightly over top edge. Frost top. Makes enough frosting for a 3-layer cake.

Cookin' & Quiltin' (Tennessee)

Old South Carrot Cake

2 cups all-purpose flour	1 teaspoon ground cinnamon
2 cups sugar	4 eggs
1 teaspoon baking powder	1 cup vegetable oil
¼ teaspoon baking soda	2 cups grated carrots
¼ teaspoon salt	

Combine dry ingredients. Stir gently and set aside. Combine eggs and oil, beating well. Fold in dry ingredients and carrots. Spoon batter into 3 greased and floured 9-inch cake pans. Bake at 375° for 25 minutes or until cake tests done (cake layers will be thin). Cool 10 minutes in pan. Remove from pans and cool completely. Yields 1 (3-layer) cake.

DELUXE CREAM CHEESE FROSTING:

½ cup butter or margarine, softened	2 teaspoons vanilla
1 (8-ounce) package cream cheese, softened	1 cup chopped pecans
1 (16-ounce) package powdered sugar	1 cup flaked coconut

Combine butter and cream cheese. Cream until light and fluffy. Add sugar and vanilla, mixing well. Stir in pecans and coconut. Spread frosting between layers and on top and side of cake.

200 Treasured Cake and Frosting Recipes (Kentucky)

Did you know…

- that carrots are not always orange? They can also be found in purple, white, red, or yellow.
- that carrots have the highest content of beta carotene (vitamin A) of all vegetables? Vitamin A is perhaps most well-known for its importance to our vision, but is also vital to other body systems and functions.
- that carrots were first grown as a medicine, not a food? Doctors in the Middle Ages prescribed carrots as a medicine for every possible affliction, from cleaning teeth to treating dog bites!

Louise's Sweet Potato Chocolate Nut Cake

**2 cups cooked and mashed
   sweet potatoes**
1½ cups vegetable oil
1½ cups sugar
1 teaspoon vanilla
4 eggs
3 cups all-purpose flour
2 teaspoons baking powder

2 teaspoons baking soda
¼ teaspoon nutmeg
¼ teaspoon ginger
2 teaspoons cinnamon
1 cup chopped walnuts
**½ cup melted unsweetened
   chocolate**

In bowl blend the first 5 items. Sift dry ingredients and add to the bowl. Add nuts to ⅔ of the batter. Add the chocolate to the remaining ⅓ of the batter. In a greased and floured tube pan, gently pour the nut batter. Pour chocolate batter on top of nut batter. Take a knife to swirl batters to get a marbleized effect. Bake at 350° for 60–70 minutes. Pick-test. Cool in pan 10 minutes. Invert onto serving dish. Frost or glaze, if desired. Serves 16.

The Best of the Sweet Potato Recipes (Pennsylvania)

Garden Eggplant Pudding Cake

**1 package yellow cake mix
   with pudding**
½ cup sour cream
¼ cup oil
**2 cups peeled and grated
   eggplant**

4 eggs
½ teaspoon nutmeg
½ teaspoon cinnamon
⅛ teaspoon ground cloves
⅛ teaspoon salt

Combine all ingredients and beat 4 minutes. Pour into greased and floured 10-inch Bundt pan. Bake 50–55 minutes in 350° oven. Sprinkle powdered sugar on top.

Iola's Gourmet Recipes in Rhapsody (Great Plains)

Squash Cake

3 cups grated squash
3 cups sugar
½ cup oil
4 eggs
1 teaspoon vanilla
3 cups all-purpose flour

2 teaspoons baking powder
2 teaspoons baking soda
1 teaspoon cinnamon
1 teaspoon salt
1 cup chopped pecans

Grate squash (or cook and strain). Beat sugar and oil. Add squash. Add eggs, one at a time, beating after each. Add vanilla. Sift together the dry ingredients. Add sifted flour; mix and beat well. Add nuts. Pour into greased and floured 9x13-inch pan.

TOPPING:
¾ cup brown sugar
3 teaspoons cinnamon

3 tablespoons butter
   or margarine, softened

Crumble together. Sprinkle on top and bake at least one hour in 350° oven. Check before removing to see if completely done in center.

The Pink Lady...in the Kitchen (Arkansas)

Zucchini Chocolate Cake

2 cups shredded or sliced
   zucchini
½ cup water
1 teaspoon salt, divided
2 cups all-purpose flour
1 teaspoon baking soda
1 teaspoon baking powder
1 teaspoon cinnamon
½ teaspoon nutmeg

4 tablespoons cocoa
3 large eggs
2 cups sugar
½ cup oil
¾ cup buttermilk
1 teaspoon vanilla
1 teaspoon grated orange peel
1 cup chopped pecans or
   walnuts

Preheat oven to 350°. Grease and flour a 9x13-inch pan. Cook zucchini 10 minutes with water and ½ teaspoon salt; drain and mash. Sift dry ingredients, including remaining salt. Beat eggs until light. Beat in sugar and oil. Combine zucchini and buttermilk. Stir flour mixture into eggs, alternating with buttermilk/zucchini. Stir in vanilla, orange peel, and nuts. Pour into prepared pan. Bake for 40–50 minutes.

Our Cherished Recipes (Alaska)

Fresh Tomato Cake

7 medium-size tomatoes
½ cup butter, softened
1 cup packed brown sugar
2 eggs
½ cup raisins
½ cup chopped dates
3 cups all-purpose flour

2 teaspoons baking powder
1 teaspoon baking soda
½ teaspoon salt
1 teaspoon allspice
½ teaspoon ground ginger
¾ teaspoon grated orange rind

Skin tomatoes; cut into quarters and remove seeds. Chop. Measure 3 cups. Drain well in sieve. Set aside.

Cream butter and brown sugar until light and fluffy. Add eggs, one at a time, beating well after each. Stir in raisins, dates, and drained tomatoes (mixture may appear curdled). Combine dry ingredients; gradually add to creamed mixture. Turn in to greased 5x9-inch loaf pan. Bake at 350° for 1 hour and 10 minutes, or until tests done. Cool in pan 5 minutes. Remove from pan and complete cooling on wire rack. Sprinkle with powdered sugar before serving, if desired.

Cookin' at Its Best (Idaho)

Blueberry Pound Cake

1 cup butter or margarine,
   softened
2 cups sugar
4 eggs
2½ teaspoons vanilla

3 cups all-purpose flour, divided
½ teaspoon salt
1 teaspoon baking powder
1 pint fresh blueberries

Cream butter or margarine and sugar. Add eggs, one at a time, beating until light and fluffy. Add vanilla. Sift 2 cups flour with salt and baking powder and mix into creamed mixture. Mix well. Use remaining flour to dredge blueberries and gently fold these into mixture. Prepare greased 10-inch tube pan and coat with sugar. Bake cake at 325° for 1 hour 15 minutes. Allow cake to cool in pan 10 minutes, then turn out onto rack. Makes 15 servings.

Tradition in the Kitchen 2 (Illinois)

Bavarian Apple Cheesecake

1⅓ cups sugar, divided
⅓ cup butter or margarine
1 tablespoon shortening
¾ teaspoon vanilla, divided
1 cup all-purpose flour
⅛ teaspoon salt
4 cups sliced, peeled, and cored
  cooking apples (Golden
  Delicious or Granny Smith)

2 (8-ounce) packages cream
  cheese, softened
2 eggs
1 teaspoon ground cinnamon
¼ cup sliced almonds

In a medium mixer bowl, beat ½ cup sugar, butter or margarine, shortening, and ¼ teaspoon vanilla on medium speed with an electric mixer until combined. Blend in flour and salt until crumbly. Pat on the bottom of a 9-inch springform pan. Set aside.

Place apple slices in a single layer in a shallow baking pan. Cover with foil. Bake in a 400° oven for 15 minutes. Meanwhile, for filling, in a large mixer bowl, beat cream cheese, ½ cup sugar, and remaining ½ teaspoon vanilla with an electric mixer until fluffy. Add eggs all at once, beating on low speed just until combined. Pour into dough-lined pan. Arrange warm apple slices atop filling. Combine remaining ⅓ cup sugar and cinnamon. Sprinkle filling with sugar mixture and the almonds.

Bake in a 400° oven for 40 minutes or until golden. Cool. Chill 4–24 hours before serving. Serves 12.

Hudson Valley German-American Society Cookbook (New York)

The apple is the official state fruit of New York, West Virginia, Washington, and Rhode Island and its blossom is the official state flower of Michigan.

★★★★★★★★★★★ ★★★★★★★★★★★

Key Lime Cheesecake
with Strawberry Sauce

CRUST:

2 cups graham cracker crumbs
¼ cup sugar

½ cup butter or margarine,
  melted

Stir together all ingredients and firmly press on bottom and 1 inch up sides of a greased 9-inch springform pan. Bake at 350° for 8 minutes; cool.

FILLING:

3 (8-ounce) packages cream
  cheese, softened
1¼ cups sugar
3 large eggs

1 (8-ounce) container sour
  cream
1½ teaspoons grated lime zest
½ cup lime juice

Beat cream cheese at medium speed with an electric mixer until fluffy; gradually add sugar; beat until blended. Add eggs, one at a time, beating well after each addition. Stir in sour cream, zest, and juice. Pour Filling into Crust. Bake at 325° for 1 hour and 5 minutes. Remove from oven and immediately run knife around edge of pan, releasing sides. Cool completely on wire rack. Cover and chill 8 hours. Garnish with strawberries. Serve with Strawberry Sauce.

STRAWBERRY SAUCE:

1¼ cups chopped fresh
  strawberries

½ cup sugar
1½ teaspoons grated lime zest

Process all ingredients in food processor until smooth.

Strawberries: From Our Family's Field to Your Family's Table
(Georgia)

★★★★★★★★★★★ ★★★★★★★★★★★

Lemon Cheesecake
with Berry Topping

¾ cup fat-free granola
1 (16-ounce) container fat-free
  cottage cheese
1 (8-ounce) package fat-free
  cream cheese, softened
¼ cup plus ½ tablespoon flour
1¼ cups sugar

4 egg whites, beaten
1 tablespoon lemon juice
1 tablespoon grated lemon rind
¼ cup fresh blueberries
¼ cup fresh strawberries
¼ cup fresh raspberries

Preheat oven to 325°. Place granola in food processor or blender, and blend until slightly ground. Lightly spray 8-inch springform pan with cooking spray and place ground granola in pan.

Combine cottage cheese and cream cheese in food processor or blender, and process until smooth. Add flour, sugar, egg whites, lemon juice, and lemon rind to cheese mixture. Pour into prepared pan and bake in preheated oven for 50 minutes. Turn oven off and let the cheesecake remain in oven for another hour, with the door slightly open. Remove pan from oven and allow cheesecake to cool completely before removing sides of pan. Top cheesecake with mixed berries and serve. Serves 12.

Nutritional Analysis Per Serving: Cal 151; Prot 9g; Carbo 29g; Chol 5mg; Sod 228mg; Dietary Fiber < 1 gram; Exchanges: 2 starch; ½ meat.

Recipes for Fat-Free Living Cookbook (Arizona)

Lemon Trivia:
- The average lemon holds about three tablespoons of juice and has about eight seeds.
- Lemons are technically berries (as are oranges, watermelons, and tomatoes).
- A lemon tree produces fruit almost year-round, and can bear as many as 3,000 lemons per year.

Flourless Chocolate Raspberry Truffle Torte

RASPBERRY SAUCE:

¾ **pound fresh raspberries**
½ **cup sugar**
1 **orange, juiced (¼ cup)**

½ **lemon, juiced (1½**
   tablespoons)

Put all ingredients in blender and process until smooth. Strain and refrigerate until ready to use. Any remaining Sauce can be frozen for months.

TORTE:

1¼ **pounds bittersweet or**
  semisweet chocolate
2 **sticks butter**

1¼ **cups Raspberry Sauce**
8 **eggs**
½ **cup sugar**

Spray a springform pan with nonstick spray. Line bottom with parchment or wax paper to fit. Spray paper with spray. Preheat oven to 425°.

Melt chocolate and butter over double-boiler. Add Raspberry Sauce when melted. Whip eggs with sugar in electric mixer until triple in volume. Pour chocolate mixture into eggs and fold until blended and smooth. Pour batter into pan and tap on counter to release any air bubbles. Set on a baking sheet tray with edges or in a baking dish with sides and pour about ¼ inch of hot water into tray or dish to create a water bath. Be careful not to get any water into the chocolate torte. Bake at 425° for 10–12 minutes until outside edges just start to pull away from pan. Torte will set once it is cooled. Refrigerate until completely cooled. Serves 8–10.

Food, Glorious Food (Ohio)

In the United States, about 90% of all raspberries sold come from Washington, California and Oregon. In Canada, the province of British Colombia produces about 80% of all raspberries sold in Canada.

Mother's Birthday Torte

A real beauty! This torte can be made with any seasonal fruit.

9 egg whites
¾ teaspoon cream of tartar
⅛ teaspoon salt
3 cups sugar

2½ teaspoons vanilla, divided
1½ teaspoons white vinegar
4 cups (2 pints) heavy cream
1 pint strawberries

Preheat oven to 325°. Lightly grease 2 (9-inch) cake pans with butter, or line pans with parchment paper.

Beat egg whites, cream of tartar, and salt until very stiff. Slowly add sugar, 1½ teaspoons vanilla, and vinegar and continue beating. Divide batter into cake pans. Bake for 60 minutes. Let cool in pans for 5 minutes; remove and cool completely.

To assemble torte, whip cream and remaining 1 teaspoon vanilla. Slice one-third of the strawberries. Place one cooled meringue on a serving plate, trimming, if necessary, to fit. Cover with about 1½ cups whipped cream and sliced strawberries. Invert second meringue, place on top of first and trim. Ice the top and sides with the remaining whipped cream; arrange whole strawberries on top and refrigerate. Yields 8–10 servings.

Note: To avoid crystallizing, leave meringue in cool oven for 2–3 hours after baking.

Five Star Sensations (Ohio)

There is a centuries-old custom that if you break a double strawberry in half and share it with someone else, the two of you will fall in love.

Peach Torte

2¼ cups all-purpose flour,
  divided
¾ cup butter
10 tablespoons powdered sugar
  (approximately ⅔ cup)
2 eggs, beaten

1½ cups sugar
¾ teaspoon baking soda
¼ teaspoon salt
½ teaspoon vanilla
4 cups fresh sliced peaches
¾ cup chopped nuts (optional)

Blend 2 cups flour, butter, and powdered sugar together with pastry blender. Pat into a greased 9x13-inch baking pan. Bake 18–20 minutes at 350°. Cream together eggs and sugar; add and blend baking soda, salt, vanilla, and remaining flour. Stir in sliced peaches and nuts, if desired. Pour over crust and bake 40–45 minutes in 350° oven. Serve with whipped cream or ice cream.

A Taste of Christ Lutheran (Wisconsin)

Did you know peach blossoms are carried by Chinese brides, as the peach tree is considered to be the tree of life, and its fruit a symbol of immortality and unity?

ELLEN LEVY FINCH, WWW.WIKIPEDIA.ORG

Orange trees are widely cultivated in tropical and subtropical climates for the delicious sweet fruit, which is peeled or cut (to avoid the bitter rind) and eaten whole, or processed to extract orange juice, and also for the fragrant peel. In 2008, 68.5 million tons of oranges were grown worldwide, primarily in Brazil and the U.S. state of Florida.

Wagon Wheel Cookies

FILLING:

1 cup water
1 cup sugar
1½ tablespoons lemon juice

2 cups chopped dates
1 cup chopped nuts

Cook Filling ingredients, except nuts, at medium heat, stirring until mixture thickens. Set Filling mixture aside to cool. When Filling mixture is cool, add nuts.

DOUGH:

1 cup shortening
2 cups brown sugar
3 eggs, well beaten
4 cups sifted all-purpose flour

1 teaspoon baking soda
1 teaspoon vanilla
½ teaspoon salt

Beat together shortening, brown sugar, and eggs. Add flour, baking soda, vanilla, and salt. Mix until well blended. Divide Dough in half. Wrap each half in plastic wrap and chill for at least 30 minutes.

Roll each section of Dough into a rectangle. Spread with Filling and roll from long side. Wrap in plastic wrap and return to refrigerator for one hour.

Remove wrap and cut into ¼-inch slices. Place on greased cookie pan and bake at 350° for 10–12 minutes.

Recipes Thru Time (Utah)

When buying dates, avoid ones that are sticky or ones that have crystallized sugar on the surface.

Fig Pinwheels

Anyone with a fig tree will love using this recipe.

1 cup figs, put through food
  chopper
¼ cup water
1 cup sugar, divided
1 cup chopped nuts
½ cup butter or margarine,
  softened
½ cup brown sugar
1 egg
2 cups all-purpose flour
½ teaspoon baking soda
¼ teaspoon salt

Combine chopped figs, water, and ½ cup sugar. Cook until thick. Cool. Fold in nuts. Cream butter, remaining ½ cup sugar, and brown sugar. Mix in egg. Sift flour, soda, and salt and add to first mixture. Roll on floured board or cloth. Spread with fig mixture; roll up like jellyroll. Chill. Cut in slices and bake at 400° for 12 minutes.

Fruits of the Desert Cookbook (Arizona)

Old-Fashioned Oatmeal Apple Cookies

¾ cup butter Crisco
1¼ cups packed brown sugar
1 egg
¼ cup milk
1½ teaspoons vanilla
1 cup all-purpose flour
1¼ teaspoons cinnamon
¼ teaspoon nutmeg
½ teaspoon baking soda
½ teaspoon salt
¾ cup chopped walnuts
1 cup peeled and diced apples
¾ cup raisins
3 cups quick cooking oats

Cream Crisco, brown sugar, egg, milk, and vanilla. Combine all dry ingredients and add to creamed mixture. Mix well; add nuts, apples, and raisins. Stir in oats. Drop by tablespoonfuls onto greased cookie sheet. Bake at 375° for 13 minutes.

Home Cookin' (Missouri)

Glazed Fresh Apple Cookies

2 cups sifted all-purpose flour
1 teaspoon baking soda
½ cup butter or margarine,
  softened
1½ cups packed brown sugar
½ teaspoon salt
1 teaspoon cinnamon
1 teaspoon ground cloves

½ teaspoon nutmeg
1 unbeaten egg
1 cup chopped walnuts
1 cup finely chopped, unpared
  apples
1 cup raisins, chopped
¼ cup apple juice, milk, or
  orange juice

Sift flour and soda together. Cream butter, sugar, salt, and spices. Add egg and mix thoroughly. Add ½ flour mixture, nuts, apples, raisins, and juice. Mix well. Add remainder of flour and mix again. Drop by rounded spoonsful on greased cookie sheet. Bake 11–14 minutes in a 400° oven. While warm, glaze with mixture below.

GLAZE:
1½ cups powdered sugar
2 tablespoons butter, softened

Enough orange juice to spread

Recipe by Mrs. Walter Myers, wife of Mayor, Virginia City, Montana
First Ladies' Cookbook (Big Sky)

An average apple contains just 75 calories, no fat, and the following nutrients: vitamins A, C, B6, and B12, thiamin, niacin, and pectin, which helps lower cholesterol.

★★★★★★★★★★★ ★★★★★★★★★★★

Apple and Cheese Pleasers

Children love these high-protein breakfast cookies.

¾ cup all-purpose flour

⅔ cup margarine, softened

⅓ cup brown sugar

1 egg

1 teaspoon vanilla

½ teaspoon cinnamon

½ teaspoon baking powder

½ teaspoon salt

1½ cups Quaker Oats

1 cup shredded Cheddar cheese

¾ cup raisins

1 cup chopped apple

Combine flour, margarine, sugar, egg, vanilla, cinnamon, baking powder, and salt in large bowl. Mix well. Add oats, cheese, and raisins. Stir in apples. Mix well. Drop by tablespoonfuls onto ungreased cookie sheet. Bake at 375° for 15 minutes or until golden brown. Store in tightly covered container in refrigerator. Yields about 24 cookies.

Educated Taste (Georgia)

Apple Orchard Easies

½ cup butter or margarine

2 cups sugar

2 tablespoons flour

¼ teaspoon salt

1 cup pared, grated, apples

3 cups quick rolled oats

1 cup chopped nuts

1 teaspoon vanilla

3 tablespoons sugar

3 teaspoons cinnamon

Melt butter in a heavy pan; stir in sugar, flour, salt, and apples. Cook to boiling; boil for 1 minute. Remove from heat; add rolled oats, nuts, and vanilla immediately. Mix thoroughly. Drop, using teaspoon, on wax paper. Cool. Roll in mixture of sugar and cinnamon. Makes 60 balls.

For Crying Out Loud...Let's Eat! (Indiana)

Peach Cookies

½ cup margarine or butter
1 cup sugar
1 large egg
2 cups all-purpose flour
½ teaspoon baking soda
¼ teaspoon nutmeg

¼ teaspoon cinnamon
⅛ teaspoon ginger
⅛ teaspoon ground cloves
⅛ teaspoon salt
3 medium fresh ripe peaches
½ cup raisins (optional)

Cream margarine or butter and sugar in a bowl. Add egg and beat until light and fluffy. In another bowl, mix flour, baking soda, and seasonings. Stir flour mixture into egg mixture, a little at a time. Peel, pit, and finely dice peaches; stir into cookie mixture. Stir in raisins, if desired. Drop dough by rounded teaspoonfuls onto cookie sheet. Bake at 375° for 20 minutes until cookies are browned on top. Cool thoroughly on wire rack before storing. Yields about 4 dozen 1½-inch cookies.

Note: These are soft, cake-like cookies. If cookies become too soft on standing, put them into a warm 250°–300° oven for a few minutes.

The Peach Sampler (South Carolina)

Christopher Columbus brought peach trees to America on both his second (1493) and third (1498) voyages.

Lemon-Zucchini Cookies

2 cups all-purpose flour
1 teaspoon baking powder
½ teaspoon salt
¾ cup butter, softened
¾ cup sugar

1 egg, beaten
Grated rind of 1 lemon
1 cup shredded zucchini
1 cup chopped walnuts or
    pecans

Combine flour, baking powder, and salt. Set aside. Cream butter and sugar. Beat in egg and lemon rind. Stir in flour mixture until smooth. Stir in zucchini mixture and nuts. Drop by rounded teaspoons on greased cookie sheets. Bake at 375° for 15–20 minutes. Drizzle with Lemon Glaze while still warm. Yields 4 dozen.

LEMON GLAZE:
1½ tablespoons freshly
    squeezed lemon juice

1 cup powdered sugar

Mix until smooth.

Picnics on the Square (Wisconsin)

Zucchini Cookies

1 cup butter or margarine
2 cups sugar
2 cups shredded zucchini
4 cups all-purpose flour
1 teaspoon ground cloves

1 cup raisins (optional)
2 teaspoons baking soda
2 teaspoons cinnamon
1 teaspoon salt
¾ cup chopped nuts

Cream together butter and sugar. Add remaining ingredients. Drop by teaspoonfuls onto cookie sheet. Bake at 375° for 10 minutes. Let cool before removing from tray. Makes 30–36 cookies.

The Manor Cookbook (Michigan)

★★★★★★★★★★★★ ★★★★★★★★★★★★

Orange Drop Cookies

1 cup margarine, softened	1 teaspoon baking soda
2 cups sugar	1 cup milk
2 eggs, beaten	4¾ cups all-purpose flour
Juice from 1 orange	2 teaspoons baking powder
Grated rind from 1 orange	

Cream margarine, sugar, and eggs. Add juice and grated rind. Mix baking soda with milk and add to margarine mixture. Add flour and baking powder. Mix well. Drop by teaspoonfuls onto an ungreased baking sheet. Bake at 375° for 12–15 minutes. When cookies are completely cool, ice with Orange Drop Cookie Icing.

ORANGE DROP COOKIE ICING:

Juice from 1 orange	1 (1-pound) box confectioners'
2 teaspoons butter, softened	sugar

Mix juice, softened butter, and confectioners' sugar together; spread on cookies.

Love, Mom: Stories and Recipes from Kingston, Ohio (Ohio)

Orange Brownies

1½ cups all-purpose flour	4 eggs
2 cups sugar	2 teaspoons orange extract
1 teaspoon salt	Grated rind of 1 orange
1 cup butter, softened	Confectioners' sugar

Preheat oven to 350° and grease a 9x13-inch pan. Mix all ingredients except confectioners' sugar together and pour into greased pan. Bake for 30 minutes. When cool, sprinkle with confectioners' sugar. Yields 48.

Just Desserts (Pennsylvania)

★★★★★★★★★★★★   ★★★★★★★★★★★★

Apple Brownies

⅔ cup margarine, softened
1¾ cups brown sugar
2 eggs
1 teaspoon vanilla
2 cups all-purpose flour
2 teaspoons baking powder

¼ teaspoon salt
1 cup chopped, peeled apples
⅓ cup chopped walnuts
⅓ cup chopped raisins
Powdered sugar

Cream margarine and brown sugar. Add eggs and beat until well mixed. Add vanilla and mix again. Add sifted dry ingredients and beat until mixture is smooth. Add apples, walnuts, and raisins and stir gently with a strong spoon. Spread batter in a greased 9x13-inch pan and bake at 350° for 30–35 minutes. Remove brownies from pan and roll each one in sifted powdered sugar. Yields 1½ dozen.

The Apple Barn Cookbook (Tennessee)

Apple Bars

2½ cups all-purpose flour
1 teaspoon salt
1 cup shortening
2 eggs, separated
Milk (about ½ cup)
1 cup cornflakes

12 apples, peeled and sliced
1–1½ cups sugar
1 teaspoon cinnamon
½ cup powdered sugar
1 tablespoon milk

Cut flour and salt into shortening. Beat egg yolks and add milk to make ⅔ cup. Mix well and add to flour mixture. Roll ½ of the dough between 2 sheets of wax paper to fit a jellyroll pan. Crush cornflakes and spread on dough. Add apples, sugar, and cinnamon. Roll the rest of the dough for top. Beat egg whites and brush on top. Bake at 350° for 50–60 minutes. Frost with mixture of powdered sugar and milk.

Incredible Edibles (Great Plains)

Apple Squares

2 eggs
1½ cups sugar
1 cup oil
3 fresh apples, peeled and
 sliced thin
1 teaspoon salt
1 teaspoon baking soda
2 teaspoons dry yeast granules

3 teaspoons cinnamon
1 teaspoon nutmeg
2½ cups all-purpose flour
1 cup chopped pecans or
 walnuts
1 (6-ounce) package
 butterscotch morsels

Combine eggs, sugar, and oil; beat well. Add apples, salt, soda, yeast, cinnamon, nutmeg, flour, and nuts. Mix well. Place in greased 9x13x2-inch pan. Cover with butterscotch morsels. Bake in 325° oven for 45 minutes. Cut into squares; serve with ice cream.

The Crowning Recipes of Kentucky (Kentucky)

The Best Date Bars

CRUST:
½ cup butter, softened
¼ cup sugar

1 cup sifted all-purpose flour

Mix butter, sugar, and flour until crumbly. Press evenly in a greased 9x9-inch or 7x11-inch pan. Bake at 400° for 10–12 minutes. Do not brown the Crust.

FILLING:
⅓ cup all-purpose flour
½ teaspoon baking powder
¼ teaspoon salt
2 eggs, beaten
1 cup brown sugar

½ cup chopped dates
1 teaspoon vanilla
½ cup chopped walnuts
Powdered sugar (optional)

Mix together the flour, baking powder, and salt. Set aside. Beat eggs with brown sugar and add dates; blend well. Add flour mixture, vanilla, and nuts. Spread over baked Crust and bake at 350° for 30 minutes. Cut into squares or bars while hot. May dust with powdered sugar, if desired.

Favorite Recipes for Islanders (Hawaii)

★★★★★★★★★★★ ★★★★★★★★★★★

Banana Bars

1½ cups sugar
½ cup margarine, softened
1 cup sour cream
2 eggs
1½ cups mashed bananas

2 teaspoons vanilla
2 cups all-purpose flour
1 teaspoon baking soda
¾ teaspoon salt
½ cup chopped nuts

Heat oven to 375°. Grease and flour jellyroll pan. Mix sugar, margarine, sour cream, and eggs for 1 minute. Beat in bananas and vanilla. Beat in flour, soda, and salt for 1 minute. Stir in nuts. Bake 20–25 minutes. Cool and frost with Butter Frosting.

BUTTER FROSTING:
¼ cup margarine
2 cups powdered sugar

1 teaspoon vanilla
3 tablespoons milk

Heat margarine over medium heat until lightly brown. Remove from heat and mix in powdered sugar. Beat in vanilla and milk until smooth.

Arizona State Fair Blue Ribbon Recipes (Arizona)

Blueberry Lemon Bars

2 sticks butter, softened
¾ cup powdered sugar
2¼ cups all-purpose flour,
   divided
½ cup finely chopped pecans,
   divided

4 eggs
1½ cups sugar
1 cup lemon juice
1 teaspoon baking powder
1½ cups fresh blueberries

Preheat oven to 350°. Beat butter with mixer until fluffy. Add powdered sugar; beat until combined. Beat in 2 cups flour. Stir in ¼ cup pecans. Press into bottom of greased 9x13-inch baking pan. Bake 20 minutes until golden.

Meanwhile, combine eggs, sugar, lemon juice, baking powder, and remaining ¼ cup flour. Beat with mixer on medium speed 2 minutes. Sprinkle berries over prepared crust. Pour filling over berries, and sprinkle with remaining pecans. Bake 30–35 minutes or until set and lightly golden. Cool. Cut into bars. Store in fridge.

Cooking Carley Style (South Carolina)

Lemon Glazed Persimmon Bars

1 cup persimmon pulp with
  1½ teaspoons lemon juice
1 teaspoon baking soda
1 egg
1 cup sugar
½ cup oil
8 ounces pitted dates, chopped

1¾ cups all-purpose flour
1 teaspoon cinnamon
1 teaspoon nutmeg
¼ teaspoon cloves
1 cup chopped pecans or
  walnuts

Mix pulp with baking soda. Lightly beat egg. Stir in sugar, oil, and dates. Combine flour with cinnamon, nutmeg, and cloves. Add to date mixture alternately with the persimmon pulp just until well blended. Stir in nuts. Spread evenly in a greased and floured jellyroll pan (10x15-inches). Bake in a 350° oven until lightly browned, about 25 minutes. Cool for 5 minutes, then spread with Lemon Glaze. Cool thoroughly, then cut into bars, about 3x1½-inches. Keep well wrapped. Makes about 30 bars.

LEMON GLAZE:
1 cup unsifted powdered sugar   2 tablespoons lemon juice

Blend until smooth.

Durham's Favorite Recipes (California)

Strawberry Squares

1 cup sifted all-purpose flour
¼ cup brown sugar
½ cup chopped black walnuts
½ cup butter, melted
2 egg whites

1 cup sugar
2 cups sliced strawberries
2 tablespoons lemon juice
1 cup whipping cream,
  whipped

Mix first 4 ingredients; bake in shallow pan at 350° for 20 minutes. Stir occasionally. Sprinkle ⅔ crumbs in 9x13x2-inch pan. Combine egg whites, sugar, berries, and lemon juice. Beat at high speed about 10 minutes. Fold in whipped cream. Pour over crumbs. Top with remaining crumbs. Freeze 6 hours. Serves 12.

The Never Ending Season (Missouri)

Date Loaf Candy

½ cup milk
2 cups sugar
¼ cup butter

1 cup chopped dates
1 teaspoon vanilla
1 cup broken pecans

In saucepan, boil milk, sugar, and butter to 240°, or until mixture forms soft ball in cold water. Remove from heat and add dates and vanilla. Heat until dates melt. Add pecans and beat until cool. Pour onto wet cheesecloth and form a ball or log. Let cool and unroll from cheesecloth. Slice candy roll or log every ½ inch or so.

First Family Favorites (Virginia II)

Persimmon Candy

5 cups sugar
½ cup light corn syrup
1 teaspoon salt
¾ cup persimmon pulp

1½ cups evaporated milk
1 teaspoon vanilla
4 tablespoons butter
½ cup chopped hickory nuts

Combine all ingredients except vanilla, butter, and nuts, in a heavy pan. Cook to a hard-ball stage (approximately 32 minutes) over medium heat. Stir continually. Blend in vanilla and butter. Set aside until cool. Beat mixture until it becomes dull. Add nuts. Pour into greased 9x13-inch dish and let stand until firm (at least 12 hours). Cut into 1-inch squares. Yields 70 pieces.

Steamboat Adventures (Missouri)

The oldest-known persimmon tree is located in Okayama, Japan, and is thought to be more than 600 years old.

Candied Orange Peel

My mother always made this for Christmas.

4 navel oranges
2½ cups sugar, reserving
  ½ cup for dipping

1 cup water
¼ cup light corn syrup

Remove orange peel in about ⅓-inch strips with a sharp knife, leaving some of the white on the orange. Cut into 3-inch lengths. Put in a large, heavy saucepan and cover with cold water. Bring to a boil and boil 3 minutes. Drain, and repeat the procedure 3 times in all, discarding the water each time and replacing it with fresh. Drain peel after last boiling and set it aside in a bowl.

Rinse out saucepan, and combine 2 cups sugar, 1 cup water, and syrup in it. Place over medium heat and cook, stirring, until sugar dissolves. Add orange peel, turning heat to simmer, and cook gently until peel is translucent, about 30 minutes. Cool in syrup about 45 minutes, then lift out each strip with a fork, draining over edge of pan, and roll in the reserved ½ cup sugar. Place on wax paper to firm up.

Raleigh House Cookbook (Texas II)

The navel orange has thick, bright orange skin that is very easy to peel. The flesh is sweet and meaty.

Pies &
Other Desserts

★★★★★★★   ★★★★★★★

USDA

The first peaches were planted in Georgia in the 18th century.
The first commercial production did not occur until the mid-19th
century. The peach is the state fruit of Georgia and South Carolina.
It is also the state flower of Delaware.

Caramel Apple Pecan Pie

¾ cup sugar
¼ cup all-purpose flour
1 teaspoon cinnamon
Dash of salt
⅛ teaspoon nutmeg

6 cups peeled and sliced
  Jonathan or Granny Smith
  apples
Pastry for a double crust pie
1 tablespoon butter

Combine sugar, flour, cinnamon, salt, and nutmeg. Toss apples and sugar-flour-cinnamon mixture. Turn into a 9-inch pastry shell. Dot with butter. Cover with top crust. Moisten, seal, and flute edges with fingers or fork. Prick or slit top crust to allow steam to escape. Bake at 450° for 10–15 minutes, then reduce heat to 350° for 40–45 minutes. Remove from oven, and allow to cool. Top with caramel topping.

CARAMEL-PECAN TOPPING:

8 ounces Kraft caramels,
  unwrapped

2 tablespoons evaporated milk
½ cup chopped pecans

Place caramels and milk in double boiler and heat, or place in a microwave-safe bowl, and melt until smooth. Add chopped pecans and spread over top of pie.

Baked with Love (Missouri)

Bourbon Apple Pie

½ cup raisins
4 tablespoons bourbon, divided
6–7 cups peeled, cored, and
  sliced apples
¾–1 cup sugar (to taste)
2 tablespoons all-purpose flour

1 teaspoon cinnamon
⅛ teaspoon nutmeg
½ cup chopped walnuts or
  pecans
Dough for 9-inch 2 crust pie

Preheat oven to 425°. Plump raisins in 2 tablespoons bourbon. Sprinkle remaining 2 tablespoons bourbon over sliced apples.

Combine sugar, flour, cinnamon, and nutmeg. Add sugar mixture, raisins, and nuts to apples and mix thoroughly. Put in crust. Bake in lower third of oven for 50–60 minutes.

Preparation Time: 30 minutes + baking. Yields 1 pie.

CordonBluegrass (Kentucky)

Blackberry and Apple Pie

1½ pounds large cooking
  apples
2 tablespoons melted butter
4 ounces sugar, divided
2 pounds fresh blackberries

Pastry for 1 crust pie
1 egg yolk, mixed with
  1 tablespoon sugar
Whipped cream for garnish

Peel, core, and slice apples. In a heavy sauté pan, melt butter and cook apples over medium heat. Sprinkle with 2 tablespoons sugar and stir well. The apples should not fall apart. Combine remaining sugar with the blackberries; taste and add more sugar if necessary.

  Spread blackberries in a 2-inch-deep pie dish. Spoon apples over top. Cover whole surface of pie with crust, sealing the edges (to edge of pie dish). Brush top with egg yolk-sugar mixture. Bake for 20–25 minutes in a 400° oven or until the crust is golden brown. Cool pie at room temperature and serve with whipped cream.

A Gathering of Recipes (Nevada)

Blueberry Cream Pie

3 (9-inch) pie shells

1 cup chopped pecans

Press pecans into pie shells and bake according to instructions. Cool shells before adding Filling.

FILLING:

1 (8-ounce) package cream
  cheese, softened
1 (1-pound) box powdered sugar

1 (12-ounce) container frozen
  Cool Whip, thawed

Cream together cream cheese and powdered sugar. Fold in Cool Whip. Pour Filling into cool pie shells.

TOPPING:

3½ cups blueberries
1 cup sugar (or less)

2 tablespoons cornstarch
1 tablespoon lemon juice

Mix blueberries, sugar, and cornstarch, and cook over low heat. Add lemon juice; continue to cook until thick. Cool and spread on top of Filling.

Family and Food–Recipes and Reminiscences (North Carolina)

★★★★★★★★★★★★ ★★★★★★★★★★★★

Buttermilk Berry Pie

3 large eggs
1 cup sugar
2 cups buttermilk
1 tablespoon butter, melted,
  cooled

1 teaspoon orange zest
¾ teaspoon cinnamon
⅛ teaspoon nutmeg
1 teaspoon vanilla extract
1 (9-inch) ready-made pie crust

Preheat oven to 425°. Beat all ingredients together. Pour batter into pie crust. Bake for 35 minutes. Serve with Berry Sauce and garnish with fresh berries.

BERRY SAUCE:
1 pint sliced strawberries
1 pint raspberries

¼ cup seedless raspberry jam

Purée berries and jam; strain. Yields 6 servings.

A Taste of the Murphin Ridge Inn (Ohio)

Sour Cream Peach Pie

CRUST:
2½ cups graham cracker
  crumbs, divided

½ cup butter, melted

Preheat oven to 350°. In bowl, combine 2 cups crumbs and melted butter. Press remaining ½ cup crumbs into 9-inch pie pan. Bake 5 minutes.

FILLING:
2 cups thinly sliced fresh
  peaches
2 eggs, beaten
½ cup sour cream

⅔ cup sugar
2 teaspoons vanilla extract
¼ teaspoon ground cinnamon

Place sliced peaches in baked Crust. Combine remaining ingredients in bowl and mix well. Pour mixture over peaches. Sprinkle reserved crumbs over top of peach mixture. Bake 45 minutes. Makes 8 servings.

The Table at Grey Gables (Tennessee)

★★★★★★★★★★★ ★★★★★★★★★★★

Sour Cream Pear Pie

This is our most popular pear dessert at the Pear Party in September. Our daughter-in-law Linda makes lots so everyone can sample.

PIE:

1 cup sour cream
1 egg
¾ cup sugar
1 teaspoon vanilla
¼ teaspoon salt

2 tablespoons all-purpose flour
4 cups peeled and diced ripe
   pears
1 (9-inch) pie shell, unbaked

Preheat oven to 375°. Blend sour cream, egg, sugar, vanilla, salt, and flour until smooth. Fold in prepared pears. Pour into pie shell. Bake for 40 minutes. Sprinkle with Pecan Streusel Topping and bake another 10 minutes. Cool slightly and serve.

PECAN STREUSEL TOPPING:

¼ cup butter, cut in small pieces
¼ cup all-purpose flour
¼ cup brown sugar

1 teaspoon cinnamon
¼ cup finely chopped pecans

Cut butter into combined flour, sugar, and cinnamon. Add pecans. Serves 6–8.

Recipe by Rasmussen Farms (Hood River)
The Fruit Loop Cookbook (Oregon)

Did you know that pear trees can produce fruit for up to 100 years?

Coconut Banana Cream Pie

PIE CRUST:

1⅓ cups flaked coconut
⅔ cup rolled oats

3 tablespoons margarine,
   melted

Mix well all ingredients in a 9-inch pie pan. Press into bottom and sides of pan. Bake at 300° for 15 minutes, or until golden.

FILLING:

3 cups milk
⅓ cup cornstarch
3 eggs, separated
¾ cup sugar, divided

2 tablespoons margarine
1½ teaspoons vanilla
2 large bananas

In large saucepan, mix milk, cornstarch, yolks, ½ cup sugar, and margarine. Cook over medium heat, stirring constantly, until it boils and thickens. Boil one minute. Stir in vanilla. Slice bananas into pie shell. Pour custard on top. Beat egg whites until stiff peaks form. Gradually stir in remaining ¼ cup sugar. Spread meringue over filling, being sure to seal edges. Bake in preheated 400° oven 10 minutes, or until meringue is golden. Cool on wire rack. Makes 8 servings.

Easy Recipes for 1, 2 or a Few (Colorado)

Cantaloupe Cream Pie

1 cup sugar
2 tablespoons all-purpose flour
3 eggs, beaten
1 cup puréed cantaloupe

1 teaspoon vanilla extract
2 tablespoons butter
1 (8-inch) pastry shell, baked
1 cup whipping cream, whipped

Combine sugar and flour in saucepan; add eggs, mixing well. Stir in cantaloupe purée and cook over medium heat 8–10 minutes, stirring constantly, until mixture boils and thickens. Remove from heat; stir in vanilla and butter. Cool. Pour filling into pastry shell; spread evenly with whipped cream. Chill. Yields 6 servings.

Heart of the Mountains (North Carolina)

Mrs. Strom Thurmond's Watermelon Pie

Senator Strom Thurmond was elected United States Senator from South Carolina in 1954.

4 cups chopped watermelon rind	½ teaspoon ground nutmeg
2 oranges, peeled and finely chopped	½ teaspoon ground cinnamon
	¼ teaspoon curry powder
2 tablespoons lemon juice	Dash of cayenne pepper
1 teaspoon grated lemon rind	1 (9-inch) pie shell, baked
2 cups brown sugar	1 cup crumbled gingersnaps
	9 egg whites, beaten

Place watermelon rind in a large saucepan and barely cover with water. Bring to a boil and add oranges, lemon juice, and lemon rind. Cook until watermelon is transparent. Stir in brown sugar and spices. Allow mixture to cool. Pour into pie shell and sprinkle with gingersnap crumbs. Spread beaten egg whites over top. Bake for 20 minutes at 325°. Serves 8.

Putting on the Grits (South Carolina)

Delightful Strawberry Pie

3 egg whites	½ cup flaked coconut
1½ cups white sugar, divided	½ cup chopped pecans
¾ teaspoon cream of tartar	2 cups whipped cream
½ cup saltine crackers, crushed	½ teaspoon unflavored gelatin
	4 cups sliced fresh strawberries

Preheat oven to 375°. In a large bowl, beat egg whites until soft peaks form. Gradually add 1 cup sugar and cream of tartar, continuing to beat until whites form stiff peaks. Gently fold in cracker crumbs, coconut, and pecans. Spread mixture onto the bottom and up sides of a 9-inch pie pan. Bake in preheated oven for 20–22 minutes, or until lightly browned. Cool completely. In a large bowl, beat cream, gelatin, and remaining ½ cup sugar until stiff peaks form. Fold in strawberries, then pour over egg white layer. Cover and refrigerate for 2 hours.

Traditional Treasures (Nevada)

★ ★ ★ ★ ★ ★ ★ ★ ★ ★ ★   ★ ★ ★ ★ ★ ★ ★ ★ ★ ★ ★

Strawberry Ice Cream Pie

1 (3-ounce) package strawberry
   gelatin
1 cup hot water
½ cup cold water
1 pint vanilla ice cream

1 cup sliced fresh or frozen
   strawberries
1 (9-inch) pie shell, baked and
   cooled

Dissolve gelatin in hot water. Add cold water; stir. Cut ice cream in 6 chunks; add to gelatin mixture. Stir until ice cream melts; chill. When mixture begins to thicken, 20–30 minutes, gently fold in berries. Pour into cooled shell. Chill until firm.

Note: Lemon gelatin and peach slices may be substituted for strawberries.

A Gathering of Recipes (Nevada)

Northwest Huckleberry Pie

Native huckleberries are a summer treat for hikers throughout the timberline areas of the Pacific Northwest. These small, firm berries are a favorite of cooks and bears alike. If you are unable to find them, blueberries are a reasonable alternative.

1 (9-inch) pie crust, unbaked

FILLING:
¾ cup sugar
¼ cup all-purpose flour
½ teaspoon nutmeg
½ teaspoon cinnamon

5 cups peeled, cored, and thinly
   sliced tart apples
1 cup huckleberries or
   blueberries

TOPPING:
1 cup all-purpose flour
½ cup butter, cut into pieces

½ cup brown sugar

Press pie crust into a 9-inch pie plate and flute edges. Combine Filling ingredients and place in pie crust. Combine Topping ingredients and mix until crumbly. Sprinkle over pie filling. Bake at 375° for 50 minutes. Cover with aluminum foil for the last 10 minutes if top browns too quickly. Serves 8.

Gold'n Delicious (Washington)

Florida Orange Pie

FILLING:

2 cups orange juice
1 cup sugar
2 tablespoons cornstarch
¼ cup water
½ teaspoon salt
1 tablespoon butter or
  margarine

3 egg yolks
3 tablespoons grated orange
  rind
1 cup orange sections
1 (9-inch) pie shell, baked

Combine orange juice and sugar, and boil until sugar dissolves. Mix cornstarch and water; add to orange juice mixture. Add salt and butter. Beat egg yolks and add a little of hot mixture and stir together, then combine and stir until thickened. Add grated orange rind and sections just before removing from heat. Pour into pie shell and let cool.

TOPPING:

3 egg whites
3 tablespoons ice water

Pinch of salt
6 tablespoons sugar

Beat egg whites until frothy; add ice water, then salt. Add sugar slowly while beating eggs until stiff, but not dry. Mound lightly on filled pie shell and spread to edge of crust. Bake at 300° for 15–20 minutes or until brown. Yields 8 servings.

Historic Spanish Point: Cooking Then and Now (Florida)

About 90% of the Florida orange crop is used to make orange juice, which is Florida's official state beverage.

Cracker Pie

3 egg whites
1 cup sugar
¼ teaspoon baking powder
Pinch of salt

20 dates, chopped
½ cup chopped nuts
12 soda crackers, rolled fine

Beat egg whites until stiff. Gradually add sugar, baking powder, and salt. Mix in other ingredients. Pour into greased pie pan and bake in 350° oven for 20 minutes. Do not overbake. Wonderful hot or cold. Whipped cream or ice cream topping can be used, but is good plain.

Cracker Barrel Old Country Stores: Old Timey Recipes & Proverbs to Live By (Tennessee)

Easy Zucchini Blender Pie

3 cups cooked and mashed
  zucchini
1 stick butter or margarine
¼ cup sugar
4 eggs

2 tablespoons all-purpose flour
2 tablespoons lemon flavoring
2 tablespoons coconut flavoring
2 teaspoons vanilla extract
1 (9-inch) pie shell, unbaked

Put all ingredients into a blender; blend well and pour into pie shell. Bake at 350° for 55 minutes or till knife inserted into center comes out clean.

The Best of the Zucchini Recipes (Pennsylvania)

Historians generally agree that almonds and dates, both mentioned in the Old Testament of the Bible, were among the earliest cultivated foods.

Leesee's Sweet Potato Pie

This has got to be one of the best pies ever, and if you like sweet potato pie to begin with, you're gonna love this one!

3 or 4 large sweet potatoes
1½ cups sugar
2 eggs (3, if small)
1 tablespoon butter, melted
Pinch of salt
½ cup milk
1 teaspoon allspice

1 teaspoon cinnamon
1 teaspoon nutmeg
2 or 3 tablespoons bourbon
  whiskey
1 (9-inch) pie shell, unbaked
3 tablespoons butter

Cook sweet potatoes and mash to make 2 cups. Mix potatoes, sugar, eggs, 1 tablespoon melted butter, salt, milk, allspice, cinnamon, nutmeg, and whiskey together well and pour into pie shell. Dot all over top with real butter. Bake at 375° for 1 hour or until knife in center comes out clean.

Gran's Gems (Mississippi)

Fresh Sweet Potato Pie

2 cups mashed, cooked sweet
  potatoes (4 medium)
3 eggs
1 cup packed brown sugar
1 teaspoon salt
½ teaspoon ground
  cinnamon

½ teaspoon ground nutmeg
¼ teaspoon ground ginger
⅛ teaspoon ground cloves
1 cup evaporated milk or light
  cream
1 (9-inch) pie shell, unbaked
Pecans for garnish

To cook sweet potatoes, bake in preheated 350° oven 40 minutes, or boil in water to cover 20 minutes, until soft. Cool, peel, and mash until smooth. In large bowl, beat eggs with sugar, salt, and spices. Add mashed sweet potatoes and evaporated milk; mix well. Turn into unbaked pie shell. Bake in preheated 350° oven 1 hour and 15 minutes or until tip of silver knife inserted in center comes out clean. Garnish with pecans. Serve with whipped cream or ice cream, if desired.

Kentucky Kitchens Volume I (Kentucky)

Fresh Pumpkin Pie

Pastry for one-crust pie
2 eggs, slightly beaten
2 cups evaporated milk
1⅓ cups fresh pumpkin purée*
¾ cup brown sugar

1 teaspoon salt
1½ teaspoons cinnamon
1½ teaspoons ginger
¼ teaspoon cloves

Line pie plate with pastry. Stir eggs and milk into pumpkin. Add sugar, salt, and spices and mix well. Pour pumpkin mixture into pastry and bake at 450° for 10 minutes, then reduce heat to 350° and bake for an additional 30 minutes, or until a knife inserted in the center comes out clean.

*Pumpkin Purée: Cut pumpkin in half and remove seeds; peel and cut into 1-inch cubes. Put cubes into a saucepan and add ½–1 cup water (only enough to keep pumpkin from burning). Cover saucepan and simmer pumpkin, stirring often, until it becomes thick and mushy. Mash pumpkin or whirl in a blender to purée.

Note: Yellow squash can be substituted for pumpkin in this recipe.

Hopi Cookery (Arizona)

There are 1.5 million pumpkins produced in the United States each year, with the majority harvested in the month of October. The top pumpkin-producing states in the nation include California, Illinois, Indiana, and Pennsylvania, with Illinois producing the most.

Lemon Chess Tarts

4 eggs, slightly beaten
1½ cups sugar
6 tablespoons butter, melted
  and cooled
¼ cup milk

1 tablespoon cornmeal
¾ teaspoon grated lemon rind
1 tablespoon lemon juice
16 tart shells, unbaked

In mixing bowl, combine eggs, sugar, butter, milk, cornmeal, lemon rind, and lemon juice, stirring well to distribute sugar. Place tart shells on cookie sheet and divide filling evenly among the 16 shells. Bake at 350° for 35–40 minutes or until knife inserted in center comes out clean. Cool on wire rack. Cover and chill to store.

Gran's Gems (Mississippi)

Crusty Peach Cobbler

3 cups sliced fresh peaches
¼ cup sugar
1 tablespoon lemon juice

1 teaspoon grated lemon peel
1 teaspoon almond extract

Arrange peaches in a greased 8-inch square baking pan. Sprinkle with mixture sugar, lemon juice, lemon peel, and almond extract. Heat in 400° oven while preparing Shortcake.

SHORTCAKE:
1½ cups all-purpose flour
½ teaspoon salt
3 teaspoons baking powder
3 tablespoons sugar, divided

⅓ cup shortening
½ cup milk
1 egg, well beaten

Sift together flour, salt, baking powder, and 1 tablespoon sugar; cut in shortening until mixture looks like coarse crumbs. Add milk and egg at once; stir just until flour is moistened. Spread dough over hot peaches. Sprinkle with remaining 2 tablespoons sugar. Bake in a 400° oven 40 minutes or until nicely browned.

Field o' Dreams Farm Cookbook II (Alabama)

Buttermilk-Crusted Blackberry Cobbler

FILLING:

1½ pounds blackberries
3½ tablespoons all-purpose
   flour

1⅓ cups sugar
1⅓ tablespoons vanilla extract

In a medium bowl, combine blackberries, flour, sugar, and vanilla. Pour into greased 8x12x2-inch pan.

CRUST:

1 tablespoon plus 2½ teaspoons
   sugar
¾ teaspoon baking powder
¼ teaspoon salt
⅓ cup shortening

½ cup buttermilk
1⅓ cups all-purpose flour,
   divided
2 tablespoons melted butter
Whipped topping

In a large bowl, stir together 1 tablespoon sugar, baking powder, salt, shortening, buttermilk, and ¾ cup flour to form a sticky dough. Spread remaining flour on a work surface and knead dough until most of the flour is incorporated and dough is manageable. Roll dough to about ¼-inch thickness and cut with a knife into large pieces. Cover blackberry filling with dough, overlapping pieces. Drizzle melted butter over dough and sprinkle with remaining 2½ teaspoons sugar.

Preheat oven to 350°. Bake until crust is golden brown and filling is bubbly, about 50 minutes. Serve with whipped topping. Serves 8–10.

Approximate values per serving (based on 8 servings): Cal 345; Fat 10g; Chol 77mg; Carbo 44g; Sod 184 mg; Cal from Fat 49%.

By Request (Arizona)

Three Berry Cobbler

Summer or winter, this is a winner.

1½ cups sugar, divided
5 cups blueberries, raspberries,
  and strawberries (if frozen
  and thawed, remove 1 cup
  liquid)
1 cup all-purpose flour

1½ teaspoons baking powder
1 teaspoon cinnamon
¼ teaspoon salt
1 cup warmed milk
½ teaspoon vanilla
1 stick butter

Sprinkle ½ cup sugar over berries and let stand. Combine remaining sugar and dry ingredients, then add milk and vanilla. Stir to moisten. Melt butter and put in large oval dish. Add batter, then top with berries. Bake at 350° for 30 minutes. Increase heat to 400° and bake an additional 15 minutes. Serves 10–12.

Three Rivers Cookbook III (Pennsylvania)

Fresh Peach Crisp

1 cup flour
½ cup sugar
½ cup firmly packed light
  brown sugar
¼ teaspoon salt
½ teaspoon cinnamon

½ cup margarine
4 cups sliced fresh peaches
¼ teaspoon almond extract
2 tablespoons water
¼ teaspoon ground nutmeg
Whipping cream

Combine first 5 ingredients. Cut in margarine with a pastry blender until mixture resembles coarse cornmeal. Set aside.

Combine peaches, almond extract, and water. Spoon into a greased 9-inch square baking dish. Sprinkle flour mixture over peaches. Sprinkle nutmeg on top. Bake covered in a 350° oven for 15 minutes. Remove cover and bake 35–45 minutes longer or until the topping is brown. Serve warm with whipped whipping cream. Serves 6–8.

Revel (Louisiana)

Raspberry Crumble

3 cups crushed raspberries
1¼ cups sugar, divided
Juice from ½ lemon
¼ cup butter or margarine,
  softened

¾ cup all-purpose flour
Pinch of salt

Preheat oven to 350°. Coat 1-quart quiche dish with vegetable spray. Sprinkle raspberries with half of sugar, add lemon juice, and stir well. Place in prepared dish.

Blend butter with remaining sugar, flour, and salt and spread over raspberries. Bake 40 minutes. Yields 4 servings.

Favorite New England Recipes (New England)

Huckleberry Quickie

2 cups huckleberries
1½ cups sugar, divided
¾ cup all-purpose flour,
  divided
¼ teaspoon salt, divided

2 tablespoons butter
1 tablespoon lemon juice
1 cup water
1¼ teaspoons baking powder
1 egg

Combine berries, 1 cup sugar, ¼ cup flour, ⅛ teaspoon salt, butter, lemon juice, and water in a saucepan. Bring to a boil and simmer 5 minutes. Pour into a greased 9-inch-square baking pan. Now mix ½ cup flour, ½ cup sugar, ⅛ teaspoon salt, and baking powder. Add egg; stir quickly and spoon over berry mixture. Bake at 350° for 25 minutes.

Huckleberries and Crabmeat (Oregon)

Huckleberries, according to studies from the United States Department of Agriculture, help prevent scurvy through high levels of vitamin C. The berries are a useful adjunct for lowering blood sugar in diabetics.

Baked Cherry Dessert

4 fresh peaches
2 quarts fresh cherries, pitted
¾ cup sugar

4 tablespoons cornstarch
3 tablespoons lemon juice

Grease a 9x13-inch baking dish. Remove skin and pits from peaches; slice. Stir together fruits, sugar, cornstarch, and lemon juice. Pour evenly into baking dish.

TOPPING:

1½ cups sugar
1½ cups oat flour or oatmeal

1 cup butter, softened

Combine ingredients, making even crumbs, then sprinkle over fruit. Bake at 350° for 40–45 minutes. Cool. Serve with vanilla ice cream.

Wheat Free Wishes (Michigan)

Cherry Soup

Some people say they come to Pommerntag just for this wonderful fruit soup!

DUMPLING MIXTURE:

1 egg, beaten
4 heaping tablespoons
  all-purpose flour

½ teaspoon baking powder
¾ cup milk
Pinch of salt

Mix together. It will look like cake batter.

4 cups water
1¾ cups sugar

3 cups pitted fresh sour
  cherries

Boil water with sugar; add cherries and cook to soften. Check sweetness and add more sugar, if necessary. Bring to a good boil. Continue boiling while dribbling (pour in slowly) Dumpling Mixture into the cherry mixture. Remove from heat. Serve warm or cold.

Favorite Recipes of Pommern Cooks (Wisconsin)

Blueberry Dumplings

SAUCE:

2 cups fresh blueberries
½ cup sugar

1 cup water
1 tablespoon lemon juice

Bring ingredients to a boil in large saucepan. Meanwhile, prepare Dumplings.

DUMPLINGS:

1 cup plain flour
2 teaspoons baking powder
Dash of salt

½ teaspoon sugar
½–¾ cup milk

Mix ingredients and drop by tablespoon into boiling Sauce. Cook 20–25 minutes over medium heat, until berries are tender. Serve warm with whipping cream. Yields 8–10 Dumplings.

Sandlapper Cooks (South Carolina)

Quick and Easy Apple Dumplings

2 medium-size Granny Smith
  apples
2 (10-count) cans Butter-Me-Not
  Biscuits

Cinnamon sugar
2 cups Sprite
2 cups sugar
2 sticks margarine

Peel and core apples and cut into 40 wedges. Pat out biscuits and wrap 2 pieces of apple in each one. Place in a greased, 9x13-inch baking pan and sprinkle with cinnamon sugar. Mix Sprite, sugar, and margarine in saucepan and bring to a boil. Pour over the dumplings and sprinkle lightly with additional cinnamon sugar. Bake at 400° for 12–15 minutes or until biscuits are a golden brown.

Munchin' with the Methodists (Mississippi)

Blackberry Dumplings

First get a stick to beat the snakes out of the bushes. Pick all the berries you can for the pot and eat just as many. My mother made Christmas wine with a lot of berries. The dumplings were our reward for picking the berries.

4 tablespoons butter	**3½ cups plain flour**
1 cup milk	**3 teaspoons baking powder**
2 eggs	**4 cups water**
3½ cups sugar, divided	**1½ quarts blackberries**
2 teaspoons vanilla	

Melt butter and allow to cool. Mix with milk, eggs, 1 cup sugar, and vanilla. Add dry ingredients. Do not overmix.

In a large saucepan, combine water, remaining 2½ cups sugar, and berries. Cook over medium heat until mixture thickens. Drop dough by the spoonful into the berry mixture. Cook until dough rises. Test with fork. When it comes out clean, remove dumplings and continue adding dumplings until all dough is used. Serve warm with blackberry mixture. Makes 3–4 dozen.

Cajun Cookin' Memories, Photos, History, Recipes (Louisiana II)

Blackberries are composed of many individual drupelets, each like a small berry with one seed, surrounding a firm core called the receptacle. These individual drupelets contribute extra skin, seeds, and pectin all adding to the dietary fiber value of the berry's nutritional content, making it among the highest fiber content plants known.

Bananas Foster

2 tablespoons brown sugar
1 tablespoon butter
1 ripe banana, peeled and sliced
  lengthwise

Dash of cinnamon
½ ounce banana liqueur
1 ounce white rum
1 large scoop vanilla ice cream

Melt brown sugar and butter in flat chafing dish. Add banana and sauté until tender. Sprinkle with cinnamon. Pour in banana liqueur and rum over all, and flame. Baste with warm liquid until flame burns out. Serve immediately over ice cream. Yields 1 serving.

Brennan's New Orleans Cookbook (Louisiana)

The Cornerstone Inc.'s Banana Éclair

HOT FUDGE SAUCE:

2 squares unsweetened
  baking chocolate
⅓ cup butter or margarine

4 tablespoons sugar
1 cup heavy cream
2 teaspoons vanilla extract

Melt chocolate and butter over low heat, stirring to blend. Add sugar and stir until completely dissolved. Add heavy cream, stirring to combine. Remove from heat. Add vanilla and stir until well mixed. Set aside.

ÉCLAIR:

1 (3-ounce) package vanilla
  cook and serve pudding

4 commercial croissants
2 bananas, sliced

Cook pudding according to package directions. Let cool. Make a pocket in croissants, and evenly divide sliced bananas among each pocket. Spoon in desired amount of vanilla pudding, and drizzle Hot Fudge Sauce over top. Serves 4.

South Carolina's Historic Restaurants (South Carolina)

Banana Split Chimichangas

8 ounces bittersweet chocolate, chopped into small pieces
6 tablespoons unsalted butter
1 cup heavy cream
4 (6-inch) flour tortillas
1 ripe banana, peeled and quartered lengthwise
½ cup chopped macadamia nuts
1 pint vanilla ice cream
1 egg, beaten
2–3 cups vegetable oil
Powdered sugar

Combine chocolate, butter, and cream in the top of a double boiler over simmering, not boiling, water. Stir occasionally until all ingredients are melted and well combined. Set aside and allow to cool.

Heat a skillet or griddle over medium-high heat. (Do not grease.) Place tortillas over heat to soften enough to become pliable. Remove from heat and arrange 1 piece of banana, about ¼ of the cooled chocolate mixture, 2 tablespoons nuts, and 2 tablespoons ice cream off center on each tortilla.

Brush inside edges of tortillas with beaten egg. Fold top edge of tortilla about a quarter of the way over filling. Repeat with bottom edge. Starting with the unfolded edge closest to the filling, roll into a shape like an egg roll. Freeze for several hours or overnight. Keep frozen until ready to serve.

Just before serving, heat oil in a skillet or deep-fryer to 400°. Fry tortilla rolls in hot oil until golden brown on all sides, about 3 minutes. Dust with powdered sugar and serve immediately. Serves 4.

Laurel's, Sheraton Park Central Hotel, Dallas
Dallas Cuisine (Texas II)

One variety of banana, the "Ice Cream Banana," is BLUE. It turns yellow like other bananas when ripe. It has a taste like vanilla custard, and the texture of a marshmallow.

Frozen Soufflé
with Hot Strawberry Sauce

½ gallon vanilla ice cream
12 almond macaroons, crumbled
5 tablespoons Grand Marnier
2 cups heavy cream

½ cup chopped toasted
   almonds
Powdered sugar

Soften ice cream slightly. Stir in crumbled macaroons and Grand Marnier. Whip cream until thick and shiny; fold into ice cream mixture. Spoon into an angel food cake pan. Sprinkle surface lightly with almonds and powdered sugar. Cover with plastic wrap. Freeze until firm, 4–5 hours or overnight. Unmold onto cold platter. Return to freezer until serving time.

HOT STRAWBERRY SAUCE:

1 quart fresh strawberries,
   cleaned and halved

Sugar (about ½ cup)
5 tablespoons Grand Marnier

Just before serving, put berries in a saucepan with sugar; simmer until soft, but not mushy. Remove from heat; stir in Grand Marnier. Serve frozen soufflé topped with sauce. Yields 12 servings.

Out of This World (Tennessee)

Berry Mousse

1½ cups fresh strawberries
1 (8-ounce) package cream
   cheese, cut in cubes
½ cup sifted powdered sugar

1 (4-ounce) container frozen
   whipped topping, thawed
Sliced almonds, toasted

In a blender, combine strawberries, cream cheese, and powdered sugar. Cover and blend until mixture is smooth. Pour into mixing bowl and fold in whipped topping. Spoon mousse mixture into 6 dessert dishes. Chill 3–4 hours, or overnight. To serve, sprinkle with toasted sliced almonds.

Carnegie Hall Cookbook (West Virginia)

White Chocolate Pear Bread Pudding

1 quart plus 1 cup heavy cream, divided
1 cup white chocolate chips
10 egg yolks
2 cups sugar
1 vanilla bean, scraped
1 pint plus 2 tablespoons whole milk, divided
8 large croissants, chopped
2 pears, peeled, cored, and finely chopped

In medium saucepan, heat 1 cup cream. Bring to a boil and pour over white chocolate chips in a bowl; whisk until smooth. In a large bowl, combine egg yolks, sugar, and vanilla bean. Add remaining cream and 1 pint milk to white chocolate mixture, whisking constantly to combine. Add remaining 2 tablespoons milk to egg mixture to thin out by whisking, then add all, and pour over chopped croissants. Mix in pears and bake in greased individual oven-proof bowls (or greased 2-quart casserole dish) at 350° for 25–35 minutes. Serves 8.

Recipe from Yia Yia's Eurocafé, Germantown
Fine Dining Tennessee Style (Tennessee)

Lemon Blueberry Bread Pudding

The tart lemon contrasts beautifully with the sweet blueberries.

6 cups torn French or Italian bread (1-inch chunks)
3 cups milk
4 eggs
¾ cup sugar, divided
Juice and grated rind of 2 lemons
1½ pints fresh blueberries
1 tablespoon butter, softened

In large bowl, soak bread in milk for 20 minutes. Preheat oven to 350°. Beat eggs with all but 2 tablespoons sugar. Beat in lemon juice and rind. Pour egg mixture over soaked bread and mix well. Add blueberries and mix. Pour into buttered shallow 3-quart baking dish. Sprinkle remaining sugar over top. Bake about 40 minutes, until top is lightly browned and crusty. Serve warm or cooled.

Lambertville Community Cookbook (Mid-Atlantic)

Avocado Pudding

This dessert is typically made in Brazilian homes, where avocados are considered a fruit. If you think of an avocado solely as a dip for tortilla chips, you will be pleasantly surprised.

2 very ripe avocados
Juice from ½ lemon
¼ cup sugar

½–¾ cup heavy cream (or yogurt)

In a glass bowl, mash avocados with lemon juice, slowly adding sugar. Blend in heavy cream; taste and adjust, if necessary. Refrigerate for 2–6 hours. Serve cold. Serves 4.

Note: Florida avocados (green with dark "splotches") are closer to those found in Brazil than the larger, lighter green California Haas variety.

La Cocina de la Familia (New York)

Banana Pudding

North Carolina natives think of banana pudding as a dessert served everywhere. It was not until I received a request for the recipe from New York City that I began to realize, it is distinctive to this section.

½ cup plus 6 tablespoons sugar, divided
Pinch of salt
3 tablespoons flour

4 eggs, divided
2 cups milk
Vanilla wafers
Bananas

Blend ½ cup sugar, salt, and flour. Add 1 whole egg and 3 yolks and mix together. Stir in milk. Cook over boiling water, stirring, until thickened. Remove from heat and cool.

In a baking dish, arrange a layer of whole vanilla wafers, a layer of sliced bananas, and a layer of custard. Continue, making 3 layers of each.

Make a meringue by beating remaining 3 egg whites till stiff, then gradually add remaining 6 tablespoons sugar. Spread over banana mixture and brown in 375° oven. Makes 8 servings. Serve cold, not chilled.

North Carolina and Old Salem Cookery (North Carolina)

Editors' Extra: For a creamier texture, make only two layers, using vanilla wafers and bananas more sparsely. Yum!

Blueberry Whiskey Sabayon

Sabayon is a mousse-like dessert sauce, the French name for the fluffy Italian zabaglione made with sweet Marsala wine. Sabayon has three primary ingredients; egg yolks, sugar, and alcohol.

½ cup fresh blueberries	2 tablespoons bourbon whiskey
4 tablespoons sugar, divided	½ cup heavy cream, whipped
2 egg yolks	

Cook blueberries with 2 tablespoons sugar in a stainless steel (non-corrosive) saucepan over low heat, stirring until sugar dissolves. Continue cooking until the berries are very soft and have released most of their juice, 5–8 minutes.

Place cooked blueberries and juice, egg yolks, remaining 2 tablespoons sugar, and whiskey in top of a double boiler. Place over gently boiling water; the upper pan should not touch the water. Cook, whisking often, until the custard has thickened and reaches 160° on an instant-read thermometer, about 10 minutes.

Prepare an ice bath: Fill a large bowl with ice and nest the bowl of cooked blueberry mixture in it. Whisk the mixture until it is cold. You can refrigerate this sabayon base, covered, for up to 6 days. Before serving, fold in the whipped cream. Makes about 1½ cups.

Note: For a sabayon to accompany chocolate nut torte, omit the blueberries and the first sugar and substitute dark rum for the whiskey. Or prepare sabayon with white wine or champagne, to use as a topping for fresh fruit.

Chocolate Snowball (Utah)

Over 200 million pounds of blueberries are grown commercially each year, making it the second most popular berry in the United States. In first place is the strawberry, with over 2 billion pounds produced annually.

Peaches with Sour Cream and Strawberries

8 ripe peaches
Brandy
Lemon juice
2 cups sour cream
1 pint strawberries, hulled, sliced
¼ cup superfine granulated sugar
2 tablespoons Grand Marnier, rum, or brandy
Macaroon crumbs

Skin peaches; halve and pit them. Sprinkle with brandy and lemon juice. Chill well. Fold sour cream into strawberries; add sugar (not too much), and Grand Marnier.

To serve, arrange peach halves in large bowl, or in individual champagne glasses. Spoon strawberry cream mixture over top and sprinkle with finely crushed macaroon crumbs. Serves 8.

The Colorado Cookbook (Colorado)

Aunt Pat's Peach Melba

4 fresh peaches, scalded in boiling water, skinned, quartered, and pitted
¼ cup sugar
2 cups water
½ teaspoon vanilla extract
Vanilla ice cream
Vanilla wafers

Combine all ingredients, except ice cream and vanilla wafers. Cook over medium heat until peaches are soft. Drain and chill. At serving time, place 1 scoop of vanilla ice cream in 4 champagne glasses. Place 4 quarters of peach around ice cream. Top with Raspberry Sauce, and serve with vanilla wafers.

RASPBERRY SAUCE:
1 cup fresh raspberries, unsweetened
⅓ cup orange juice
1½ tablespoons sugar
2 teaspoons cornstarch

Combine all ingredients in saucepan. Cook over medium heat, stirring constantly, until sauce is thickened and bubbling. Cook at least 1 minute extra. Strain sauce to remove seeds. Cover and chill. Makes 4 servings.

What's This Green Stuff, Flo? (Big Sky)

Grapes in Sour Cream

Green seedless grapes   **Dark brown sugar**
Sour cream

Prepare this the morning of serving. Pick over clusters of seedless grapes and pick each one off individually; discard any soft or bad ones. Cover them in enough whipped sour cream to really coat each grape, then sprinkle with dark brown sugar to taste. Refrigerate and keep stirring whenever you're at the refrigerator.

 Just before serving, spread grapes on baking sheet and sprinkle brown sugar (¼ cup) over the top of grapes. Place under the broiler very briefly, just enough to caramelize the sugar.

Hawaii Cooks Throughout the Year (Hawaii)

Pears de Noel

2 cups dry red wine   **1 tablespoon vanilla**
1 cup water   **6 large firm pears**
¾ cup sugar   **1½ cups chocolate syrup**
6 whole cloves   **1 tablespoon orange-flavored**
1 cinnamon stick, broken in half **liqueur**
1 tablespoon grated orange peel **Mint leaves for garnish**

Cook wine, water, sugar, cloves, cinnamon stick, orange peel, and vanilla over medium-high heat for 10 minutes in a large saucepan. While this is cooking, peel the pears, leaving stem on. Place pears in wine mixture, reduce heat to simmer, and poach pears for 10 minutes. Remove pan from heat and let pears cool to room temperature in syrup. Remove pears from syrup and chill in refrigerator at least an hour.

 Mix chocolate syrup with orange liqueur and spoon onto dessert plates. Place a pear on top of chocolate; garnish with mint leaves. Serves 6.

Christmas in Arizona Cook Book (Arizona)

Raspberry Pizza

CRUST:

1 cup all-purpose flour
1 stick butter or margarine,
  softened

½ cup powdered sugar

Blend ingredients and knead into dough. Spread on pizza pan and bake 10 minutes at 350°.

FILLING:

1 (8-ounce) package cream
  cheese, softened
1 (14-ounce) can sweetened
  condensed milk

1 teaspoon vanilla
⅓ cup lemon juice
1 pint fresh raspberries

Combine cream cheese, milk, vanilla, and lemon juice. Spread over cooled crust. Top with raspberries and cover with Raspberry Glaze.

RASPBERRY GLAZE:

1 cup fresh raspberries
1 cup sugar, divided

1 cup water
2½ tablespoons cornstarch

In a saucepan, combine raspberries, ¾ cup sugar, and water. Cook until berries are soft. Add mixture of remaining ¼ cup sugar and cornstarch. Cook until thick and glazed.

Contributed by New Mexico Congressman Joe Skeen
The Very Special Raspberry Cookbook (New Mexico)

Sweetheart Pizza

CRUST:

1 cup all-purpose flour
¼ cup powdered sugar

1 stick margarine, room
  temperature

Mix together and press into heart shape on a 12-inch pizza pan that has been sprayed with Pam (or oiled). Bake at 325° for 15–20 minutes. Cool completely.

CREAM CHEESE LAYER:

1 (8-ounce) package cream
  cheese, softened

½ cup sugar

Blend together and spread on cooled Crust.

STRAWBERRY GLAZE:

1 cup sugar
1 cup water
3 tablespoons cornstarch

3 tablespoons strawberry
  Jell-O (dry mix)
1 pint strawberries, sliced

Combine sugar, water, cornstarch and Jell-O in saucepan and cook, stirring constantly, until thick and clear. When cool, add sliced strawberries and pour on top of Cream Cheese Layer. Chill before serving.

Note: If using a 16-inch pizza pan, double recipe.

Family Celebrations Cookbook (Illinois)

Caramel Apple Pizza

1 package sugar cookie dough
1 cup peanut butter
1 large Granny Smith apple

1 bottle caramel syrup
¼ cup chopped peanuts

Let cookie dough come to room temperature; spread evenly onto pizza pan. Bake at 350° for 15 minutes or until lightly browned. Cool. Spread with a thin layer of peanut butter. Layer with thinly sliced apple and drizzle with caramel syrup. Sprinkle with chopped nuts.

Feeding the Flock—MOPs of Westminister (West Virginia)

Pan-Fried June Apples

After long winters, my family yearned for fresh fruit. Mother fried the fresh June apples and served them with hot biscuits, freshly churned butter, and milk. Yum!

2 tablespoons bacon drippings
4 cups sliced apples,
  peeled (or unpeeled)

1½ cups sugar
½ teaspoon cinnamon
½ teaspoon salt

Heat bacon drippings in skillet and add apples. Stir in sugar, cinnamon, and salt, then cover and cook for about 5 minutes, or until the sugar liquefies. Remove lid and fry, stirring occasionally, until apples are tender, and the liquid is cooked away. Serves 4–6.

More than Moonshine: Appalachian Recipes and Recollections
(Kentucky)

Peach Buttermilk Ice Cream

1 tablespoon unflavored gelatin
  (1 envelope)
1¼ cups sugar, divided
2 cups buttermilk
1 egg, beaten

¼ teaspoon salt
4 cups whipping cream
1 tablespoon vanilla extract
2 cups fresh peaches, mashed

In saucepan, combine gelatin, 1 cup sugar, and buttermilk. Dissolve gelatin mixture over low heat, stirring occasionally. Gradually add hot mixture to egg, stirring constantly. Stir in salt, cream, and vanilla. Combine mashed peaches and remaining ¼ cup sugar; add to mixture. Chill and churn-freeze. Yields approximately 3 quarts.

Note: Regular milk may be substituted for buttermilk.

Giant Houseparty Cookbook (Mississippi)

Watermelon Popsicles

½ Missouri watermelon
2 teaspoons fresh lemon
  juice

½ cup sugar
½ cup distilled water

Cut watermelon into cubes and rub through a strainer to remove seeds, making 3 cups watermelon juice.

In small saucepan mix together sugar and water; simmer 3 minutes. Remove from heat; stir in watermelon juice and lemon juice. Turn into 2 ice trays. Freeze until very mushy, then insert a popsicle stick in each cube. Freeze. Makes about 36 small popsicles.

The Never Ending Season (Missouri)

Maine Blueberry Gingerbread

½ cup shortening
1 cup plus 3 tablespoons sugar,
  divided
1 egg
2 cups sifted all-purpose flour
½ teaspoon ginger

1 teaspoon cinnamon
½ teaspoon salt
1 cup sour milk or buttermilk
1 teaspoon baking soda
3 tablespoons molasses
1 cup fresh blueberries

Cream shortening and 1 cup sugar. Add egg, and mix well. Mix and sift together flour, ginger, cinnamon, and salt. Add to creamed mixture alternately with sour milk, in which soda has been dissolved. Add molasses. Carefully fold in blueberries, and pour batter into a greased and floured 9x9-inch pan. Sprinkle remaining 3 tablespoons sugar over batter. Bake in preheated 350° oven for 50 minutes to 1 hour. (Sugar makes sweet, crusty topping when cake is baked.) Makes 9–12 servings.

Merrymeeting Merry Eating (New England)

★★★★★★★★★★★ ★★★★★★★★★★★

Koktuli Fruit Galette

While the Koktuli doesn't have any fruit trees, anglers do delight in the river's rainbow trout fishery. The light nature of this dessert suggests the best way to float this river: pack a minimal amount of gear, a lightweight flyrod and plenty of gossamer tippets for these tail-dancing rainbows.

1 (9-inch) round of puff pastry, well-chilled
2 tablespoons all-purpose flour
½ cup sugar, divided
4 firm, ripe unpeeled nectarines, halved, pitted, and thinly sliced

1 egg yolk
1 tablespoon heavy cream
1 tablespoon cold unsalted butter, cut into small pieces

Preheat oven to 400°. Place the circle of puff pastry (available in frozen food section of grocery store) on a parchment-lined baking sheet. With the tines of a fork, prick the pastry surface except for a ½-inch rim. Sprinkle only the punctured area of the circle with flour and ¼ cup sugar.

Starting just inside the unpunched edge, arrange the nectarine slices, with cut edges toward the center, in concentric circles covering the pastry entirely.

Beat egg yolk with heavy cream to make a glaze. Brush egg yolk glaze on just the exposed rim of puff pastry, sprinkle the remaining ¼ cup sugar on top of the fruit and dot with butter. Bake for 18–20 minutes at 400° until the fruit is tender and the pastry has puffed and turned golden brown. Serve immediately. Serves 6.

Recipe from Iliamna Lake Resort
Best Recipes of Alaska's Fishing Lodges (Alaska)

A nectarine is a fuzzless variety of peach. It is NOT a cross between a peach and a plum.

Indiana Raspberry Tart

A unique recipe combining cooked and uncooked berries with exceptional results.

PASTRY:

1 cup all-purpose flour	**½ cup (1 stick) butter or**
2 tablespoons sugar	**margarine, cold**
⅛ teaspoon salt	**2–3 tablespoons cold water**

Preheat oven to 400°.

   In medium bowl, combine flour, sugar, and salt. Cut in butter until crumbly. Sprinkle water, 1 tablespoon at a time, until pastry mixture is just moist and holds together. Press pastry into the bottom and 1-inch up the side of a 9-inch springform pan. Set aside.

FILLING:

¼ teaspoon ground	**6 cups fresh raspberries,**
cinnamon	**divided**
⅔ cup sugar	**Whipping cream**
¼ cup all-purpose flour	

Combine cinnamon, sugar, and flour in small bowl. Sprinkle half the flour mixture over the bottom of pastry. Top with 4 cups raspberries. Sprinkle remaining flour mixture over raspberries.

   Bake tart on lowest oven rack, 50–60 minutes, or until golden and bubbly. Remove from oven; cool on wire rack. After tart has completely cooled, carefully remove side of springform pan. Top with remaining 2 cups raspberries. Cut into wedges.

   To serve, pour 2 tablespoons cream on individual plate; arrange a tart wedge on cream. Serves 10.

Back Home Again (Indiana)

Spumoni
(Luxurious Ice Cream Whip)

1 quart strawberries or
  raspberries
Juice of 1 lemon
3 tablespoons sugar

1 cup chopped walnuts
1 cup chopped pistachio nuts
½ cup powdered sugar
3 cups whipped cream

Mash berries with lemon juice and sugar. Let them marinate ½ hour. Add nuts and powdered sugar, and stir vigorously. Fold into whipped cream. Pour into loaf pans or round ice cream mold, and freeze. Cut into inch slices to serve.

Herrin's Favorite Italian Recipes Cookbook (Illinois)

Storing Fruits and Vegetables

How you store produce can greatly impact their taste and texture. Most should remain unwashed until ready to use to avoid premature spoilage.

STORE IN REFRIGERATOR:
Apples* (under 7 days)
Apricots*
Artichokes
Asparagus
Beets
Blackberries
Blueberries
Broccoli
Brussels sprouts
Cabbage
Carrots
Cauliflower
Celery
Cherries
Corn
Figs*
Grapes
Green beans
Green onions
Herbs (except basil)
Lima beans
Leafy vegetables
Leeks
Lettuce
Mushrooms
Okra
Peas
Plums
Radishes
Raspberries
Spinach
Sprouts
Strawberries
Summer squash
Yellow squash
Zucchini

STORE ON COUNTERTOP:
Apples* (over 7 days)
Bananas*
Basil
Cucumbers
Eggplant
Garlic
Ginger
Grapefruit
Jicama
Lemons
Limes
Mangoes
Oranges
Papayas
Peppers
Persimmons
Pineapple
Tomatoes*
Watermelon

STORE IN COOL, DRY PLACE:
Acorn squash
Butternut squash
Onions (away from potatoes)
Potatoes (away from onions)
Pumpkins
Spaghetti squash
Sweet potatoes
Winter squash

**RIPEN ON COUNTERTOP,
THEN REFRIGERATE**
Avocados*
Nectarines*
Melons* (Cantaloupe, Honeydew)
Peaches*
Pears*
Plums*

*Keep away from other produce

Selecting Fruits and Vegetables

When possible, it is best to shop for fresh produce often and buy only what you will use within a few days. This will cut down on the amount wasted because of spoilage.

All fruits and vegetables should be thoroughly rinsed (avoid detergents) just before eating, cutting, or cooking. Dry with a clean paper towel. (*See previous page for storing tips.*) Even if you plan to peel the produce before eating, it is still important to wash it first.

Apples: Good color usually indicates full flavor.

Asparagus: Stalks should be tender and firm; tips closed and compact.

Bananas: Should be firm, fresh in appearance and unscarred.

Beans: Select pods that are well-filled but not bulging. Avoid dried, spotted, yellowed, or flabby pods.

Beets, Carrots, Parsnips, Radishes, Rutabagas, Turnips: Choose smooth, firm vegetables. Oversized ones may have a woody stem or pithy texture.

Berries: Select plump, solid berries with good color. They will not ripen after you buy them.

Broccoli, Brussels Sprouts, Cabbage, Cauliflower: Heads should be firm, have a good bright color, and be free of yellow spots and softness.

Cantaloupes: You can spot an unripe melon by its green tones. Instead, look for a cream-colored skin (with no green patches) that has a slightly soft end (the end opposite the stem).

Cherries: The stems should be attached. Cherries should be firm and plump.

Corn: Good quality has fresh, green husks. The silk should be stiff, dark and moist. Ears are well-filled with plump, firm, milky kernels.

Cucumbers, Okra, Peppers: Look for bright, even color, plump and firm. Avoid ones with blemishes, wrinkles, and soft spots.

Eggplant: Smaller, immature eggplants are best. Choose a firm, smooth-skinned eggplant that is heavy for its size; avoid those with soft or brown spots.

Grapes: Should be plump and firmly attached to stems.

Green Onions: Choose onions with small bulb ends and firm green tops.

Lettuce: Look for springy, healthy-looking leaves and no sign of bugs.

Mushrooms: Choose ones with firm, white, smooth skins. Avoid overripe mushrooms (shown by wide-open caps and dark, discolored gills underneath) and those with pitted or seriously discolored caps.

Onions: Size and color do not affect flavor or quality. Clean, hard, well-shaped onions with dry skins are usually of good quality. They should have absolutely no smell. If they do, they are probably bruised somewhere under the skin.

Oranges, Grapefruit, Lemons: Choose ones heavy for their size. Smooth, thick skins usually indicate more juice. Greenish tinge does not affect quality.

Peaches, Nectarines: Best quality are slightly firm, not bruised, with yellow or red color over entire surface.

Pears: Winter varieties are marketed slightly underripe. When ripe and ready to eat, they yield slightly to pressure.

Peas: Select pods that are well-filled but not bulging. Avoid dried, spotted, yellowed or flabby pods.

Pineapples: Ripe pineapples have a fragrant, fruity aroma. Leaves should still be intact. Usually the heavier the fruit, the better the quality.

Plums: Look for smooth-skinned fruit that is not too soft.

Potatoes: Best quality are firm, smooth, well-shaped, free from cuts, blemishes, and decay, and reasonably clean. Potatoes with green skins may be bitter; cut away before using.

Strawberries: Look for a deep red color with a shiny skin. Avoid buying any with green or yellow patches, as they're unripe (and won't ripen any further). Very large strawberries often have inferior flavor to smaller berries.

Tomatoes: Choose tomatoes that are plump, firm, and uniform in color. Fragrance is a good indicator of a good tomato. Smell the stem end. It should retain the garden aroma of the plant itself.

Watermelons: Have somewhat dull surface and creamy color underneath when ripe. Be sure it has a well-defined yellow area on one side. This is the spot where the watermelon has been resting while ripening, and if it's not there it means it may have been harvested too soon.

Winter Squash, Sweet Potatoes: Choose vegetables that are clean, smooth, well-shaped, and firm. Damp or soft spots may indicate decay.

Zucchini, Summer Squash: Stem should not be shriveled or discolored. Select squash with bright, glossy skin. Smaller squashes are younger and more tender than larger ones.

Seasonal Produce

Shopping for produce when in season will provide the best quality at the best prices. While most produce is now available year-round, the seasonal items on this list will have a better chance of being locally grown. *Please note: seasons may vary according to region.*

SPRING:
(March, April, May)
Apricots
Asparagus
Cherries
Grapefruit
Lemons
Lettuce
Mustard Greens
Onions
Oranges
Peas
Pineapples
Radishes
Rhubarb
Strawberries
Turnips

SUMMER:
(June, July, August)
Apricots
Beans
Berries:
   Blackberries
   Blueberries
   Raspberries
   Strawberries
Cantaloupes
Cauliflower
Cherries
Corn
Cucumbers
Eggplants
Figs
Grapes
Huckleberries
Limes

Mangos
Melons
Okra
Onions
Peaches, Nectarines
Peas
Peppers
Plums
Potatoes
Rhubarb
Summer Squash
Tomatoes
Watermelons
Zucchini

FALL:
(September, October, November)
Apples
Beans
Broccoli
Brussel Sprouts
Cabbage
Carrots
Cauliflower
Celery
Collard Greens
Corn
Cranberries
Cucumbers
Eggplants
Figs
Grapes
Huckleberries
Lettuce
Limes
Melons

Okra
Onions
Pears
Peas
Peppers
Potatoes
Pumpkins
Rutabagas
Sweet Potatoes
Turnips
Winter Squash

WINTER:
(December, January, February)
Broccoli
Brussel Sprouts
Cabbage
Cauliflower
Celery
Grapefruit
Lemons
Oranges
Radishes
Rutabagas
Sweet Potatoes
Tangerines
Turnips
Winter Squash

YEAR-ROUND:
Avocados
Bananas
Beets
Carrots
Mushrooms
Spinach

List of Contributors

JOE SOLEM / HAWAII VISITORS AND CONVENTION BUREAU

James Dole paid $1.1 million or $12 an acre for the island of Lana'i in 1922, and planted 16,000 acres of pineapples there. Today more than one-third of the world's commercial supply of pineapples comes from Hawaii.

★★★★★★★★★★★ ★★★★★★★★★★★

Listed below are the cookbooks that have contributed recipes to the *Recipe Hall of Fame Farmers Market Cookbook*, along with copyright, author, publisher, city, and state. The information in parentheses indicates the BEST OF THE BEST cookbook in which the recipe originally appeared.

Alabama Blueberry Festival Recipes, Greater Brewton Area Chamber of Commerce, Brewton, AL (Alabama)

Alabama's Historic Restaurants and Their Recipes ©1998 by Gay N. Martin, 2nd edition, John F. Blair, Publisher, Winston-Salem, NC (Alabama)

Alaska's Gourmet Breakfasts, by Leicha Welton, Fairbanks, AK (Alaska)

All-Alaska Women in Timber Cookbook, Alaska Women in Timber, Ketchikan, AK (Alaska)

Allons Manger, St. Jules Catholic Church, Belle Rose, LA (Louisiana)

America Celebrates Columbus ©1999 The Junior League of Columbus, OH (Ohio)

An Amish Kitchen ©1998 Harold Press, by A Committee of Amish Women, Scottdale, PA (Pennsylvania)

An Apple a Day ©1996 Rea Douglas, San Diego, CA (California)

Another Sunrise in Kentucky, by Tracy and Phyllis Winters, Winters Publishing, Greensburg, IN (Kentucky)

The Apple Barn Cookbook ©1983 The Apple Barn and Cider Mill, Sevierville, TN (Tennessee)

Apples, Apples, Apples ©1991 by Ann Clark, Marionville, MO (Missouri)

Apples, Brie & Chocolate ©1996 Nell Stehr, Amherst Press, Amherst, WI (Wisconsin)

Aren't You Going to Taste It, Honey? ©1995 The Toledo Blade Company, Toledo, OH (Ohio)

Arizona Chefs: Dine-In Dine-Out Cookbook ©1997 Arizona Chefs, by Elin Jeffords, Phoenix, AZ (Arizona)

Arizona State Fair Blue Ribbon Recipes ©1996 Coliseum and Exposition Center Board, Golden West Publishers, Phoenix, AZ (Arizona)

Armstrong Centennial Cookbook, Armstrong Heritage Museum, Armstrong, IA (Iowa)

Asthma Walk Cook Book, American Lung Association of Ohio, Norwalk, OH (Ohio)

Atlanta Cooknotes ©1982 The Junior League of Atlanta, GA (Georgia)

Aunt Freddie's Pantry ©1984 by Freddie Bailey, Natchez, MS (Mississippi)

Back Home Again ©1993 The Junior League of Indianapolis, IN (Indiana)

Baked with Love, Blue Owl Restaurant & Bakery, Kimmswick, MO (Missouri)

Basque Cooking and Love ©1991 by Darcy Williamson, Caxton Press, Caldwell, ID (Idaho)

Be Our Guest ©2000 The Juneau Convention and Visitors Bureau, Juneau, AK (Alaska)

Becky's Brunch & Breakfast Book ©1983 by Rebecca Walker, Austin, TX (Texas)

Begged, Borrowed and Stöllen Recipes, by Jean Ritter Smith, Eugene, OR (Oregon)

Best Bets ©1993 Nathan Adelson Hospice, Las Vegas, NV (Nevada)

The Best from New Mexico Kitchens ©1978 by New Mexico Magazine, Sheila MacNivan Cameron, Sante Fe, NM (New Mexico)

Best Kept Secrets, Homeland Park Fire Department, Anderson, SC (South Carolina)

The Best of Down-Home Cooking ©2003 Holy Trinity AME Church, The Holy Trinity AME Church Courtesy Club, North Las Vegas, NV (Nevada)

The Best of the Sweet Potato Recipes ©1992 E.B. Danbar, Penndel, PA (Pennsylvania)

The Best of the Zucchini Recipes ©1992 E.B. Danbar, Penndel, PA (Pennsylvania)

The Best of Wheeling ©1994 The Junior League of Wheeling, WV (West Virginia)

Blackened Mountain Seasonings, by Kemper Bornman, Linda Warren, and Suzanne Goodell, Black Mountain, NC (North Carolina)

Blessed Be the Cook, St. Anne's Altar Society, Camp Douglas, WI (Wisconsin)

The Bloomin' Cookbook, DuBoistown Garden Club, South Williamsport, PA (Pennsylvania)

The Blue Willow Inn Bible of Southern Cooking ©2005 by Billie and Louis Van Dyke, Social Circle, GA (Georgia)

The Blueberry Lover's Cookbook, by Muriel C. Pelham, Village Mills, TX (Texas)

Bountiful Blessings from the Bauknight Table, by H. Felder & Margaret D. Bauknight Family, Central, SC (South Carolina)

The Bounty of Chester County Heritage Edition ©2001 Chester County Agricultural Development Council, West Chester, PA (Pennsylvania)

Bouquet Garni ©1983 Pascagoula-Moss Point Mississippi Junior Auxiliary, Pascagoula, MS (Mississippi)

Bravo, Chef! ©1983 The Dallas Opera Guild, Dallas, TX (Texas)

Breads and Spreads ©1992 Carol Rees Publications, Edward C. Rees, Waycross, GA (Georgia)

Brennan's New Orleans Cookbook ©1961 Brennan's Restaurant and Hermann B. Deutsch, Pelican Publishing Company, Gretna, LA (Louisiana)

By Request ©1998 Betsy Mann / Photos ©1998 Northland Publishing, Flagstaff, AZ (Arizona)

Cajun Cookin' Memories, Photos, History, Recipes, Franklin Golden Age Club, Franklin, LA (Louisiana)

Calling All Cooks, Two ©1998 Telephone Pioneers of America, Alabama Chapter #34,Telephone Pioneers of America, Alabama Chapter #34, Birmingham, AL (Alabama)

Cape May Fare, Mid-Atlantic Center for the Arts, Cape May, NJ (Mid-Atlantic)

Caring and Sharing, Center for Care and Counseling, North Augusta, SC (South Carolina)

Caring is Sharing, Nurses of Highland Park Hospital, Highland Park, IL (Illinois)

Carnegie Hall Cookbook ©1997, 2001 Carnegie Hall, West Virginia, Lewisburg, WV (West Virginia)

Catering to Shrimp, by Carol Cate, Winchester, OR (Oregon)

Celebrations ©1999 Telephone Pioneers of America, Alabama Chapter #34, Birmingham, AL (Alabama)

Celebrations on the Bayou ©1989 The Junior League of Monroe, LA (Louisiana)

Centennial Cookbook, Spring Glen United Methodist Church, Jacksonville, FL (Florida)

A Century of Recipes, Hospice Visions, Inc., Twin Falls, ID (Idaho)

A Century of Recipes Through the Windows of Time, East Congregational United Church of Christ, Grand Rapids, MI (Michigan)

Champagne...Uncorked! The Insider's Guide to Champagne ©1996 RMZ Publications, by Rosemary Zarly, New York, NY (New York)

Chickadee Cottage Cookbook, by Donna Hawkins, Mahtomedi, MN (Minnesota)

Chicken Expressions ©1992 Dome Publishing Co, Inc., by Normand Leclair, N. Kingston, RI (New England)

Chocolate Snowball ©1999 Letty Holloran Flatt, Globe Pequott Press, Guilford, CT (Utah)

Christmas in Arizona Cook Book, by Lynn Nusom, Golden West Publishers, Phoenix, AZ (Arizona)

Collectibles III, by Mary Pittman, Van Alstyne, TX (Texas)

Colorado Collage ©1995 The Junior League of Denver, CO (Colorado)

The Colorado Cookbook ©1981 University of Colorado Norlin Library, Friends of the Libraries/University of Colorado at Boulder, Boulder, CO (Colorado)

Cook Book: Favorite Recipes from Our Best Cooks, Central Illinois Tourism Council, Springfield, IL (Illinois)

The Cookbook AAUW, American Association of University Women, Jamestown, NY (New York)

The Cookbook II ©1985 Worcester Art Museum, Worcester, MA (New England)

The Cookin' Cajun Cooking School Cookbook ©1997 by Lisette Verlander and Susan Murphy, Gibbs Smith, Publisher, New Orleans, LA (Louisiana)

Contributors

Cookin' & Quiltin', by The Jolly Dozen Quilters, Linden, TN (Tennessee)

Cookin' at Its Best, New Meadows Senior Citizens Center, New Meadows, ID (Idaho)

Cookin' in Paradise, Paradise Valley Volunteer Fire Department Auxiliary, Bonners Ferry, ID (Idaho)

Cookin' in the Spa, Hot Springs Junior Auxiliary, Hot Springs, AR (Arkansas)

The Cooking Book ©1978 The Junior League of Louisville, KY (Kentucky)

Cooking Carley Style, McMaster Family Fund, Aiken, SC (South Carolina)

Cooking in Clover, Jewish Hospital Auxiliary, St. Louis, MO (Missouri)

Cooking in Clover II, Jewish Hospital Auxiliary-Parkview Chapter, St. Louis, MO (Missouri)

Cooking Wild Game & Fish Southern Style ©2000 by Billy Joe Cross, Brandon, MS (Mississippi)

Cooking with 257, Boy Scout Troop 257, North Port, FL (Florida)

Cooking with Classmates, Teachers, Family & Friends, Garr Christian Academy and Preschool, Charlotte, NC (North Carolina)

Cooking with Cops, Too, Pocatello Police Department, Pocatello, ID (Idaho)

Cooking with My Friends ©2003 by LaVece Ganter Hughes, Wind Publications, Nicholasville, KY (Kentucky)

Cooking with Watkinsville First Christian Church, Christian Woman's Fellowship at Watkinsville First Christian Church, Watkinsville, GA (Georgia)

Cooks Extraordinaires ©1993 Service League of Green Bay, WI (Wisconsin)

A Cook's Tour of Iowa ©1988 University of Iowa Press, Chicago, IL (Iowa)

CordonBluegrass ©1988 The Junior League of Louisville, KY (Kentucky)

Costco Wholesale Employee Association Cookbook, Costco Employee Association, Kennewick, WA (Washington)

Country Chic's Home Cookin, by Christine C. Milligan, Preston, MD (Mid-Atlantic)

Country Lady Nibbling and Scribbling ©1994 by Alice Howard, Country Lace Productions, Elgin, IA (Iowa)

Cracker Barrel Old Country Stores: Old Timey Recipes & Proverbs to Live By ©1983 by Phila Hach, Clarksville, TN (Tennessee)

The Crooked Lake Volunteer Fire Department Cookbook, Ladies Auxiliary, Crivitz, WI (Wisconsin)

The Crowning Recipes of Kentucky ©1986 by Madonna Smith Echols, Marathon International Book Company, Madison, IN (Kentucky)

Culinary Memories of Merridun, Volume 2 ©2003 by Peggy Waller, JD and White Dog Publications, Union, SC (South Carolina)

Culinary Secrets of Great Virginia Chefs ©1995 by Martha Hollis Robinson, Thomas Nelson Publishers, Nashville, TN (Virginia)

Dallas Cowboy's Wives' Family Cookbook ©1993 Happy Hill Farm Academy/Home, Granbury, TX (Texas)

Dallas Cuisine ©1993 Two Lane Press, Dallas, TX (Texas)

Delectable Dishes from Termite Hall ©1982 by Eugene Walter, The Willoughby Institute, Inc., Mobile, AL (Alabama)

The Dexter Cider Mill Apple Cookbook ©1995 Katherine Merkel Koziski, Chelsea, MI (Michigan)

Dining by Fireflies ©1994 Junior League of Charlotte, NC (North Carolina)

Dining with Pioneers Volume II ©1992 Telephone Pioneers of America, Tennessee Chapter No. 21, BellSouth Pioneers, Nashville, TN (Tennessee)

The Dinner Bell Rings Again!, Lancaster County Society of Farm Women #22, Millersville, PA (Pennsylvania)

Dinner on the Ground ©1990 Stoke Gabriel Enterprises, Alexandria, IA (Louisiana)

Dishing It Out ©2000 New Paltz Ballet Theatre, Inc., New Paltz, NY (New York)

Duck Soup & Other Fowl Recipes ©1994 by Lyndia Vold, Valleyford, WA (Washington)

264

Dungeness Crabs and Blackberry Cobblers ©1991 by Janie Hibler (Oregon)

Durham's Favorite Recipes, Durham Woman's Club, Durham, CA (California)

Dutch Oven Delites ©1995 by Val and Marie Cowley, Logan, UT (Utah)

Dutch Pantry Cookin' Volume II, Dutch Pantry Family Restaurant, Williamstown, WV (West Virginia)

Easy Recipes for 1, 2 or a Few ©1994 by Anna Aughenbaugh, Fort Collins, CO (Colorado)

Eat to Your Heart's Content!, by Woody and Betty Armour, Hot Springs, AR (Arkansas)

Eat to Your Heart's Content, Too!, by Woody and Betty Armour, Hot Springs, AR (Arkansas)

Educated Taste, LaGrange College Alumni Association, LaGrange, GA (Georgia)

Elsah Landing Heartland Cooking ©1984 The Elsah Landing Restaurant, Inc., Helen Crafton and Dorothy Lindgren, Grafton, IL (Illinois)

Encore ©1981 Walker School Association, Dot Gibson Publications, Waycross, GA (Georgia)

Enjoy, by Martha Harrison, Toledo, IA (Iowa)

Even More Special ©1986 The Junior League of Durham and Orange Counties, Inc., Durham, NC (North Carolina)

Family and Food–Recipes and Reminiscences ©1999 Mosabele Publications, by Mollie M. Ward, Sara M. Riley, Betty M. Sanderson, and Lela M. Harrell, Harrells, NC (North Carolina)

Family Celebrations Cookbook, Saline County Homemakers Extension Assn., Harrisburg, IL (Illinois)

Family Fare, by Arleth Erickson, Grantsburg, WI (Wisconsin)

The Farmer's Daughters ©1987 S-M-L, Inc., by Flora R. Sisemore, Martha R. Merritt, and Mary R. Mayfield, Dewitt, AR (Arkansas)

Favorite New England Recipes ©1993 by Sara B.B. Stamm, Country Roads Press, Castine, ME (New England)

Favorite Recipes for Islanders, Hilo Extension Homemakers Council, Inc., Hilo, HI (Hawaii)

Favorite Recipes from Alaska's Bed and Breakfasts, Fairbanks Association of B & Bs, Fairbanks, AK (Alaska)

Favorite Recipes of Pommern Cooks ©1992 Favorite Recipes of Pommern Cooks, Pommerscher Verein Freistadt, Germantown, WI (Wisconsin)

Feeding the Flock (First Baptist Church, Boiling Spring Lake), First Baptist Church, Southport, NC (North Carolina)

Feeding the Flock (Shiloh Baptist Church), Shiloh Baptist Church, Ramseur, NC (North Carolina)

Feeding the Flock—MOP's of Westminister, MOPS of Westminister, Bluefield, WV (West Virginia)

Feeding the Herd, Jackson Hole CowBelles, Jackson, WY (Big Sky)

The Festival Cookbook ©1987 Good Books, by Phyllis Pellman Good, Intercourse, PA (Pennsylvania)

Field O' Dreams Farm Cookbook II ©1996 LaVa Publications, by Ann Varnum and Martha Lavallet, Webb, AL (Alabama)

Fiftieth Anniversary Cookbook, Northeast Louisiana Telephone Co, Inc., Collinston, LA (Louisiana)

Fine Dining Mississippi Style ©1999 by John M. Bailey, Quail Ridge Press, Brandon, MS (Mississippi)

Fine Dining Tennessee Style ©2000 by John M. Bailey, Quail Ridge Press, Brandon, MS (Tennessee)

First Family Favorites, First Baptist Church of Woodbridge Women's Ministry, Woodbridge, VA (Virginia)

First Ladies' Cookbook ©1996 by Betty L. Babcock, Shodair Children's Hospital, Helena, MT (Big Sky)

Five Star Sensations ©1991 Auxiliary of University Hospitals of Cleveland, OH (Ohio)

Flatlanders Cook Book, by Helen Lanier Strickland, Lakeland, GA (Georgia)

Flavors of the Gardens ©2000 Callaway Gardens Resort, Inc., Pine Mountain, GA (Georgia)

Food, Glorious Food, First Unitarian Universalist Church of Columbus, OH (Ohio)

For Crying Out Loud…Let's Eat! ©1988 The Service League of Hammond, IN (Indiana)

Fresh Market Wisconsin ©1993 Terese Allen, Amherst Press, Amherst, WI (Wisconsin)

Friends and Celebrities Cookbook II, Castle Performing Arts Center, Kaneohe, HI (Hawaii)

From Amish and Mennonite Kitchens ©1984 Good Books, Good Books, Intercourse, PA (Pennsylvania)

From the High Country of Wyoming, Flying A Guest Ranch, Pinedale, WY (Big Sky)

The Fruit Loop Cookbook ©2001 Hood River County Fruit Loop, Hood River, OR (Oregon)

Fruits of the Desert Cookbook ©1981 The Arizona Daily Star, by Sandal English at The Arizona Daily Star, Tucson, AZ (Arizona)

The Garden Patch, by Kay Hauser, St. John's, AZ (Arizona)

A Gathering of Recipes, Western Folklife Center, Elko, NV (Nevada)

Generations ©1994 Junior League of Rockford, IL (Illinois)

Georgia on my Menu ©1988 League Publications/Junior League of Cobb-Marietta, GA (Georgia)

Giant Houseparty Cookbook ©1981 Chamber of Commerce, Chamber of Commerce, Philadelphia, MS (Mississippi)

Golden Moments ©1996 by Arlene Giesel Koehn, Golden Moments Publishing, West Point, MS (Mississippi)

Gold'n Delicious ©1995 The Junior League of Spokane, WA (Washington)

Grandmother's Cookbook ©1990 by Elizabeth Rose von Hohen and Carrie J. Gamble, Doylestown, PA (Pennsylvania)

Gran's Gems, by Jane Rayburn Hardin, Birmingham, AL (Mississippi)

Great Flavors of Texas ©1992 Southern Flavors, Pine Bluff, AR (Texas)

A Great Taste of Arkansas ©1986 Southern Flavors, Inc., Pine Bluff, AR (Arkansas)

Guess Who's Coming to Dinner ©1986 by Mary Beth Busbee and Jan Busbee Curtis, Atlanta, GA (Georgia)

The Ham Book ©1977 by Robert W. Harrell and Monette R. Harrell, Harrell Hams, Suffolk, VA (Virginia)

Hawaii Cooks Throughout the Year ©1990 by Maili Yardley, Honolulu, HI (Hawaii)

Heart of the Mountains ©1987 Buncombe County Extension Homemakers, Asheville, NC (North Carolina)

Heavenly Delights, United Methodist Women, Page, AZ (Arizona)

Heavenly Hostess, St. John's Episcopal Church Women, Monroeville, AL (Alabama)

Herbs in a Minnesota Kitchen, by Jan Benskin and Bonnie Dehn, Ramsey, MN (Minnesota)

Here's to Your Heart: Cooking Smart, The Heart Care Center, Waukesha, WI (Wisconsin)

Herrin's Favorite Italian Recipes Cookbook, Herrin Hospital Auxiliary, Herrin, IL (Illinois)

HERSHEY'S Fabulous Desserts ©1989 Hershey Food Corporation, Ronks, PA (Pennsylvania)

High Cotton Cookin' ©1978 Marvell Academy Mothers' Association, Marvell, AR (Arkansas)

Historic Kentucky Recipes, Mercer County Humane Society, Harrodsburg, KY (Kentucky)

The Historic Roswell Cook Book ©1982 The Roswell Historical Society, Inc., Roswell, GA (Georgia)

Historic Spanish Point: Cooking Then and Now, Gulf Coast Heritage Association, Inc., Osprey, FL (Florida)

Historically Delicious ©1994 Tri-Cities Historical Society, Grand Haven, MI (Michigan)

Holiday Treats, by Theone L. Neel, Bastian, VA (Virginia)

Home Cookin', by Kathy Beckner, Missouri Apple Growers, Wellington, MO (Missouri)

★★★★★★★★★★★ ★★★★★★★★★★★

Home Cookin' Is a Family Affair, by Emily Swisher, Sayre, OK (Oklahoma)

Home Cooking with the Cummer Family, Dubuque, IA (Iowa)

Hooked on Fish on the Grill, Pig Out Publications, Inc., Kansas City, MO (Missouri)

Hopi Cookery ©1980 The Arizona Board of Regents, by Juanita Tiger Kavena at University of Arizona Press, Tucson, AZ (Arizona)

Hospitality Heirlooms ©1983 South Jackson Civic League, Jackson, MS (Mississippi)

How to Enjoy Zucchini ©1983 Josie's Kitchen, by Josie Carlsen, Carlsen Printing, Ogden, UT (Utah)

How to Make A Steamship Float ©1985 American Steamship Company, Harbor House Publishers, Boyne City, MI (Michigan)

Huckleberries and Crabmeat, by Carol Cate, Winchester, OR (Oregon)

Hudson Valley German-American Society Cookbook ©1995, 1998 Waldy Malouf, Hudson Valley German-American Society, Kingston, NY (New York)

Hullabaloo in the Kitchen ©1983 Dallas A&M University Mother's Club, Dallas, TX (Texas)

In Good Taste ©1983 Department of Nutrition, School of Public Health of the University of North Carolina, Chapel Hill, NC (North Carolina)

Incredible Edibles, Lake Region Heritage Corporation, Inc., Devils Lake, ND (Great Lakes)

Inverness Cook Book ©1963 All Saints Episcopal Guild, Inverness, MS (Mississippi)

Iola's Gourmet Recipes in Rhapsody, by Iola Egle, McCook, NE (Great Plains)

Irene's Country Cooking ©2002 by Irene D. Wakefield, Anticipation Press, Cheyenne, WY (Big Sky)

It's a Long Way to Guacamole ©1978 by Rue Judd and Ann Worley, Arlington, VA (Texas)

It's Our Serve, Junior League of Long Island, Roslyn, NY (New York)

Jambalaya ©1983 Junior League of New Orleans, LA (Louisiana)

The Junior League of Grand Rapids Cookbook I ©1976 The Junior League of Grand Rapids, MI (Michigan)

The Junior Welfare League 50th Anniversary Cookbook, Mayfield-Graves County Junior Welfare League, Annie Gardner Foundation, Mayfield, KY (Kentucky)

Just Desserts ©1998 The Shipley School, Bryn Mawr, PA (Pennsylvania)

Kentucky Authors Cooks ©2004 by Barbara Papyach, Nicholasville, KY (Kentucky)

The Kentucky Derby Museum Cook Book ©1986 Kentucky Derby Museum Corporation, Louisville, KY (Kentucky)

Kentucky Kitchens Volume I ©1989 Telephone Pioneers of America, Kentucky Chapter No. 32, Bellsouth Telephone Pioneers, Louisville, KY (Kentucky)

Kingman Welcome Wagon Club Cookbook, Welcome Wagon Club of Kingman, Kingman, AZ (Arizona)

Kitchen Chatter, by Pat Duran, Henderson, NV (Nevada)

Kitchen Keepsakes, The Houselog Family, Ellsworth, MN (Minnesota)

La Cocina de la Familia ©1998 The Vera Institute of Justice, La Bodega de la Familia, New York, NY (New York)

LaConner Palates ©1998 by Patricia Flynn and Patricia McClane, Bookends Publishing, Oak Harbor, WA (Washington)

Lambertville Community Cookbook ©1995 Kalmia Club of Lambertville, Kalmia Club of Lambertville, Lambertville, NJ (Mid-Atlantic)

Lehigh Public Library Cookbook, Lehigh Public Library, Lehigh, IA (Iowa)

Let Freedom Ring, In Touch Foundation, Windsor Heights, IA (Nevada)

Let's Talk Food from A to Z, by Doris Reynolds, Naples, FL (Florida)

License to Cook Minnesota Style ©1996 Penfield Press, by Gerry Kangas, Iowa City, IA (Minnesota)

Lion House Entertaining ©2003 Hotel Temple Square Corporations, Deseret Book Company, Salt Lake City, UT (Utah)

Lone Star Legacy ©1981 Austin Junior Forum, Inc., Austin Junior Forum Publications, Austin, TX (Texas)

Long Lost Recipes of Aunt Susan, M-PRESS, Hot Springs Villa, AR (Oklahoma)

Louisiana LEGACY ©1982 The Thibodeaux Service League, Thibodaux, LA (Louisiana)

Love, Mom: Stories and Recipes from Kingston, Ohio ©2001 by Brenda McGuire, Columbus, OH (Ohio)

Lowcountry Delights II ©2003 by Maxine Pinson and Malyssa Pinson, SSD, Inc., Savannah, GA (South Carolina)

The Lowfat Grill ©1996 by Donna Rodnitzky, Prima Publishing, Roseville, CA (Iowa)

M.D. Anderson Volunteers Cooking for Fun ©1991 M.D. Anderson Cancer Center Volunteers, M.D. Anderson Volunteer Service, Houston, TX (Texas)

Mackay Heritage Cookbook, by Charlotte McKelvey for South Custer Historical Society, Mackay, ID (Idaho)

The Manor Cookbook, The Manor, Jonesville, MI (Michigan)

Marion Brown's Southern Cook Book ©1980 The University of North Carolina Press, by Marion Brown, Chapel Hill, NC (North Carolina)

Measures of Love, by Beverly White and Terri Foster, Springville, NY (New York)

Merrymeeting Merry Eating ©Regional Memorial Hospital, Mid Coast Hospital, Brunswick Auxiliary, Brunswick, ME (New England)

The Mississippi Cookbook ©1972 University Press of Mississippi, Home Economics Division of the Mississippi Cooperative Extension Service, Jackson, MS (Mississippi)

The Mongo Mango Cookbook ©2001 by Cynthia Thuma, Pineapple Press, Inc., Sarasota, FL (Florida)

Montana Celebrity Cookbook ©1992 American and World Geographic Publishing, by Susie Graetz at Intermountain Children's Home and Services, Helena, MT (Big Sky)

More Hoosier Cooking ©1982 Indiana University Press, Edited by Elaine Lumbra, Bloomington, IN (Indiana)

More of What's Cooking ©1995 Apples to Zucchini, Inc, Dallas, TX (Texas)

More Tastes & Tales ©1987 by Peggy E. Hein, Heinco, Inc., Austin, TX (Texas)

More than Beans and Cornbread ©1993 by Barbara McCallum, Pictorial Histories Distribution, Charleston, WV (West Virginia)

More than Moonshine: Appalachian Recipes and Recollections ©1983 University of Pittsburg Press, Pittsburg, PA (Kentucky)

More Than Soup Bean Cookbook ©1990 by Anna Aughenbaugh, Fort Collins, CO (Colorado)

Munchin' with the Methodists ©2001 Carolina United Methodist Women, Booneville, MS (Mississippi)

Mushrooms, Turnip Greens & Pickled Eggs ©1971 by Frances Carr Parker, TapPar Ltd., Kinston, NC (North Carolina)

The Never Ending Season, Missouri 4-H Foundation, Columbia, MO (Missouri)

North Carolina and Old Salem Cookery ©1955 Elizabeth Hedgecock Sparks, by Beth Tartan, TarPar Ltd., Kernersville, NC (North Carolina)

Northern Lites ©1997 Lites Ltd., by Rose Chaney and Connie (Berghan) Church, Sandpoint, ID (Idaho)

Noted Cookery ©1969 The Junior Group of the Dallas Symphony Orchestra League, Dallas, TX (Texas)

Of Tide & Thyme ©1995 The Junior League of Annapolis, MD (Mid-Atlantic)

Offerings for Your Plate, First Baptist Church, Tremont, MS (Mississippi)

Ohio State Grange Cookbook (Gold), Ohio State Grange, Fredericktown, OH (Ohio)

Oma's (Grandma's) Family Secrets, by Linda F. Selzer, Homestead, IA (Iowa)

101 Great Lowfat Desserts ©1995 by Donna Rodnitzky, Prima Publishing, Roseville, CA (Iowa)

Onions Make the Meal Cookbook, Idaho-Eastern Oregon Onion Committee, Parma, ID (Idaho)

Oregon Cook Book ©1995 Golden West Publishers, by Janet Walker, Phoenix, AZ (Oregon)

Oregon Farmers' Markets Cookbook and Guide ©1998 by Kris Wetherbee, Maverick Publications, Oakland, OR (Oregon)

Oregon: The Other Side, Beta Omicron Chapter - ESA, Hines, OR (Oregon)

Our Cherished Recipes, First Presbyterian Church Deacons, Skagway, AK (Alaska)

Out of this World ©1983 The Oak Hill School Parents' Association, Nashville, TN (Tennessee)

Outdoor Cooking: From Backyard to Backpack ©1991 Department of Transportation, State of Arizona, Arizona Highways Magazine, Phoenix, AZ (Arizona)

Palate Pleasers, Forest Hills United Methodist Church, Brentwood, TN (Tennessee)

Par 3: Tea-Time at the Masters® ©2005 Junior League of Augusta, GA (Georgia)

Paul Naquin's French Collection II - Meats & Poultry ©1980 Paul Naquin, Baton Rouge, LA (Louisiana)

The Peach Sampler ©1983 by Eliza Mears Horton, West Columbia, SC (South Carolina)

Philadelphia Main Line Classics ©1982 Junior Saturday Club, Wayne, PA (Pennsylvania)

The Philadelphia Orchestra Cookbook ©1980 West Philadelphia Women's Committee for the Philadelphia Orchestra, Bryn Mawr, PA (Pennsylvania)

Picnics on the Square ©1994 Wisconsin Chamber Orchestra, Inc., Madison, WI (Wisconsin)

The Pink Lady…in the Kitchen, Medical Center of South Arkansas Auxiliary, El Dorado, AR (Arkansas)

Pioneer Pantry, Telephone Pioneers of America, Lucent Technologies Chapter #135, Lisle, IL (Illinois)

Pleasures from the Good Earth, Rock of Ages LWML, Sedona, AZ (Arizona)

Presentations ©1993 Friends of Lied, Lied Center for Performing Arts, Lincoln, NE (Great Plains)

Pungo Strawberry Festival Cookbook, Pungo Strawberry Festival, Virginia Beach, VA (Virginia)

Pupus from Paradise, Assistance League of Hawaii, Honolulu, HI (Hawaii)

Putting On the Grits ©1984 The Junior League of Columbia, SC (South Carolina)

Queen Anne's Table, Edenton Historical Commission, Edenton, NC (North Carolina)

Raleigh House Cookbook ©1991 Raleigh House, by Martha R. Johnson, Kerrville, TX (Texas)

Recipes & Memories ©1996 The Bessie Chamblee Family and Providence Baptist Church, by Lee McCaskill, Fort Pierce, FL (South Carolina)

Recipes and Remembrances, GFWC Santa Rosa Woman's Club, Gulf Breeze, FL (Florida)

Recipes for Fat Free Living Cookbook 2 ©1998 Fat Free Living, Inc., by Jyl Steinback, Scottsdale, AZ (Arizona)

Recipes for the House that Love Built, Ronald McDonald House of Durham, NC (North Carolina)

Recipes from Big Sky Country: A Collection of Montana's Finest Beds & Breakfast Recipes ©2001 Tracy Winters, Montana Bed & Breakfast Association, Winters Publishing, Greensburg, IN (Big Sky)

Recipes from the Children's Museum at Saratoga, The Children's Museum at Saratoga, Saratoga Springs, NY (New York)

Recipes from the Heart, St. Mark Lutheran Church and Preschool, Elko, NC (Nevada)

Recipes of Note for Entertaining, Rochester Civic Music Guild, Rochester, MN (Minnesota)

Recipes Thru Time, Tooele County Daughters of Utah Pioneers, Stansbury Park, UT (Utah)

Red Flannel Town Recipes, Red Flannel Festival, Cedar Springs, MI (Michigan)

Red River Valley Potato Growers Auxiliary Cookbook, R.R.V.P.G. Auxiliary, East Grand Forks, MN (Great Plains)

Revel ©1980 Junior League of Shreveport, LA (Louisiana)

River Brethren Recipes, Sonlight River Brethren School, Mount Joy, PA (Pennsylvania)

The Rocky Mountain Wild Foods Cookbook ©1995 by Darcy Williamson, Caxton Press, Caldwell, ID (Idaho)

A Samford Celebration Cookbook, Samford University Auxiliary, Birmingham, AL (Alabama)

Sample West Kentucky ©1985 Paula Cunningham, Kuttawa, KY (Kentucky)

Sandlapper Cooks ©1998 Sandlapper Society, Inc., Lexington, SC (South Carolina)

Savor the Flavor, Holy Cross Ladies Society, Buffalo, NY (New York)

Savor the Flavor of Oregon ©1990 The Junior League of Eugene, OR (Oregon)

Seasoned with Aloha Vol. 2, VP-9 Officer Spouses' Club, Kailua, HI (Hawaii)

Seems Like I Done It This A-Way III, by Cleo Stiles Bryan, Tahlequah, OK (Oklahoma)

Shaloha Cookbook ©2002 Congregation Kona Beth Shalom, Kailua-Kona, HI (Hawaii)

Shared Treasures, First Baptist Church, Monroe, LA (Louisiana)

Sharing Our Best ©2003 Morris Press Cookbooks, United Methodist Women of First United Methodist Church, Bay Minette, AL (Alabama)

Sharing Our Best-Franklin ©2002 Franklin Community Church, Apples of Gold Women's Ministry of Franklin Community Church, Franklin, TN (Tennessee)

Ship to Shore II ©1985 Ship to Shore, Inc., by Jan Robinson, Charlotte, NC (North Carolina)

Ships of the Great Lakes Cookbook ©2001 Creative Characters Publishing, Central Lake, MI (Michigan)

Simply in Season ©2005 Herald Press, by Mary Beth Lind & Cathleen Hockman-Wert, Herald Press, Scottdale, PA (Pennsylvania)

Simply Scrumptious Microwaving ©1982 Simply Scrumptious, Kitchen Classics, Stone Mountain, GA (Georgia)

Simply the Best Recipes, Matanuska Telephone Association, Inc, Palmer, AK (Alaska)

Singing in the Kitchen ©1992 by Mavis Punt, Sioux Center, IA (Iowa)

A Slice of Paradise ©1996 The Junior League of the Palm Beaches, West Palm Beach, FL (Florida)

The Smithfield Cookbook ©1978 The Woman's Club of Smithfield, VA (Virginia)

Smokehouse Ham, Spoon Bread, & Scuppernong Wine ©1998 by Joseph Dabney, Cumberland House Publishing, Nashville, TN (Tennessee)

Someone's in the Kitchen with Melanie ©2004 by Melanie Reid Soles, Greensboro, NC (North Carolina)

Soul Food, Ascension Lutheran Church, East Lansing, MI (Michigan)

Sounds Tasty!, KAZU-FM, Pacific Grove (California)

Soupçon II ©1982 The Junior League of Chicago, IL (Illinois)

Soups, Stews, Gumbos, Chilis, Chowders, and Bisques, by John Colquhoun (South Carolina)

South Carolina's Historic Restaurants ©1984 Dawn O'Brien and Karen Mulford, John F. Blair, Publisher, Winston-Salem, NC (South Carolina)

The Southern Gospel Music Cookbook ©1998 by Bethni Hemphill, Brenda McClain, and Jim Clark, Cumberland House Publishing, Nashville, TN (Tennessee)

Southern Vegetable Cooking ©1981 Sandlapper Publishing Co, Inc., Orangeburg, SC (South Carolina)

The South's Legendary Frances Virginia Tea Room Cookbook ©1981, 1996 by Mildred Huff Coleman, Atlanta, GA (Georgia)

St. Francis in the Foothills 30th Anniversary Cookbook, St. Francis in the Foothills UMC, Tucson, AZ (Arizona)

St. Mary's Family Cookbook, St. Mary's Council of Catholic Women, Bloomington, WI (Wisconsin)

Standing Room Only, New Stage Theatre, Jackson, MS (Mississippi)

★★★★★★★★★★★★ ★★★★★★★★★★★★

Steamboat Adventures, by Kenneth C. Weyand, Discovery Publications, Kansas City, MO (Missouri)

Still Gathering, Auxiliary to the American Osteopathic Assn., Chicago, IL (Illinois)

Strawberries: From Our Family's Field to Your Family's Table ©2005 Calhoun Produce, Inc., Ashburn, GA (Georgia)

The Table at Grey Gables ©1998 by Linda Brooks Jones, Cumberland House Publishing, Nashville, TN (Tennessee)

Take Two & Butter 'Em While They're Hot! ©1998 Native Ground Music, Inc., by Barbara Swell, Asheville, NC (West Virginia)

Taste and See, St. Phillip Neri Catholic Church, Milwaukee, WI (Wisconsin)

A Taste of Archaeology ©1995 Archaeological Society of South Carolina, Inc., by John Ehrenhard, Columbia, SC (South Carolina)

A Taste of Christ Lutheran, Mabel E. Jackson, Celebration Committee, Sharon, WI (Wisconsin)

A Taste of Columbus Vol III ©1987 by Beth and David Chilcoat, Worthington, OH (Ohio)

A Taste of Fayette County, New River Convention & Visitors Bureau, Oak Hill, WV (West Virginia)

A Taste of Montana: A Collection of Our Best Recipes ©1999 Tracy Winters, Montana Bed & Breakfast Association, Winters Publishing, Greensburg, IN (Big Sky)

A Taste of Prairie Life ©1996 Loaun Werner Vaad, Chamberlain, SD (Great Plains)

A Taste of the Murphin Ridge Inn ©2004 by Sherry McKenney, West Union, OH (Ohio)

A Taste of Twin Pines, Twin Pines Alumni, W. Lafayette, IN (Indiana)

Taste the Good Life! Nebraska Cookbook, Cookbooks by Morris Press, Kearney, NE (Great Plains)

Taste Trek!, Heimdal Science Fiction Club, Rustburg, VA (Virginia)

Tastes from the Country, Skullbone Community Center, Cordova, TN (Tennessee)

Third Wednesday Homemakers Volume II, Fraziers Bottom Pliny Extension Homemakers, Fraziers Bottom, WV (West Virginia)

Three Rivers Cookbook III ©1990 Child Health Association of Sewickley, PA (Pennsylvania)

Today's Herbal Kitchen ©1995 The Memphis Herb Society, Memphis Herb Society, Wimmer Companies, Memphis, TN (Tennessee)

Tradition in the Kitchen 2 ©1993 North Suburban Beth El Sisterhood, Highland Park, IL (Illinois)

Traditional Treasures, Sun City Aquacize Club, Las Vegas, NV (Nevada)

A Traveler's Table ©2002 by John Izard, Tampa, FL (Georgia)

Treasured Alabama Recipes ©1967 Kathryn Tucker Windham, Selma, AL (Alabama)

Treasured Greek Recipes, Philoptochos Society of St. Sophia Greek Orthodox Church, Albany, NY (New York)

Treasured Recipes from Mason, Ohio, Mason Historical Society, Mason, OH (Ohio)

A Treasury of Recipes for Mind, Body & Soul ©2000 by Laurie Hostetler, Grand Rapids, OH (Ohio)

Tucson Treasures ©1999 Tucson Medical Auxiliary, Tucson, AZ (Arizona)

Turnip Greens in the Bathtub ©1981 Genie Taylor Harrison, Baton Rouge, LA (Louisiana)

200 Treasured Cake and Frosting Recipes, by Fayetta Blair, Vitgie, KY (Kentucky)

Unbearably Good! Sharing Our Best, Waushara County Homemakers, Wautoma, WI (Wisconsin)

Upper Crust: A Slice of the South ©1986 The Junior League of Johnson City, TN (Tennessee)

The Very Special Raspberry Cookbook ©1993 The Very Special Raspberry Cookbook Committee, Carrie Tingley Hospital Foundation, Albuquerque, NM (New Mexico)

Vintage Virginia ©2000 Virginia Dietetic Association, Centreville, VA (Virginia)

The VIP Cookbook: A Potpourri of Virginia Cooking ©1989 edition, The American Cancer Society, Glen Allen, VA (Virginia)

Virginia's Historic Restaurants and Their Recipes ©1984 by Dawn O'Brien, John F. Blair, Publisher, Winston-Salem, NC (Virginia)

West Virginia Country Cooking, by Janese Tennant, Parkersburg, WV (West Virginia)

What's Cookin' in Melon Country, Rocky Ford Chamber of Commerce, Rocky Ford, CO (Colorado)

What's for Dinner? ©1999 by Brenda Abelein & Kelly Wilkerson, Portland, OR (Oregon)

What's New in Wedding Food ©1985 by Marigold P. Sparks and Beth Tartan, TarPar Ltd., Kinston, NC (North Carolina)

What's This Green Stuff, Flo?, by Jerry Palen, Laffing Cow Press, Saratoga, WY (Big Sky)

Wheat Free Wishes, by Lori K. Smith, Muskegon, MI (Michigan)

When Dinnerbells Ring ©1978 Talladega Junior Welfare League, Talladega, AL (Alabama)

White Grass Café Cross Country Cooking ©1996 White Grass Ski Touring Center, by Laurie Little and Mary Beth Gwyer, Davis, WV (West Virginia)

Wild Fare & Wise Words ©2005 S.C. Outdoor Press Association, by Jim and Ann Casada, Rock Hill, SC (South Carolina)

Wild Thyme and Other Temptations ©2000 Junior League of Tucson, AZ (Arizona)

Wildlife Harvest Game Cookbook ©1988 by Wildlife Harvest Publications, Inc., Wildlife Harvest Publications, Inc., Goose Lake, IA (Iowa)

Winners ©1985 The Junior League of Indianapolis, IN (Indiana)

With Great Gusto ©1987 The Junior League of Youngstown, OH (Ohio)

Without a Doubt ©2000 St. Thomas Episcopal Church, Greenville, AL (Alabama)

The Wyman Sisters Cookbook, by Laura F. Tesseneer, Crescent Springs, KY (Kentucky)

WWW.WIKIPEDIA.ORG

Wisconsin is the leading producer of cranberries, accounting for more than half of U.S. production. To harvest cranberries, the beds are flooded with six to eight inches of water above the vines. A harvester is driven through the beds to remove the fruit from the vines. Harvested cranberries float in the water and can be conveyed or pumped from the bed.

Index

Index

Index

Index

Index

Index

Index